Iran at the Crossroads

Iran at the Crossroads

Global Relations
in a Turbulent Decade

EDITED BY
Miron Rezun

Westview Press
BOULDER • SAN FRANCISCO • OXFORD

Westview Special Studies on the Middle East

The epigraph on p. vii is taken from "Sword of a Relentless Revolution" in the June 12, 1989, issue of *Time*. It is copyright © 1989 by The Time Inc. Magazine Company and is reprinted with permission.

This Westview softcover edition is printed on acid-free paper and bound in library-quality, coated covers that carry the highest rating of the National Association of State Textbook Administrators, in consultation with the Association of American Publishers and the Book Manufacturers' Institute.

Published in 1990 in the United States of America by Westview Press, Inc., 5500 Central Avenue, Boulder, Colorado 80301, and in the United Kingdom by Westview Press, 36 Lonsdale Road, Summertown, Oxford OX2 7EW

Library of Congress Cataloging-in-Publication Data
Iran at the crossroads : global relations in a turbulent decade /
edited by Miron Rezun.
    p. cm.—(Westview special studies on the Middle East)
  Includes bibliographical references and index.
  ISBN 0-8133-7854-0
  1. Iran—Foreign relations—1979–   . I. Rezun, Miron. II. Series.
DS318.83.I73   1990
327.55—dc20

90-12426
CIP

Printed and bound in the United States of America

The paper used in this publication meets the requirements of the American National Standard for Permanence of Paper for Printed Library Materials Z39.48-1984.

10   9   8   7   6   5   4   3   2   1

In memory of my mother, Lea,
who always strove for peace

He who establishes a dictatorship and does not kill Brutus, or he who founds a republic and does not kill the sons of Brutus, will only reign a short time.

—Machiavelli, *Discorsi*

He came to symbolize everything the West found incomprehensible and baffling about the East: his intense, ascetic spirituality and air of other-worldly detachment; his medieval, theocratic mind-set, which drew its parallels and precedents from the Islamic world of the 7th century; the mystical certitude that he spoke in the name of God, his country and Muslims everywhere.

—*Time* (in a June 12, 1989,
comment on Khomeini's death)

Contents

ix

PART FOUR
FOCUS ON THE IRAN-IRAQ WAR

PART FIVE
IRAN AND THE SUPERPOWERS

PART SIX
CONCLUSION

Preface and Acknowledgments

The chapters in this book were written by me or solicited from renowned experts to produce a work that anticipated an imminent post-Khomeini period in Iranian history. The first draft was not ready until June 1989, practically coinciding with the death of Khomeini and the tenth anniversary of the Iranian Revolution—an important milestone after a decade of turmoil.

The book you are about to read took some time to put together. Based on extensive research, the project was undertaken in early 1988 and ended about the spring of 1990. A sincere debt of gratitude is naturally owed to all of my contributors. But the preparation of any book does not take place in a financial void. My gratitude is especially extended to the academic vice-president of my university, Dr. Robert Burridge, for granting me the seed money from the university's Development Fund. Substantial financial assistance to cover the bulk of the logistical expenses was offered by the Canadian Institute of International Peace and Security in Ottawa and by the Social Sciences and Humanities Research Council of Canada through its program of aid to scholarly conferences.

I am particularly indebted to Barbara Ellington of Westview Press; her insightful suggestions considerably improved the editorial work involved. The research assistance of one of my students, Robert Trifts, is also gladly acknowledged, particularly in connection with the concluding chapter.

Finally, I owe an immense debt to my secretary, Melynda Jarratt, for proofreading the entire manuscript, to Angela Williams for producing a convenient index, to Christine Arden for the fine copy editing, and to Debbie Sloan, Rheta MacElwain, and Angela Williams for putting the whole manuscript on memory disks and for being so patient with me while I did my best to ensure that all the chapters were as up-to-date as possible.

Miron Rezun
New Brunswick, Canada

About the Contributors

Shaul Bakhash is Robinson Professor of History at George Mason University. He was born in Teheran and was educated at Harvard and Oxford universities. He worked for many years as a journalist in Iran, where he was a correspondent and editor for *Kayhan* newspapers, and he reported on Iran for such publications as the *Economist*, the *London Times*, the *Financial Times*, and *Newsweek* magazine. He also taught history at Iranian universities. Since returning to the United States in 1980, he taught at Princeton University before joining the faculty of George Mason University. His articles have appeared in the *New York Review of Books*, the *New Republic*, the *Washington Post*, the *New York Times*, the *Los Angeles Times*, and the *Boston Globe*. He is the author of two books, the more recent of which is *The Reign of the Ayatollahs: Iran and the Islamic Revolution* (1982).

William O. Beeman is an Associate Professor of Anthropology at Brown University and is also Associate Editor of the *Pacific News Service* based in San Francisco. He has served as occasional consultant to the U.S. State Department on Middle East Affairs and has authored several books, most notably *Language, Status and Power in Iran*, as well as numerous scholarly and popular articles on Middle East culture and politics. He received his B.A. from Wesleyan University, in Middletown, Connecticut, and his M.A. and Ph.D. at the University of Chicago, all in anthropology.

Fuat Borovali was born in Turkey and studied in England and Canada. He received his B.A. from Manchester University in England and his Ph.D. at Queen's University in Kingston, Ontario. He has extensively researched the role of the military in Turkish and Middle East politics. His current research interests include the Iran-Iraq peace process, the role of ethnicity in the region's politics (with respect to the Kurds, for example), the Cyprus issue, and the paths to greater understanding between the Middle East and the West. He has published several articles in Canadian and U.S. journals. Fuat Borovali teaches International Relations at Bilkent University in Ankara.

Shahram Chubin, an Iranian national, is currently at Geneva's Graduate Institute of International Studies and was formerly on the staff of the International Institute of Strategic Studies in London. His most recent publication is *Iran and Iraq at War* (Tauris and Westview, 1988). His other books include *The Persian Gulf: The Role of the Outside Powers* (1981) and *Iran's Foreign Relations* (1974). He has written extensively on regional conflicts, including such articles as "Reflections on the Gulf War," *Survival*, July-August 1986; "The Conduct of Military Operations," in *Politique Etrangère*, No. 2 (June 1987), Special Issue on the Iran-Iraq War; and "The Superpowers and Regional Conflicts: Trends and Outlook," *Adelphi Paper* (Spring 1989). Dr. Chubin is a graduate of Oberlin College and Columbia University, and he has taught at universities in the United States and Europe.

Shireen T. Hunter, born in Iran, is Deputy Director of the Middle East Project at the Center for Strategic and International Studies. She is the author of *OPEC and the Third World: The Politics of Aid* (1987) and has edited and contributed a chapter on Iran to *The Politics of Islamic Revivalism* (1989). She is currently working on a book on Iran's foreign relations since the revolution. Dr. Hunter has written numerous book chapters as well as op-ed and journal articles. Her articles have appeared in *SAIS Review, The Middle East Journal, Foreign Policy, The Washington Quarterly, OPEC Review, Middle East Insight, American-Arab Affairs*, and the *Third World Quarterly*. Her op-ed pieces have appeared in major newspapers, including the *International Herald Tribune*, the *New York Times*, and the *Christian Science Monitor*. She appears regularly on television in the United States and the United Kingdom and makes radio commentaries worldwide.

Ashok Kapur was born in India and is a Professor of Political Science at the University of Waterloo, in Ontario, Canada. He received his Ph.D. in political science at Carleton University in Ottawa. He is the author of *India's Nuclear Option* (1976), *International Nuclear Proliferation* (1979), *The Indian Ocean* (1983), and *Pakistan's Development* (1987). Dr. Kapur is currently writing about South Asian international relations.

Miron Rezun was born in Israel and is an Associate Professor in the Department of Political Science at the University of New Brunswick in Canada. He received his Ph.D. from the University of Geneva, Switzerland, and has travelled in and published widely on the Soviet Union and the Middle East. His current areas of interest are Soviet science and technology and the problems of the Soviet nationalities. His articles have appeared in *Etudes Internationales*, the *International Journal, Queen's Quarterly*, and *Problems of Communism*. He has written in French for *AGORA* and *Le Monde* and has published a collection of articles for the Centre Québécois des Relations Internationales in Quebec City. One of his books, *The Soviet Union and Iran*

(Westview, 1988), has become the definitive study of Soviet-Iranian relations during the Reza Shah period. He has also authored a book entitled *The Great Struggle* (1990) and another on Canadian-Iranian relations (forthcoming in 1991) and is currently working on a book dealing with ethnicity and the nationalities in the USSR.

Carol R. Saivetz has taught at Northeastern University and Simmons College and was an Associate Professor of Political Science at Tufts University. In addition, she is a Visiting Scholar at Harvard University's Russian Research Center. She is the author of numerous articles on Soviet policy in the Third World and the co-author of *Soviet–Third World Relations* (Westview, 1985). Her most recent publication is *The Soviet Union and the Gulf in the 1980s* (Westview, 1989). She has also recently edited *The Soviet Union in the Third World* (Westview, 1989).

Roger M. Savory is Professor Emeritus in the Department of Middle East and Islamic Studies at the University of Toronto and a Fellow of Trinity College. Born in Peterborough, England, he received his B.A. in Oriental studies (Arabic and Persian) from Oxford University and his Ph.D. in Persian studies from the University of London. From 1950 to 1960 he held a Lectureship in Persian at the School of Oriental and African Studies, University of London, and from 1960 until his retirement in 1987 he was a member of the teaching staff of the University of Toronto. From 1954 to 1956 he worked as an editorial assistant on the new edition of *The Encyclopaedia of Islam*, and from 1956 to 1960 he was the Editorial Secretary of the English edition of this work. He has been a member of the Board of Directors (1969–1971) and Vice-President (1973–1974) of the Middle East Studies Association of North America. In 1972 he was elected a Fellow of the Royal Society of Canada.

His major work in the field of Persian history is a two-volume translation of a seventeenth-century Persian text, *The History of Shah 'Abbas the Great*, published in 1979 as part of the Persian Heritage Series. This work was selected by *Choice*, the journal of the American Library Association, as an outstanding academic book of 1979. He has also published another book on Safavid history, *Iran Under the Safavids* (1980), as well as a collection of articles entitled *Studies on the History of Safavid Iran* (1987).

John Sigler is a Professor of Political Science and International Affairs at Carleton University in Ottawa, Ontario. He is co-editor with Charles Doran of *Canada and the United States: Enduring Friendship, Persistent Stress* (1985). His most recent articles on U.S. foreign policy and the Middle East have appeared in *International Journal* and *Circa, 1984–85* and in previous volumes of the *Conflict Yearbook* published by the Centre Québécois des Relations Internationales.

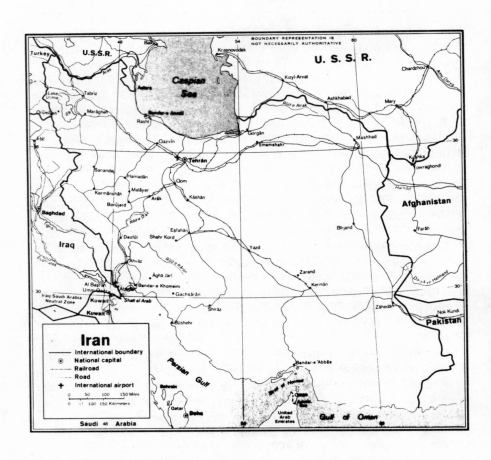

Iran

Introduction

Miron Rezun

This book is the result of extensive research and inquiry into the manifold problems facing the Islamic Republic of Iran in the area of international affairs. The implicit assumption is that Iran, from the perspective of both internal and external politics, continues to be the most intriguing and perplexing country in a world that is currently undergoing unprecedented change. The Iran-Iraq war is presumably over; Khomeini has passed from the scene; the USSR has pulled out of Afghanistan. Ironically, the Gulf itself may cease to be as important as it has been until now; the problem of oil supply and the threat of an energy crisis may no longer loom as large as it once did. Without Khomeini, surely post-Khomeini Iran may not be as assertive internationally as it once was. But there is no gainsaying that what occurred in Iran in the first decade of the existence of the Islamic Republic will attract the attention of both world scholarship and the public at large. Every effort is being made to understand this country and to determine the direction in which it is going. Arguably, the degree of interest shown in things Iranian is a highly uncommon one for any Third World state.

There is a cornucopia of materials on Iran, some good and some bad, some critical and some laudatory—depending, of course, on the political perceptions of the authors and/or their institutional affiliations. On the whole, however, there appears to be a great deal of disagreement in this growing body of literature regarding the Iranian Revolution and its aftermath. One is drawn to a remark made in the most recent Soviet study of the Islamic Republic to the effect that the United States has produced the bulk of this historiography.[1] Soviet scholars today admit that theirs cannot be the only "objective" analysis of events in Iran, pointing to the myriad schools of thought that exist on this subject in the West and the East and to the many "Western writings" that are in fact balanced, objective, and often critical of Western dealings with

1

Iran in a way that perhaps Soviet scholarship has not been. A similar admission appears in the West, in a book critical of U.S. policies in Iran, namely Robin Wright's *In the Name of God* (Simon and Schuster, 1989). But this treatment is journalistic, unduly leavened with personal observations, highly idiosyncratic and, therefore, misses the mark as a serious scholarly study. It is a facile statement to admit that Iran is at a turning point, as we are in fact making in our inquiry, and then not analyze where the country is actually headed. We must somehow try to weigh all the possibilities.

It was the personality and will of the Ayatollah Khomeini that presided to a spectacular degree over the rise in post-1979 Iran of a theocratic state order—one that could easily be likened to any church-state in medieval Europe. In such a state, theology has generally been considered the revealed truth from which it is heretical for a subject to deviate in thought, word, and deed. With the passing of Khomeini, there are many questions that must now be asked, and not only on the subject of the succession. Will there be an Iranian Thermidor, as is the pattern peculiar to most revolutions? To what extent can Iran be expected to continue making an impact on international affairs? Is Iran unexpectedly drawing closer to the Soviet Union? Is it preparing—in fact, will it be willing and able—to have another war with Iraq? And what about Iran's broken relations with most of Western Europe and the United States?

This book has accordingly been conceived and written in light of the Gulf war and in anticipation of the post-Khomeini period that now follows. The twelve governments of the European community officially withdrew their senior diplomats from Iran and are accusing its Government of unacceptable violations of the most elementary principles of international conduct. This was a reaction to the Ayatollah's call for the death of the British author, Salman Rushdie, who wrote a novel that is considered offensive to Islam. Iran and the United States, moreover, still have no diplomatic relations, and Khomeini's last will and testament specifically mentioned that Iran should always be wary of the United States.

As the title suggests, this book is concerned more with Iran's foreign relations than with its domestic environment. But the discriminating reader will undoubtedly discover that a great many foreign policy imperatives are linked to the current domestic, social, political, and economic constraints of the Islamic Republic. In addressing these questions of international import, the contributors to this project came from diverse academic backgrounds; most of them were born and educated outside of North America. The authors include one anthropologist, an historian, and a sociologist. Several are experts in international relations and strategic studies; as Iranian-area specialists, some could be called "Iranists" in the literal sense. Much of the material in this book could be regarded as controversial and contentious; and much would be perceived as portentous. Analyses differ from writer to writer, for there are no two identical methods of inquiry or unanimous critical judgement. Indeed, the themes themselves define the broadness and ambivalence of Iran's foreign relationships. Even the last chapter is a self-contained summary that does not necessarily reflect the views of the preceding ones.

In Chapters 1 and 2, we are offered contending but not necessarily antithetical perspectives on Iranian foreign policy. To be sure, both Miron Rezun and Roger Savory arrive at the general conclusion that Iran's behaviour has been irrational. But the similarity ends there. Savory contends that this behaviour is the result of inherent, internal factors, informed by economic and political imperatives, and characterized by an Islamic culture that is unlike any other Moslem state in the world. Savory believes that Khomeini's regime is based on unrealistic policies—a situation that is the antithesis of *Realpolitik*—and not on the realities of world politics. As such, this regime has created a framework for policy formulation that sees the world as an apocalyptic struggle between the forces of good and evil. Rezun, by contrast, only partly views Iran's "irrational" policies as a product of its own making. He places the blame for the turmoil of the past decade on the other powers as well, regional and external alike. Rezun's argument focuses primarily on the process by which the United States, in reacting to Iran's lack of political realism, resolutely, and just as incoherently, decided to support the Iraqis and other Arabs out of an exaggerated fear of Iran's military threat to its Arab neighbors and to the stability of the Gulf region. He leaves open the question of a pariah nation's eventual reinstatement into the community of states but maintains that, if Iran were to come back to the fold, it would have to repair its relationship with the United States.

In Chapter 3, Ashok Kapur deals with Pakistan's and India's relations with Iran. He examines the subcontinent in light of the preconditions and developments of the Iranian Revolution and in the larger context of regional and global forces. He notes that Iran's attitude toward India is not the same as its attitude toward Pakistan, and that the tenor of relations between Islamabad and Teheran has been determined as much by their respective regional and strategic concerns, particularly their attitudes in regard to the United States, as by the reciprocal dynamics between the Khomeini regime and the now-defunct Zia regime.

In Chapter 4, Fuat Borovali engages in a political comparison of Turkey and Iran, arguing that while there have been structural similarities between the two states, the Iranian Revolution denoted a certain divergence in the paths travelled by them. Since that Revolution, the ideological distinction between Kemalist Westernism and Shi'i Islamism has been compounded by differing perspectives in regard to the Kurdish issue. But on the whole, the two nations have maintained a pragmatic economic rapport. If, however, it is true that the war is over, Borovali argues, then any trade advantage that resulted from it and that normally redounded to Turkey—notwithstanding the Rushdie Affair—may now be in jeopardy.

In Chapter 5, Shireen Hunter argues that while Iran's relations with the Arabs have undergone considerable changes since the Revolution, the underlying pattern of Arab-Iranian interaction has remained remarkably the same. In her analysis of Iran's relations with both moderate and radical Arab regimes throughout the entire war period, Hunter concludes that despite Islamic Iran's professed ideal of Islamic unity and brotherhood, the Revolution and the war had the paradoxical effect of deepening long-time ethno-religious, Arab-Iranian cleavages.

This book would be somewhat elliptical if it did not deal with Iranian policies toward Israel and the Arab-Israeli conflict. In Chapter 6, Shaul Bakhash examines the evolution of Iran's relations with Israel, Syria, and Lebanon in terms of shifts in foreign policy since the Revolution. Bakhash argues that these shifts are the result of an almost instinctive determination to repudiate the policies of former years. He attributes these shifts in part to revolutionary ideology and turmoil and in part to an Iranian opportunity to influence the politics of Lebanon. Citing the influence of key individuals, including Abol-Hasan Bani-Sadr and the Ayatollah himself, he arrives at the conclusion that Iran will never be an important player in the Palestinian-Israeli conflict, although it will be a serious force in the Arab-Israeli dispute that goes beyond Palestine. He also concludes that with the end to the Iran-Iraq war, both Iran and Syria will have to rethink the basis of their alliance. And, with the Iran-Iraq cease-fire in effect, Iranian activities in Lebanon may be curtailed as Iran weighs the real and potential gains that can be derived against real and potential losses.

In Chapter 7, Shahram Chubin presents a detailed assessment of the forces that precipitated the Iran-Iraq war and accounted for its lengthy stalemate. He also discusses the elements that have been instrumental in bringing about the cease-fire. He is critical of the Iranian leaders for their inept conduct of the war, for their inability to discard their implausible romanticism and to come to grips with the stark military logistics and diplomatic realities that have developed since 1986. He also addresses some critical remarks to the community of analysts and scholars who have predicted the course of the war, whilst tacitly admitting that Iraq's use of chemical weapons to such devastating effects could not easily have been foreseen.

In Chapter 8, John Sigler provides an historiographical survey of the more prominent works done so far on the Iran-Iraq war. He divides the prevailing debates into three contending schools of international relations: the realists, the liberal internationalists, and the radical school. Sigler concludes that if there is a lesson to be learned from this war, it is that there are essentially no clear-cut winners or losers. He also advances the view that victory and defeat are changing concepts that can alter with time and perspective.

In Chapter 9, William Beeman probes the U.S.-Iranian relationship from both an anthropological and a psychological perspective. He argues that the decade from 1978 to 1989 was an exceptional one insofar as it underscored the extent to which the two nations lacked a coherent understanding of the cultural bases motivating one another's external and internal policies. Hence each nation developed a mythological image of the other that served to demonize the other party and coloured the respective foreign policy considerations. Beeman is especially critical of the United States' narrow point of view toward the Iranians and its labelling of Iran as an "outlaw" nation because the Islamic state could not conform to the U.S. mythology of foreign relations. He sees this cultural intolerance as the basis of many of the world's problems today. And he concludes that the experience with Iran constitutes an invaluable lesson for the United States. In short, the United States needs to take into consideration the cultural sensibilities of other nations.

In Chapter 10, Carol Saivetz introduces us to a new relationship that has been unfolding between Iran and the Soviet Union. She attributes this new beginning to Gorbachev's *novoe myshlenie* ("new thinking") in Soviet foreign policy—a foreign policy that is deliberately cautious, diplomatic and polished. In her treatment of these bilateral relations Saivetz takes the Soviet point of view, but she skillfully explains the positive reaction of the Iranian leadership, all the while wondering whether, from the Iranian point of view, there is such a thing as a "Little Satan."

In the last chapter, Miron Rezun offers a summary that explains the motivations behind and the impact of internal factionalism in Iran, its influence on the Rushdie Affair, and the consequences of that for Iran and the world. He attempts to prognosticate the future of Iran, now that the spiritual leader of the country has died. His general predictions suggest that there will be renewed violence of short duration, but that the country must sooner or later turn to the West.

Iran is at the crossroads in its history because its Revolution may soon be spent. If its leaders intend to consolidate the gains of that

Revolution, they will have to do so without Khomeini's guiding hand; or they must let go altogether, thus causing a repudiation of Khomeini sometime in the future. More than anything else, however, Iran must rebuild its war-torn economy and look toward a future of economic growth and political stability. The stark alternative would be the total collapse of the state. The Iranian people have sacrificed so much; and, oddly enough, they still revere Khomeini as a deity. Whether or not Iran continues on the same path initially chosen by the Ayatollah, several interrelated political decisions will long remain crucial to the survival of the Iranian Government in its present form—particularly those decisions relating to Iran's position in the Middle East, its future relationship with Iraq and the superpowers, its reintegration into the international political (and economic) order, and the course of the political and spiritual succession to the Ayatollah Khomeini.

NOTES

1. A. Z. Arabajian, ed. *Iranskaia Revoliutsia* (Moscow: Institute of Oriental Studies, 1989).

PART ONE

Two Perspectives on Iranian Foreign Policy

1

The "Pariah" Syndrome:
The Complexities of the
Iranian Predicament

Miron Rezun

The pace of events in Iran is moving so fast and the changes are so unprecedented that it is difficult to say anything conclusive. As recently as the early spring of 1987 it seemed that Iran was drawing closer to victory over Iraq and accepting it at enormous sacrifice, all the while inflaming the entire region. Then the pendulum began to swing back: By the spring of 1988 Ayatollah Khomeini's troops had been heavily battered on land, on the sea, and in the air. To make matters even worse, in the first week of July 1988 an Iran Air passenger plane was mistakenly shot down by a U.S. warship over the Strait of Hormuz, with the loss of 290 innocent persons on board. For a brief time after that Iran opened and then closed itself again toward the world at the height of the Rushdie Affair. By early June 1989 Khomeini had died, mourned by millions in his country.

What had come to pass in the brief period between early spring of 1987 and the summer of 1989 was a series of circumstantial, military, and diplomatic shifts as well as some sober rethinking of the power struggle by all the players involved. The turn of events had brought Iran to the brink of disaster. But I feel that one cannot always find fault with Iran for what had happened, although Iran could certainly be credited for being the prime mover in these epoch-making events. It would be fitting at this point to state as well that in any relationship between Iran and another country, there are not only ideological interests and concerns but also important geopolitical and strategic considerations that must be weighed. For the United States, especially, these are paramount; U.S. policies and security interests in the Gulf region have been central to the entire Iranian equation. That is why I wish

to leave the heady events of 1988 to the Conclusion, where it is my
intention to illustrate the extent of America's ignorance of Iran—culturally by far the largest and economically the most important nation
in the Gulf region. Need we plead that history has an incongruity
about it? History is full of surprises, so much so that Iran may yet
come full circle, from America's once-powerful ally, to open hostility,
and then back again. For an entire decade one could see Iran only as
a pariah. The reasons for this are rooted in the complexities of our
time and in the ambiguities of power politics, for which the starting
point was triggered by the demise of the U.S.-Iranian relationship. If
relations with the United States, and for that matter even with Western
Europe, are not mended in the post-Khomeini period, the direction of
Iranian history will be altered for many years to come.

IMPERIAL IRAN

The land of Zoroaster had been conquered by the Arab Moslems in
the seventh century. Even when the Pahlavi monarchy was first established, its leading intellectuals never really forgot the nation's pre-Islamic
past. "Pahlavism" made official a national mythology that began in the
nineteenth century under a weaker Qajar rule. It was a vigorous
nationalism aimed at glorifying the pre-Islamic past and Iranian king-
ship dating from the fifth century B.C. Its high point was reached in
the celebration of 2,500 years of monarchy at Persepolis in 1971. By
regenerating dynastic rule, the idea of Islamic ideology was discarded
from the moment the first Pahlavi monarch, Reza Shah, ascended the
Persian throne in 1925.[1]

The architect of this secular, nationalist society was not really Reza
Shah, however;[2] rather, it was a man who helped put him on the throne
and conducted the diplomacy of the nation by himself—Reza's Minister
of the Court, Teymourtash.[3] Teymourtash and the triumvirate he headed
had Iranian history rewritten to such a point that it played down the
Islamic period. A nationalist campaign was promoted to galvanize the
support of the Iranian people beyond the intellectual strata, evoking
and emphasizing an Aryan civilization since antiquity in the symbols
of *Iran-e-Bastan* and in the purity of the Persian language, *Farsi ye
ser'e*, which set Iran apart from its immediate neighbours, both Arab
and non-Arab, but more particularly from the Arabs whom Iranian
leaders regarded as "barbarian" (*"Vahshigari arab"*).

These invocations were one of the reasons behind Iran's desire for
expansionism and territorial aggrandizement. One notable incident took
place at the time King Amnanullah of Afghanistan was deposed in
1929 during a surge of Moslem fundamentalism. In fact, Teymourtash

sent a whole army to the Afghan border in a bid to wrest the Afghan province of Herat in a moment of Afghan weakness.[4] Mutual accommodations between Iran and Afghanistan followed only after Soviet and Turkish mediation. But similar territorial claims were made in this period on Bahrain and on territories in the Gulf that were perceived to be inhabited by Arabs of Persian stock. Claims to Soviet territory—particularly to Soviet Azerbaijan and parts of Central Asia—were also made in private to Nazi officials at a time of great sympathy in Iran for the German (Aryan) cause prior to and during World War II.[5]

However, it was not until the advent of Mohammed Reza Shah, Reza Shah's son, that Iran seriously began propagating its age-old national mythology and was able to arrogate to itself a preeminent role in the affairs of the Gulf. In the latter 1960s and throughout the 1970s, oil revenues had made Iran a second-ranking power in international politics, the "gendarme" of Gulf security—on a par with such states as India, despite the fact that India supports a population twenty times as large and occupies an area that is only twice as large as Iran's. Iranian nationalism opposed Arab Nasserism; Iran sent troops to help the Royalists in North Yemen while Nasser helped the Arab nationalists who were trying to set up a republic. The Shah was able to explain this action by maintaining that Nasserism was heavily influenced and even controlled by Soviet ideological imperatives, although Nasser's entire diplomatic record proved quite the contrary. The Shah's own high-handed, nationalistic commitments compelled him, on November 30, 1971, to occupy three tiny, strategically important islands (Abu Musa and the Tumbs) in the narrow entrance to the Persian Gulf. The Shah did his utmost to influence the Arab rulers of all the Gulf littoral states from Oman to Kuwait: After all, Iran had become the strongest military power in the region, and there were more than 1 million people of Iranian descent living there. The largest military operation in which Iranian forces were involved also took place in 1971, when Iran sent troops to the Sultan of Oman to put down the rebellion in Oman's southern province of Dhofar. The Shah's greatest diplomatic maneuver came even earlier—that is, in 1955, when he adhered to the short-lived Baghdad Pact to form a "Northern Tier" alliance among Iran, Turkey, Pakistan, and Iraq (which Great Britain subsequently joined). The purpose of this defensive barrier was to contain the USSR in the north, as a kind of connecting link between the North Atlantic Treaty Organization (NATO) in the West and the Southeast Asia Treaty Organization (SEATO) in the East. But in 1958 Iraq withdrew from the Pact, and from then on it ceased to be called the Baghdad Pact. It was renamed the Central Treaty Organization (CENTO), without Baghdad,[6] and it lasted until 1979, when Iran withdrew after the revolution.

This leads us to the most critical issue in Iran's desire to dominate West Asia: its rivalry in the region with Iraq. This rivalry appeared to end only when the Shah and Saddam Hussein signed the Treaty of Algiers in 1975, having reached total agreement on all outstanding disputes. But the disputes themselves, including that pertaining to the border demarcation of the Shat-al-Arab river estuary, were far too deep to lay to rest with the mere stroke of a pen. While the Iran of the Pahlavis was a state advocating national regeneration, this disagreement was not in the least inconsistent with the official religion of this nation, which is Shi'ite Islam as opposed to Sunni Islam. The leaders of Iraq had always been Sunni Moslems ruling an Arab country that is predominantly (more than one-half) Shi'ite. Iran under the Shah was therefore not loath to play on Shi'ite sentiments in the diplomatic disputes with Iraq that persisted up to 1975 and were to reappear more vehemently when the Islamic Republic of Iran was established in 1979. During the propaganda war between the two countries in the 1960s and 1970s, Iran identified Iraqi leadership with Yazid—the ruler of Iraq who, in the seventh century, killed Hossein, the grandson of the prophet Mohammed and one of the founders and martyred heroes of Shi'i Islam. It is in Iran's relations with Iraq that we clearly see how the ancient animosity between Arabs and Persians is directly transcended by their respective interpretations of Islam. On more than one occasion the Pahlavi monarch was implicated in several unsuccessful coups against the ruling Ba'athist regime in Iraq, occurring even before Khomeini called for the overthrow of Saddam Hussein.

"My enemy's enemy is my friend" is an old dictum that never escaped the attention of the Pahlavi ruler. Not only the Iraqi Kurds, whom the Shah and the Iranian Government assisted financially and militarily to fight the regime in Baghdad, but also, and more specifically, the Israelis are being referred to here. Iran's relationship with Israel goes as far back as 1950 (according to some, all the way back to the *Book of Esther*)—only two years after the establishment of *Eretz Yisrael*, when Iran extended to it a *de facto* recognition. A tacit understanding has existed since then, with the implication that Iran was to dominate West Asia while Israel would be supreme in the Middle East proper. Although this attitude toward Israel changed somewhat after the 1967 and 1973 wars, Imperial Iran never did endorse the idea of a Palestinian state—not even when relations with Egypt improved after 1973. Countless Iranian officers received training in Israel or had visited that country; both countries exchanged military supplies, and Israel's Mossad and Iran's Savak have cooperated in the field of secret intelligence since 1950; the Mossad consistently trained Savak operatives. Iran even became Israel's chief supplier of oil. After the 1967 war, Iran financed the Israeli-built 162-mile pipeline from Eilat on the Red Sea to Ashkelon on the Mediterranean.[7]

Apparently Iranian foreign policy of this period was intent not so much on penetrating neighbouring areas as on influencing them, literally recreating a Persian Empire that only an advanced state like Germany, Britain, or Russia would have attempted, or dared, in previous decades. That is probably one of the most innovative features of the Pahlavi regime.

For instance, because the landmass of Western Asia is vast and sparsely populated, Iran entered the old "Great Game" by improving on the rail links of the Indo-Persian Corridor, the instrument of land penetration that the Shah hoped would ultimately extend to the vast railway network of former British India. Railways in the developing world are still, after all, the sinews of political and economic penetration. Reza Shah (with the help of German engineers) had been able to complete the 1,400-kilometer Trans-Iranian Railway, which is a north-south line. What his son had been striving for was an east-west line that would have redirected the flow of Afghan trade away from the Soviet border back to the markets of South Asia and the Middle East. To do this he had to link up the Iranian and Pakistani rail systems. Work finally began and a spur from Qom, passing through Yazd, reached Kerman in 1977. The main Afghan cities—Herat, Kandahar, and Kabul—were supposed to be connected to this railroad, and it was thence to be extended to connect with China. The People's Republic of China had just been finishing the 1,200-kilometer Karakoram Highway crossing the Himalayas from Kashoger to Islamabad.[8] The Iranian dream was thus to establish a Teheran-Kabul-Islamabad (perhaps even a Beijing) axis and project Iranian influence over this new transportation infrastructure—an event of major geostrategic significance for both India and the USSR. For this purpose, the Shah actually gave Afghan President Mohammed Daoud a $2 billion line of credit.

It was principally for this reason that Iran was so dismayed over the recurring Indo-Pakistani wars, which drained Pakistan of resources to a greater extent than India. The Shah, in this respect, was disillusioned with the CENTO alliance. Indeed, in the first 1965 war between India and Pakistan, the United States not only failed to assist Pakistan (a member of CENTO); it even refused to allow Iran to come to Pakistan's aid with arms purchased from the United States. The Shah increasingly saw his country as the linchpin of a Moslem, non-Arab alliance, with or without the support of the United States and Britain. And again, in the wake of the Indo-Pakistan War of 1971, Iran publicly announced that it was opposed to any further weakening of Pakistan, from without or within. Economic aid and military support was subsequently given to the Pakistani army in support of Pakistan's counter insurgency campaign against the risings of the Baluch tribesmen in 1973.[9] The Pakistani province of Baluchistan borders on Iranian Baluchistan (where the Baluch are also a suppressed nationality), and Imperial Iran was anxious that irredentism of this kind from neighbouring countries did not spill over to similar movements inside Iran. In general, too, Iran invested heavily in Pakistan and India with a view toward creating future sources of materials—consumer and otherwise—for an Iranian economic expansion that never really materialized.

It is a moot point, however, as to whether economic pressures of any sort, especially those related to dwindling oil output, would have transformed the Iran of the Pahlavi monarch into an even more aggressive power than it was. The seemingly prophetic views of one observer, Fred Halliday, were simply not borne out in the Shah's lifetime. Before the fall of Imperial Iran, Halliday wrote:

> From the mid-1980s onwards, as Iran's oil output falls, the temptation will be strong for Iran to make up for the fall in its domestic output by using its armed forces to seize the wells of neighbouring states, which still have considerable reserves and an income in excess of their requirements: Kuwait, Qatar and Saudi Arabia all fall into this category.[10]

But was Iran in those days genuinely the overwhelmingly powerful nation in the region that so many have led us to believe? Iran had acquired more military hardware than it could possibly use or even knew how to use. One must inevitably ask whether in the Shah's day a combined Arab force, equipped with Soviet and U.S. arms, could not have held their own against a supremely equipped Iranian Army and Navy? For the records all too eloquently indicate that the Iranian forces were primarily used to suppress the Iranian people, to discipline them, as a show of force and to maintain the Pahlavi dynasty in power. Certainly the mantle of would-be Iranian supremacy was destined to fall on Khomeini's Islamic Republic, in much the same way that Soviet Russia had inherited many of the features of foreign policy characteristic of Tsarist Russia before it (with some notable differences, of course).

THE ISLAMIC REPUBLIC

The Iranian Revolution of 1979–1980 was ten years old as of 1990. Under the guidance of Moslem fundamentalist Ayatollah Khomeini, Islam suddenly captured world attention. To understand why the revolution in Iran took place under the guise of religious fervor, it is necessary to examine the traditional role of religion in Iranian society and politics. Historically, the mosque has maintained a close contact with the Iranian masses. It has also served to articulate criticism against unpopular monarchs, as was the case in the late 1970s. Now that the Iranian Islamic Republic has a Constitution as well as a Parliament (the Majlis), the capacity in which this clergy has served is clear.

Never before in Iranian history had the clergy served in any executive capacity. The decentralized, informal hierarchy of Islam never provided for a clear-cut political framework. Finding a successor to Khomeini, who was the indisputable unifying force of the Iranian people, has already become an imminent problem.

It was not the clergy's Indo-European origins, to be sure, but the creed of Ithna 'Ashari Shi'ism that constituted the real difference between Khomeini's Iran and that of the Shah. Shi'is throughout the centuries regard as usurpers all the successors of Mohammad, whether Arab caliphs or Persian and Arab monarchs, recognizing only the descendants of Ali's (Mohammad's cousin and son-in-law) line as the "infallible" and "sinless" Imams. There were twelve such Imams; Khomeini himself was said to be a temporary incarnation of the last Imam, pending the Imam's second coming on the last Day of Judgement as the "Mahdi," a messiah of the world, who would come to redeem the faithful.

In 1501 the Safavid dynasty established a new Iranian state and declared this Ithna 'Ashari form of Shi'ism to be the official religion of the state. But because Shi'i doctrine does not recognize temporal rulers as legitimate, it makes no separation between religion and politics. In this respect, Khomeini was at one with the founder of the Moslem Brotherhood, Hassan el-Banna, who said: "Islam is a home and a nationality, a religion and a state, a spirit and a word, and a book and a sword."

But the Shi'ite perception of that fundamentalism went even further in its scheme of things. The ideology of the Islamic Republic of Iran was born of an external as well as an internal dimension, as were the *Zahir* (exoteric) and *Batin* (esoteric) Shi'i precepts of this branch of Islam. The internal dimension is rooted in the Ithna 'Ashari Shi'i belief that Islam is an impetus for evolution. For centuries the Shi'ite sect of Islam had been the religion of dissent in Iran, with the clergy acting as the most vocal opponents of unpopular monarchs; and because of persecution suffered at the hands of the Sunnis, the concepts of martyrdom became deeply ingrained in the Iranian psyche. Externally, Shi'i Iran was regarded as fundamentally anti-Western; it was then exportable to all other Moslem states, primarily to all secular states in the region, whether to a pseudo-socialist state such as the Ba'athist regime in Iraq, or to military dictatorships using Islam as a pretext, such as Pakistan.

Khomeini had not only become leader of 100 million Shi'is in the world; he had been designated by the Ithna 'Ashari Shi'i theory of government as the leader of all the 800 million Moslems in the world, comprising both Sunnis and Shi'is. This precept was actually written into the Constitution of the Islamic Republic. Article 10 of that Constitution reads: "All Moslems form a single nation, and the Government of the Islamic Republic of Iran has the duty of formulating its general policies with a view to the merging and union of all Moslem peoples, and it must constantly strive to bring about the political, economic and cultural unity of the Islamic world."[11]

Particularly in foreign policy, this theocratic worldview amounted to a rejection of the contemporary international system as it existed. To deal with that system, however, Iran had brought about "a deliberate transformation of the major alignments of Iran's foreign relations as they existed previously."[12] According to R. K. Ramazani, Khomeini's worldview was based on six general principles: (1) no dependence on East or West, (2) a belief that the United States was the main enemy, (3) continuous struggle against the Zionist power, (4) the liberation of Jerusalem, (5) anti-imperialism, and most important of all, (6) support for all oppressed peoples everywhere, particularly for Moslems.[13] There was evidently an element of populism, even of socialism, in such references to oppressed peoples; and the Soviet Union was of course never depicted as negatively as the United States. While there may have been a convergence of views between Iran and the USSR in regard to the "imperialism" of the Western powers, the Soviet Union never considered itself culturally "antiwestern"—unlike Iran. Nor does Shi'ism acknowledge the Marxist division of the world into socialist and capitalist states; instead, it refers to the traditional Islamic division of the world into *dar al-Islam* (house of Islam) and *dar al-harb* (house of war).

But nowhere does Shi'ism apply more critically than in relation to the Arab states, and to those of the Gulf in particular; in the Iranian mind, these states had defected from true Islam. From the very outset, Ayatollah Montazeri, Khomeini's one-time religious successor, explained Iran's attitude to other Moslems as follows:

One of the characteristics of Iran's Islamic Revolution is that its mundane scope cannot be confined to certain geographical and continental areas. Indeed, our revolution is an Islamic revolution, not an Iranian revolution. . . . Final victory will be achieved when there is no trace of colonialism and exploitation left throughout the entire Islamic world. . . . All Muslims and defenceless persons in the world who are living under dictatorship and colonialism have certain expectations from the Muslim nation of

Iran, and our glorious revolution is duty-bound toward these people. The Iranian government and people, to the extent they can, must give material and psychological support and assistance to all freedom movements, especially to the Palestinian revolution.[14]

Clearly these remarks were made in the year of Khomeini's accession to power. In February 1979, Yasir Arafat, leader of the Palestine Liberation Organization (PLO) had been the first foreign dignitary to officially visit the Islamic Republic. Khomeini's good-will gesture to Arafat was to allow him to expropriate the vacated Israeli Embassy in Teheran.

However, when war broke out between Iran and Iraq in September 1980, this astute Palestinian leader suddenly found that he had to choose between his allegiance to the Arab nationalism of an emerging Iraq and his sympathy for the Islamic Revolution. It was not really a difficult decision for a Palestinian nationalist. Few Palestinians (except those who were rioting against Israeli administration in the Gaza Strip and the West Bank) were ever sympathetic to Iranian Shi'ism. Many Palestinians volunteered to fight on the Iraqi side; and it came as no surprise in the end when Arafat abandoned his short-lived alliance with Khomeini. Since then, the PLO has been in conflict with nearly all the fundamentalist Moslem groups. Khomeini belatedly realized that Arafat's objective chiefly lay in the creation of a secular Palestinian State. In Lebanon, for instance, pro-Khomeini Shi'i militiamen have been fiercely battling PLO forces; in early 1985 Shi'i forces loyal to the Lebanese Hizb'Allah (the Party of God) made an aborted attempt to destroy the PLO camps in the Beirut area. Throughout Lebanon, Hizb'Allah's exploits have included kidnappings of Americans and Europeans, suicide attacks, and hijackings (witness the case of the *Air Afrique* jet in which a French passenger was murdered in July 1987). At that time, the media reported that Khomeini "spends anywhere from $15 million to $50 million a year to finance Hizb'Allah activities in Lebanon."[15]

In addition to Lebanon, the Iranians were adroitly exploiting their kinship with the Shi'i minorities of the Gulf Arab states. These minorities constituted 30–40 percent of the population in Kuwait, 30 percent in Dubai, and 20 percent in Qatar. More important to Teheran are the Gulf States, where the Shi'is either constitute one-half of the population or form an actual majority but are living under a Sunni government: 50 percent in Oman, 60 percent in Iraq, 75 percent in Bahrain. In Lebanon, Shi'is today are more numerous than Sunni Moslems and Maronite and Orthodox Christians. To all these Shi'i elements Iran had made repeated calls to rise in revolt against their "illegitimate" Sunni governments.

The subversive methods employed by Iran became the subject of the world's headlines. In some Gulf States, agents of the Islamic Republic set up secret cells known as "Hussainiyyas" that masqueraded as religious study groups. Sometimes they went unnoticed, escaping the vigilant eye of the local police; sometimes they were detected by the Arab security agencies and suppressed. Iran was already on record for trying to overthrow the Bahrein government in December 1981, and it was responsible for an abortive coup in Qatar in the autumn of 1983. In September 1982 an Iranian Shi'i leader, Hujjat Al-Islam Musavi Khuayni, led a group of Shi'is to Mecca during the ceremonial *Hajj* and publicly announced that his goal was to dispose of the "corrupt" Saudi royal family. A much larger variation on the same theme occurred in the first week of August 1987, when thousands of Iranian pilgrims rioted and attempted to seize the Sacred Mosque at Mecca; their aim was to topple the Sunni-ruled kingdom and proclaim Khomeini the leader of all Islam. The bid was foiled by Saudi security forces (possibly with the assistance of U.S. military and naval intelligence); but the event left well over 400 persons dead. Moreover, Saudi-Iranian relations had soured to the point where the Saudis, helpless and bewildered, decided it was time to cut all diplomatic ties with Teheran.

Not surprisingly, the most novel aspect of the Iranian Revolution (aside from the Soviet invasion of Afghanistan, that is) is that it inflicted the final blow to CENTO—an alliance as we observed earlier, about which the Shah had so many misgivings. The threat of an exportable Ithna 'Ashari Shi'i led to the establishment in 1981 of the Gulf Cooperation Council (GCC), a kind of collective security belt composed of Saudi Arabia, Bahrein, Oman, Kuwait, Qatar, and the United Arab Emirates. The GCC's defense budget rose above $40 billion per year. This figure included U.S. AWAC planes and other sophisticated military equipment totalling more than half of what the whole Third World earmarks for defense spending. But this whole outlay was still no deterrent to the Iranian threat: The only state really concerned over it was Israel, not Iran. Arguably the only viable deterrent against Iran in the Gulf region was and remains the U.S. Rapid Deployment Joint Task Force (RDF), which, in January 1983, was renamed the U.S. Central Command, or USCENTCOM—with a power-projection second only to NATO in Europe.[16]

What is surprising, however, was Iran's relationship with Syria, an Arab country ruled by Moslem Alawites who trace their allegiance to Ismailism, one of the offshoots of the Shi'i movement. Syrian Alawites therefore had had more affinity with the Shi'is in Iran than with Sunni

Arabs elsewhere. But Syria is, above all, a nationalist Arab country ruled by a single-party Ba'athist regime. No doubt, too, Syria's rivalry with Iraq brought it closer to Iran and, together with Libya, it was the only Arab country supporting the Iranian war effort. Many were of the opinion that Iran maintained friendly ties only with those Arab countries that belonged to the "rejectionist front" in relation to Israel. This is still the case. But the Syrian-Iranian relationship cannot be that easily pigeonholed. Syria, after all, has had its own problems with Moslem fundamentalists such as the Moslem Brotherhood. Why then should Syria, both when the war was going in Iran's favour and, later, when Iranian fortunes were down, have wanted a fundamentalist regime in Iraq? The Syrians themselves had fought and reportedly cleared the Bekaa Valley of Khomeini supporters[17]—namely, the members of the Hizb'Allah Party. In mid-August 1987, in a conciliatory gesture toward the United States, the Syrians helped free the U.S. journalist, Charles Glass, from his Shi'i kidnappers. This is not to say that Hafez Assad of Syria would suddenly have changed sides in the Gulf War on the grounds of a belated recognition of commitment to the Arab cause. His ties with Iran had been of a purely practical nature: Syria was receiving special concessions on oil purchases in Iran.

Indeed, now that the Gulf War is over, Syria may be loosening its ties with Iran. First there is the lingering problem that rival Shi'ite militias battled for West Beirut's southern slums. With its proxy, the Pro-Syrian Shi'i Terrorist Group (Amal), Syria was trying to gain control of these southern suburbs in order to maintain credibility in Lebanon, a country Damascus has thus far considered well within its sphere of influence. But Iran, even after the war with Iraq, may be all the more determined to support Hezbollah, the only organization that had gained a significant foreign foothold for Iran's Iranian Revolution. If that support should come to pass, Syria and Iran could come to a complete parting of the ways. Syria may even be compelled to use the same scorched-earth tactics it employed to quell fundamentalist dissenters in Hamra, inside Syria, where, when it all ended, 15,000 people were murdered by Syrian government troops.

THE GULF WAR

The most dramatic impact on Iranian foreign policy was the seemingly endless war with Iraq. After eight years this war has exceeded in casualties all the Arab-Israeli wars combined, ranking sixth in terms of damage and death among all interstate wars in the world since 1815. Iraq started the conflict with a preemptive strike in September 1980, but it also came about because Iran called on the Shi'is in Iraq to revolt and overthrow the Ba'ath Government and the ruling *Tekriti* clique of Saddam Hussein. The Voice of Revolutionary Iran often exhorted the more than 5 million sons of Ali to rise up against the sons of Yazid, invocations reminiscent of Iranian propaganda at the time of the Shah. Financial assistance was sent to the *al-Da'wa* underground Shi'i movement in Iraq, and in 1980 members of this group tried to assassinate Tariq Aziz, Iraq's foreign minister. All the Arab Gulf States that were bankrolling Iraq (primarily Saudi Arabia and Kuwait) and those that sent pilots and arms (Jordan and Egypt) also became the targets of Iran's fury. Thus the war was not confined to the battlefields along their common border but, rather, was carried on by proxy to Lebanon, Abu Dhabi, Turkey, Libya, and even Paris and London.

In the meantime, the Saudis and their Arab allies were coordinating their OPEC oil-price stance at meetings of the Arab League heads-of-government, where Iran was repeatedly condemned for occupying Iraqi territory. At the important Arab summit in Algiers in June 1988, the leaders declared that the 21-member Arab league was in total solidarity with Iraq and its defense of its national territories. Alone among the Arabs, Syria raised an objection to qualify its posture; but it did so rather mildly.

In a certain sense, until 1990 Iran had little dialogue, and little diplomacy for that matter, with any Arab states except Libya, Algeria, and Syria. Its ties with Pakistan were tenuous at best; and it tolerated but never actually recognized the Soviet-supported Marxist regime in Afghanistan. Although there are many Shi'ites living in Afghanistan's border region of Herat, the population of Afghanistan is for the most part Sunni. In the eighteenth century the Iranian Safavid dynasty was temporarily overthrown by an invasion of Afghans who tried to impose Sunnism on Iran—an event that was not forgotten by the current Shi'i leadership who regarded the Afghan refugees in Iran as third-class citizens. Relations with Afghanistan have nevertheless been improving as a result of the proposed new rail links and out of gratitude for the Afghan manpower that had freed many able-bodied Iranians for the war. When all Soviet troops are finally withdrawn from Afghanistan, it is likely that Iran will play a more important role in Afghan affairs and acquire a new market for its goods. But it is wrong to believe that the Shi'i regime was incapable of evolution from within or impervious to change from without. Let us examine the evidence.

First, the internal situation in Iran was never an optimistic one. There was high inflation; rampant corruption had reached an intolerable level; food, fuel, and electricity were in short supply; and defections and treason in the military were numerous. The general dissatisfaction with the war was obvious, although by the summer of 1988, even as events were taking a bad turn, the Iranian Central Bank still had more than $5.1 billion in foreign reserves with which to finance the war and import consumer goods. But oil revenues go up and down as the international market dictates. For Iran this was not good; as the only pariah in the region, it could obtain nothing on credit. Second, Iraq's superiority over Iran in military hardware was and still is approximately 5 to 1. Third, there was and still appears to be a fierce power struggle in the government between moderates and hardliners, between the supporters of the deposed Ayatollah Montazeri (who was supported in 1986 by Hashemi and the Revolutionary Guards) and Hojatolislam Hashemi Rafsanjani (the speaker of the Parliament). After the revelations and scandal that erupted in connection with the secret McFarlane mission to Teheran in 1986 and indirect bargaining with the United States and Israel for necessary military equipment and spare parts, the more moderate Rafsanjani publicly declared:

> There are at present two relatively powerful factions in our country with differences of view on how the country should be run and on the role of the government and that of the private sector in affairs. These two tendencies also exist in the Majlis, in the government, within the clergy, within the universities and across society as a whole. . . . They may in fact be regarded as two parties without names.[18]

Finally, in 1986 there were many in Teheran who felt that for the sake of the war some secret accommodation might be reached with the United States out of sheer necessity. But Khomeini reacted angrily and began supporting the hardliners in this internal struggle. Although he was visibly ailing, Khomeini was quite capable throughout 1987 of running the whole country. His will was obeyed.

Not fanaticism, to be sure, but an astute example of histrionics is what grandiloquently characterized the Shi'i riots in Mecca in the summer of 1987. No doubt Khomeini mounted this spectacle to deflect public opinion from the internal problems and to help cement the unity of the country. His behaviour in effect exemplified the Iranian way of dealing with crisis management; it was every bit a part of Iranian statecraft that had never been discarded. Propaganda created in the public mind a chronic sense of crisis during the Mecca pilgrimage. Then the State showed its mettle and determination by taking bold and decisive actions (i.e., war games in the Gulf code-named "martyrdom") displaying its own kind of brinkmanship. According to a prominent Western observer, "the revolutionary regime in Teheran aspires, as did the Shah before it, to be recognized as the dominant power of the region. . . . Iran's tactical performance has been shrewd and tough. The new regime has used whatever leverage available to seize the initiative and to keep its many adversaries off balance."[19] Interestingly, most other Western commentators, who persistently ignored the relationship between internal conditions and external actions, seemed to believe that when Iran acted pragmatically it acted realistically, adopting a pro-Western, pro-U.S. attitude. That is how Rafsanjani's pro-U.S. lobby was usually explained. But the only noticeable pragmatism that one was able to detect among the Iranians is the ability to play one power off against another—a constant in the behaviour of any small, Third-World nation, so often subordinated to foreign influences and powers in the past.

Teheran had astutely signed an important trade pact that included a sizeable arms deal with China for the sale of tanks, planes, Silkworm missiles, and spare parts. It was a desperate move because no one seemed to be willing to sell the Iranians weapons any more. A new period of friendliness toward Moscow commenced around the beginning of 1987. But the turning point did not come until February 1986, with the arrival in Teheran of Georgi Kornienko (First Deputy Foreign Minister) to begin talks on natural gas deliveries and to establish an Aeroflot route between the Iranian capital and Moscow. That visit was reciprocated by the Iranian Foreign Minister, Ali Akbar Velayati, in February 1987. Amid the upheavals of August 1987, Soviet Deputy Minister Yuli Vorontsov visited Teheran and asked that Iran stop obstructing the search for a negotiated settlement of the Afghan crisis. He intimated that the USSR, in return, would not support a United Nations resolution that would impose sanctions or a global arms embargo against Iran if the latter failed to observe a cease-fire in the Iran-Iraq War. Considering that, four years before, Iran had suppressed the Communist Tudeh Party, jailing or executing the local Communist leaders, this rapprochement with Moscow came as a surprise. Warming up to the Soviets allowed Iran to procrastinate on any new UN Security Council resolution and Secretary-General Perez de Cuellar's efforts to end the war.[20] For as long as it could, Iran tried to continue the war for both national and religious reasons, and accordingly did not want to be cut off from potential arms suppliers. The Soviet news agency, TASS, repeatedly announced that "Moscow and Teheran are mutually concerned over the unprecedented buildup of the U.S. military presence in the region." And, if anything, Moscow reacted strongly to the Iraqi resumption of the tanker war in the fall of 1987.

Iran and the Soviet Union then began to reopen oil pipelines, and their talks centered on building a second rail link from Iran to Soviet Central Asia. Because of the Gulf War, Iran expanded port facilities at

Bandar Abbas and Shah Bahar. Teheran even took up the Pahlavi monarch's railway schemes and expressed an interest in establishing a rail link to Bandar Abbas, from either Kerman or the Gulf Command (BAFQ), over a distance of roughly 750 kilometers. (Work is currently moving ahead along the Bam-Shur Gaz alignment toward Zaheday.[21]) Again, as in the days of the Shah—though not for the same reasons— this rail link was probably motivated by the prospect of geostrategic expedience, the object being to bring Iran closer to an Asian infrastructure and to Asian markets rather than to the West, thus utilizing to its fullest the advantages of its geographical location. Iran may have been turning in 1987 toward the USSR for another reason as well: Over the previous five years Pakistan had received more than $3 million in U.S. military and economic aid, thereby becoming the most important U.S. ally in Southwest Asia. There was some talk that Pakistan was toying with the possibility of giving up the U.S. air bases in Pakistan's province of Baluchistan, together with the use of port facilities near Karachi.[22] In such a scenario Pakistan would likely emerge as something of a proxy fighting force in the Gulf, and a vital link in the entire USCENTCOM defense perimeter—an outcome that would further threaten the basic commitments of the Iranian Revolution. (For these and many other reasons it came as no surprise to anyone when Rafsanjani met and spoke with Gorbachev in Moscow in June 1989, so soon after Khomeini's death.)

Yet not all Iranians reacted in this way toward Pakistan. Many moderates felt that, precisely because of Pakistan's growing importance to the region, and partly because Pakistan now possessed the bomb, there ought to be some sort of partnership between Islamabad and Teheran. True, Pakistan is Sunni and Iran is Shi'ite. But the "creature" of the "Great Satan" (a title ascribed to Pakistan by Iran, given its relations with the United States) is a country that is more like the Middle East than the Indian subcontinent. True, many Pakistanis living near Iran's border speak Farsi and are curiously drawn to the splendour of a superior Persian culture. These Iranians have reasoned that Pakistan's contribution to a powerful Pakistan-Iran, Moslem non-Arab axis would be technological expertise. But this assistance related to the war effort against Iraq, an effort that, in view of U.S. support for Iraq, was already beginning to fall apart in early 1988. With it went the fortunes of war, as well as Shi'i supremacy in the whole region.

THE UNITED STATES SIDES WITH THE ARABS

On the one hand, the U.S. Government had maintained a strict neutrality in this conflict from the very start. U.S. public opinion, on the other hand, was anti-Iranian all along. Still fresh in the United States was the memory of nightly television coverage of surging anti-U.S. crowds during the early days of the revolution when the Iranians, breaching international law and protocol, held U.S. Embassy personnel as hostages for more than a year. But faced with the likelihood of an Iranian victory spilling over into the friendly Arab States of the Gulf, U.S. officials began to take better stock of the situation. Moreover, the leaders of the six-nation Gulf Cooperation Council, which met in Riyadh in early January 1988, decided to coordinate their defense strategies and appealed to the Americans for help.

There was an all-out panic in the Gulf when Iran began launching Chinese-built Silkworm missiles against Kuwait, a member of the GCC. At the GCC summit, King Fahd of Saudi Arabia reportedly said that the Iranians "were pointing their arrows to our chests instead of helping us to liberate Jerusalem from Zionist domination. There is no reasonable justification for this other than the desire for expansion."[23] The situation was becoming so serious that the GCC raised the possibility of direct Egyptian military assistance in the wake of a new solidarity between Egypt and the Arab states.[24]

It seemed that the whole world was ostracizing Iran for not complying with UN Resolution 598, which called upon the belligerents to agree to a cease-fire. In late December 1987, all the members of the UN Security Council, including China and the Soviet Union, signed a statement saying they would impose an arms embargo if Iran did not comply; and work on a draft of the actual embargo resolution was expected to begin in late January 1988. But that never got anywhere; resolutions are only pieces of paper, and Iran was not fooled. Behind the scenes, the Soviet Union, making a bid to get into the act, issued a proposal to the Reagan Administration according to which both the Soviets and the Americans would enforce the embargo under UN auspices, primarily by blockading the entire Gulf region. The White House rejected the idea on the grounds that it involved an increased Soviet presence in the Gulf, thus possibly threatening U.S. interests. For their part, the Arabs would still have preferred stationing Egyptian troops; but Egypt, short of helping the Iraqis with pilot training, refused to have anything to do with the Gulf.[25]

It was at this point, in February 1988, that the U.S. Government, without making the issue formal and public, decided to throw in its lot with Iraq. The sequence of events that led me to this compelling conclusion is related as follows.

On several occasions in the 1980s President Saddam Hussein of Iraq expressed his interest in expanding diplomatic contacts with the United States. The Reagan Administration responded positively to these overtures, and in 1984 diplomatic relations were reestablished. Iraq was then immediately removed from the list of countries accused of aiding and abetting terrorism; and, without much further ado, such as criticisms within Congress, all U.S. restrictions on exports to Iraq were lifted. In fact, when the existence of Iraq as a state was at risk, Saddam Hussein made every effort to emphasize to the U.S. Government the value of his regime's survival. France, too, had been supporting the Iraqi war effort with *Etendard* fighter planes and had an interest in preventing an Iraqi military defeat. But it was the United States that was becoming Iraq's protector; there is sufficient evidence to suggest that, by 1984, Iraq was receiving intelligence information from U.S. satellites passing over the battlefronts and from Saudi Arabian AWACS. In a study likely to endure as the best of its kind on this subject, there are many direct and subtle references to this U.S. interference; nor is any evidence lacking in support of the argument that the Iraqis began using poison gas against the Iranian offensives as early as 1984, and then again in 1985 and 1986.[26] The UN Security Council was the first to condemn the use of chemical weapons by Iraq in 1986, even though Iraq was clearly on the defensive at that time.

Feeling emboldened, and with Egyptian backing (as well as Saudi and Kuwaiti financing), Saddam Hussein decided that Iraq should finally move to the offensive in early 1988. A conference debating this subject was actually held in Baghdad.[27] At the end of February, Iraqi Foreign Minister Tariq Aziz asked the United States to delay any diplomatic action designed to impose an arms embargo. Iraq then began pressing its "war of the cities" with constant missile barrages lasting from late February until mid-April. The demonstrated superiority in missile stockpiles during the last round of this exchange paid off for Iraq inasmuch as Iran stopped its own missile attacks on Baghdad and gave up the long-range artillery attacks against Basra, the Iraqi strategic city in the south that Iran had failed to capture in 1987 after several human-wave offensives that cost more than 80,000 lives. The next step in the Iraqi strategic plan was to launch a series of offensives in order to regain all the territory occupied by Iran. But this could not have been accomplished without careful military planning in logistics and intelligence-gathering, thus suggesting that Iraq could not have brought off its startling victories if the United States had not provided the Iraqi Army the necessary satellite intelligence that helped turn the tide against attacking Iranian forces. Surprisingly, the Iraqi ground attack aimed at regaining the Fao Peninsula coincided with the heaviest fighting between U.S. naval forces and Iran in the Gulf. While the Iraqis were recapturing the Fao Peninsula (on April 18, 1986), after only thirty-four hours of fighting, the U.S. Navy attacked two Iranian oil platforms, disabled two Iranian frigates, and sank at least four gunboats. While this was going on, Iran claimed that U.S. helicopters were helping Iraqi troops on Fao. Iran had indeed launched missiles against U.S. warships in what appeared to be a simultaneous two-front battle—one on land, the other at sea. From then on there followed a string of Iraqi attacks on Iranian positions, leading to the recapture on May 25 of Iraqi territory east of Basra near Shalamcheh after only nine hours of fighting, and to the recapture on June 25 of the oil-rich Majnoon islands after only eight hours of fighting.[28] Having pushed Iran from virtually all significant Iranian footholds in southern Iraq, the better-equipped, better-trained, and now more highly motivated Iraqi armed forces—spearheaded by the 90,000-man elite Republican Guard—had no problems in reconquering Iraq's northern Kurdish area, forcing back the last major concentration of Iranian troops, and liberating the Kurdish town of Halabja where the Iraqis resorted to chemical weapons. Thus all developments on the war front in 1988 favoured Iraq.

Realizing that a rapprochement with the Soviet Union was not enough, and that to win the war against Iraq, relations with the United States must somehow also be normalized and restored, the more moderate factions in Iran made repeated overtures to U.S. State Department officials in an effort to reestablish some relationship. This took place during the same six-month period in which U.S. policy was tilting toward Iraq, from about the end of December 1987 until just before the sad destruction of the Iranian airliner by the U.S. cruiser *Vincennes* in July 1988.

An intermediary in these Iranian initiatives, an Iranian-American scholar (identity unknown), maintained that there were three such probes made by Iran; the first two were rejected by suspicious U.S. officials in the State Department and the third overture simply collapsed. The *Los Angeles Times*, which had come to know about them, was soon able to report that: "the fruitless effort to establish a dialogue between the United States and Iran has been marked by misunderstandings, missed opportunities and suspicion on the part of American officials badly burned in the Iran-Contra scandal."[29]

U.S. government officials warned Teheran that because of former White House aide Oliver North's abortive negotiations with Iran in the past, any future dialogue could not remain confidential. The Iranians wanted to keep the talks secret. One of the contacts through the go-between was Iran's Deputy Foreign Minister himself, Mohammad Javad Larijani. But the Reagan Administration shrugged him off out of fear that he was acting on his own or as an ally of Hashemi Rafsanjani; he was not considered a representative of the entire Khomeini regime. Some months later, however, Rafsanjani became Commander-in-Chief

of the Iranian armed forces in addition to retaining his official title as
Speaker of Iran's Parliament. It seemed that U.S. decision-makers did
not wish to parley with the Iranians at all. Another envoy described
by the Iranian-American middleman was a confidential adviser to
Khomeini and Rafsanjani, a man referred to as "Rafsanjani's Kissinger."[30] He held a doctorate in political science from the Sorbonne; but,
as it happened, the Americans mistook him for an anti-Western radical
who had been expelled from France and refused to grant him a visa
to come to Washington. He, too, had been sent by Rafsanjani to open
a narrow channel of communication with the U.S. Government before
Khomeini died.[31]

This is not to say that the Reagan Administration never wanted to
parley with the Iranian regime. Rather, the question in the State Department, as well as on Capitol Hill, was *to whom* exactly should one
speak in Iran? The Iran-Contra scandal revealed altogether too well
how Reagan and his security advisers had wanted to do something for
Iran in 1985–1986, when a working relationship with Iranian moderates
resulted in the United States' delivery of arms to Iran in exchange for
hostages. Doing business of this type ended in disaster, shaking the
U.S. security establishment to it foundations and making a mockery of
U.S. policies that tried to buy the good will of the Iranians by rewarding
kidnappers with secret ransom.

A CRITIQUE OF U.S. POLICIES IN THE GULF

My general conclusion regarding U.S. involvement in the Gulf is
that, at best, it was hazardous (witness the problems associated with
escorting Kuwaiti oil tankers out of the Gulf and sweeping the waters
for mines laid by Iran); and, at worst, it was a dangerously irresponsible
policy.

The Gulf and the narrow Strait of Hormuz are not U.S. waterways:
They are sea-lanes leading to the Indian Ocean. In the crucible of war
that pitted Iran against Iraq, a number of things went wrong that ought
not to have embroiled the U.S. Navy at all. The argument that the
Americans were protecting the Southern Gulf's Arab Sheikdoms is, to
my mind, not a convincing one; nor is the argument that without
USCENTCOM's presence, (note that $20 million a month was being
spent for the Gulf deployment) the Soviets would have seized the oil
fields and warm-water ports of the Gulf.

The U.S. naval presence in this region was well beyond that maintained by any other nation. At this writing, the U.S. deployment consists
of one command ship, four destroyers or frigates, one cruiser, and four
escorts for the cruiser. There is also an aircraft carrier group from

Diego Garcia in the Indian Ocean in case of an emergency requiring
sustained air support. The French, the British, and the Italians are
there in far reduced numbers. By contrast, the Soviets, in this decade
and in the last, have had no large warships in the Gulf at all, save one
or two frigates for reconnaissance to monitor U.S. activities and for
minesweeping operations, although most of Iraq's weapons were Soviet-
built and sold by the Soviet Union.

By early 1988 the Gulf War had already taken on aspects of a high-
speed, high-tech video game. In order to protect the sea-lanes and
those reflagged Kuwaiti tankers, U.S. men-of-war challenged unidentified
boats and aircraft almost daily. These warships forced them to state
their intentions, warning that failure to do so would put their aircraft
at great peril. That became the essence and justification of U.S. defensive
measures. And that precisely was what had happened to the Iranian
jet liner with civilian passengers on board, an aircraft that was following
a regular flight and flying within its own air corridor.

The "Aegis System," an ultra-sophisticated, electronic command and
control system, which the cruiser *Vincennes* was using to detect the
civil jet transport, mistook it for a hostile Iranian F-14 jet fighter and
shot it out of the sky. Americans, afterward, asked themselves what
had gone wrong with the Aegis system. This was America's reply to
the consequences of a tragic accident. President Reagan himself stated
in no ambiguous terms that the U.S. Navy's error in shooting down
the airliner was somewhat more reasonable than the Soviet mistake in
shooting down a Korean passenger airliner in 1983.[32] The U.S. Government was spending billions of dollars on exotic weapons of dubious
technical capability, and very few in the Administration could bring
themselves to acknowledge not only that a U.S. "star-wars-at-sea" ar-
mada should be brought into question but also that the moral standards
of U.S. involvement were seriously flawed, that U.S. policies in the Gulf
were awkward and incoherent.

Worse still, George Bush, just three and a half months away from
election, called Iran a "barbaric nation" at the UN's Security Council
in the aftermath of the tragedy designed to determine the extent of
U.S. responsibility. *New York Times* columnist William Safire explained
away the *Vincennes* captain's decision to fire the missiles as the only
possible course of action in view of the stressful "pucker factor" that
he was supposedly subjected to—mindful, no doubt, of the 37 American
sailors who died when the frigate *Stark* was accidentally attacked by
an Iraqi jet in 1987.[33] Even conspiracy theorists blamed Iran for the
air disaster, morbidly suggesting that the Iranian aircraft had been
stuffed with naked bodies and then aimed toward the *Vincennes* in a
bid to get itself shot down, Kamikaze-fashion.[34] Another far-fetched

theory was advanced by Neil Livingstone, president of the Institute of Terrorism and Subnational Conflict, who said that the Iranians had actually "doctored the crash site to produce quick, vivid pictures."[35] This psychology was clearly the reflection of a decade-long antipathy for Iran among the American general public—an antipathy triggered by the irrational seizure of 50 U.S. Embassy personnel in Teheran back in 1979, during an ordeal that lasted 444 days.

IRAN PURSUES THE PRAGMATIC LINE

To be sure, the predictable cries for revenge reverberated across Iran. But despite the air tragedy, Iranian leaders never ruled out the possibility of accepting UN Resolution 598. Iran simply could not confront the U.S. fleet directly. Moreover, Rafsanjani showed extraordinary restraint in his public pronouncements after the tragedy. In an attempt to break out of Iran's international isolation, Rafsanjani set about garnering sympathy for the Iranian cause as the victim of U.S. aggression, saying that Iran had often made enemies needlessly. At the same time a friendly gesture that had been cut short by the aircraft disaster was eagerly being pursued: improved contact with the West, notably Britain and France. Then, on July 18, 1988, came another surprise: Iran finally accepted the terms of the UN Resolution 598. Within a matter of hours the Iranian leadership announced the resumption of diplomatic relations with Canada—relations that had been severed for eight years.[36] Renewing its relationship with Canada was widely seen as an effort by Teheran to negotiate with the United States.

At this point we should stop and ask ourselves, What combination of forces was at work that prompted Iran to comply with the cease-fire resolutions and bring an end to the war? Was it Khomeini's impending death? Was it entirely due to Iraq's battle successes on the ground and the Iranian public's lack-lustre support for Khomeini's war effort? Could one not point to a delaying tactic by Teheran's leadership? Certainly U.S. Administration officials could gloatingly claim that Iran's turnabout vindicated the decision by both Washington and the other Western naval powers to build up their Gulf fleets.

But there was no longer any doubt about Iranian intentions when Khomeini himself made the decision to extricate his country from the war. "Making this decision was more deadly than drinking poison," the Imam reportedly said. According to U.S. intelligence sources, on the evening of July 16, 1988, there was a meeting in Teheran of senior political officials, including Montazeri, Rafsanjani, Prime Minister Mir Hussein Moussavi, and Ahmed Khomeini, the Ayatollah's oldest son. Montazeri supported Rafsanjani, recommending that, in the interests of the revolution, the elder Khomeini should confirm the Iranian leadership's agreement to a cease-fire. Khomeini's announcement was welcomed in every Arab capital of the Middle East, but with caution. Only Israel voiced misgivings about an end to the fighting between its two implacable foes, Iraq and Iran.

It seemed unlike Iran to suddenly want to put an end to the war. Moreover, if Iran needed a respite—which many Arab leaders claimed it did—this was a sure way of getting it. Even while negotiations were proceeding as to the type of UN-monitored cease-fire to be put in place, it did not take long for hostilities to break out again, and the din of battle did not subside until the two countries felt they had gained enough leverage in the peace negotiations. In a keynote address to the Iranian Parliament, Rafsanjani at one point actually raised the somewhat ambiguous prospect of a new relationship with the United States, suggesting that Iran would be willing to help secure the release of nine American hostages held by pro-Iranian factions in Lebanon. That too could be interpreted as another overture to Washington, although it was qualified with the request that the Americans release Iranian assets held in the United States for a decade, including $400 million worth of armaments left undelivered to Iran during that period. This might be seen as a clear illustration that, despite all the rhetoric about the "Great Satan," it would prove wise for Iran to seek some accommodation with the United States—if only because it is the leader of the Western world. But it is still far too early to conclude whether a lasting peace with Saddam Hussein's Iraq is something Iran will take seriously. Nor is it timely to assess the impact of the Iranian Revolution on the future course of events in the Gulf and on Soviet-Iranian relations, let alone the impact it might have on any foreseeable Shi'i expansionism after Khomeini's death and following a period of internal economic reconstruction and political soul-searching.

Let me conclude by saying that Iran's threat to its neighbouring Gulf States has always been something of an exaggeration. With U.S. support, the combined effort of CENTCOM and the Gulf Cooperation Council was enough to deter any exalted Iranian adventurism or alleged Soviet ambitions in the Gulf. The United States has in the last few years encouraged joint exercise and joint defense efforts by the Gulf Cooperation Council. Saudi Arabia has an AWAC-supported air defense system to defend itself. In addition, the Reagan Administration had bolstered Turkey's defenses by helping that country—and $7 billion a year is no small sum—to modernize its airfields and to build new ones at Batman and Mus in Eastern Anatolia. Thus NATO contingencies were now likewise tied to the security of the Gulf region. Apparently—and here is the rub—Washington did not believe that all these measures were quite enough to deter Iran's continued advance in Iraq in 1987; otherwise it would not have lent significant support to Iraq in 1988.

One question regarding military tactics still lingers in my mind, however: Why did Iran not try to open another front against Iraq by attacking that country from across the Syrian border, to which Iraq had sent only 100,000 troops, a number insufficient to hold down a massive attack over very extensive lines of communication? The Iraqis would have been overwhelmed and forced to shift fresh troops from the south to that new and far weaker front.

A more rational player in such a game of power politics and regional alliances, when the stakes are stacked against it, would not have eschewed military cooperation with a state like Israel, whose enemies have traditionally been the same as Iran's: In vain the Israelis made several overtures to the Iranians to assist in the struggle against Iraq. The Israelis had always attempted to form something of a tacit Israel–Iran–Saudi Arabia alliance, trying to involve the less credulous Americans in this scheme. Back in October 1982 then Israeli Ambassador to the United States, Moshe Arens, long before the "Irangate" scandal burst forth on the world, informed the press that Israel was providing arms to Iran "in coordination with the U.S. government"—in the hope of establishing relations with Iranian officers who would carry out a military coup, or who might be in a position of power in Iran during the post-Khomeini succession.[37] In this way, the Israelis, ever concerned about the outcome of the Iran-Iraq War, helped keep channels open to moderate or pragmatic elements in Iran among both the clerics and the military—elements who might one day overthrow or inherit the power of the Shi'i leadership.

Yet the Iranians—too principled, too fanatical, often irrational, and equally distrustful of the Zionist state—just could not bring themselves to make a pact with another devil, and, with little material wherewithal to achieve their goals, they made enormous and, in the end, needless, human sacrifices, without gaining much either for their ideology or for their revolution.

NOTES

1. The Reza Shah period in Iran's history is far more controversial than that of his son, Mohammad Reza Shah. Both Western and Iranian studies on this subject are extremely poor, whereas Soviet writings have proven to be more objective.

2. Reza Shah was basically illiterate and spent most of his time grooming an army, suppressing internal orders, and appropriating feudal estates.

3. For a full account of Teymourtash, see Miron Rezun, "Reza Shah's Court Minister: Teymourtash," *International Journal of Middle Eastern Studies*, No. 12, 1980, pp. 119–137. See also Miron Rezun, *The Soviet Union and Iran*, Sijthoff Leiden, The Netherlands, 1981. (This book was reissued by Westview Press in 1988.)

4. Miron Rezun, op. cit., 1981, pp. 139–140.

5. Ibid. See the last chapter in this book as well as Miron Rezun, *The Iranian Crisis of 1941*, Böhlau Verlag, Vienna/Cologne, 1982.

6. The forerunner of the Baghdad Pact was the Saadabad pact of 1937 in which the Arabs were not represented at all, although at the time Iraq (Mesopotamia) was a British protectorate.

7. Fred Halliday, *Iran, Dictatorship and Development*, Penguin Books, Middlesex, England, 1979, p. 279.

8. Milan Hauner, "The USSR and the Indo-Persian Corridor," *Problems of Communism*, January–February 1987, pp. 29–30.

9. Iran sent more than thirty Chinook helicopter gunships to the Pakistani armed forces. It also provided logistic support.

10. Fred Halliday, op. cit., p. 269.

11. Hamid Algar (trans.), *Constitution of the Islamic Republic of Iran*, Mizan Press, Berkeley, 1980, p. 31.

12. W. G. Millward, "The Principles of Foreign Policy and the Vision of World Order Expounded by Imam Khomeini and the Islamic Republic of Iran," in Nikki R. Keddie and Eric Hooglund (eds.), *The Iranian Revolution and the Islamic Republic*, Yale University Press, New Haven, 1982, p. 189.

13. R. K. Ramazani, "Khomeini's Islam in Iran's Foreign Policy," in K. Dawisha (ed.), *Islam in Foreign Policy*, Cambridge University Press, Cambridge, 1983, p. 21.

14. *Iran Voice*, September 3, 1979, p. 1.

15. *Time*, August 17, 1987.

16. CENTCOM is intended to be on a par with NATO in Europe and with CINCPAC (Commander-in-Chief, Pacific Fleet, the American alliance) in the Pacific. As of 1990, it can land an intervention force of 450,000 troops in Southwest Asia.

17. At one time Menahem Begin of Israel was actually supplying arms to the Iranian Revolutionary Guards in the Bekaa Valley of Lebanon.

18. FBIS, South Asia, June 11, 1986; cited by Gary Sick, "Iran's Quest for Superpower Status," *Foreign Affairs*, Vol. 65, No. 4, Spring 1987, p. 704.

19. Ibid., p. 713.

20. UN Security Council Resolution 598, adopted on July 20, 1987, called for a cease-fire, an exchange of prisoners, and withdrawal of belligerents' forces to prewar boundaries.

21. See Milan Hauner, op. cit., p. 30.

22. See Lawrence Lifschultz, "From the U-2 to the P-3, . . ." *Commentary*, No. 3, 1982.

23. *Christian Science Monitor*, July 8, 1988.

24. *Time*, January 11, 1988.

25. The Gulf Cooperation Council broke with Egypt when Cairo and Tel-Aviv made peace in 1979. Only Oman maintained its links with Egypt.

26. Shahram Chubin and Charles Tripp, *Iran and Iraq at War*, Westview, Boulder, 1988.

27. *Time*, January 11, 1988.

28. *Christian Science Monitor*, July 8, 1982.

29. *Los Angeles Times*, July 7, 1988.

30. Ibid.

31. Ibid.

32. *The New York Times*, July 5, 1988.

33. *The New York Times*, July 7, 1988.

34. *San Francisco Chronicle*, July 8, 1988.

35. Ibid.

36. Canada's Ambassador to Iran in 1980, Ken Taylor, helped several U.S. Embassy officials escape the country. Iran thereafter broke off diplomatic relations with Canada and demanded an apology for the act. In 1988 the request for an apology was dropped.

37. For an interesting discussion of clandestine Israeli and U.S. activities in Iran, see Noam Chomsky, *The Culture of Terrorism*, Ch. 8, Black Rose Books, Montreal/New York, 1988.

2

Religious Dogma
and the Economic and Political
Imperatives of Iranian Foreign Policy

Roger M. Savory

INTRODUCTION

My main purpose in this chapter is to determine the underlying political and economic principles, or "imperatives," of Iranian foreign policy prior to the Iranian Revolution in 1979, what the imperatives have been since that time, and what degree of continuity or change there is between the two.

1. One point of view is that in Iran, the internal political situation and foreign policy go hand in hand. To a degree, of course, this is true of all countries, but it is true of Iran to an extreme degree. Restoration of self-respect abroad is inextricably interrelated to redefinition of self at home.[1]
2. Another view is that if internal conditions and the external environment cannot be placed in separate compartments in the formulation of Iranian foreign policy, neither can political imperatives and economic imperatives. The key to Persian independence was financial reform, which in turn presupposed administrative reform.[2]
3. Freedom of action in foreign affairs is seen by most Third World and developing countries as the *sine qua non* of political independence and sovereignty. This was the view of the late Shah of Iran,[3] and it is the view of the Khomeini regime.

Rouhollah K. Ramazani, in his two-volume study of Iranian foreign policy from 1500 to 1973,[4] detected a "tendency of its [Iran's] policy

35

makers to adopt objectives beyond their means."⁵ From the sixteenth
to the eighteenth centuries, "policy makers" meant, in effect, the shah,
who played a dominant role in foreign policy decisions. In the nineteenth century, this situation changed little. In other words, foreign
policy–making in Iran, until the Constitutional Revolution of 1906–
1907, was merely an extension of the power of the shah. "The means
[of attaining foreign policy objectives] most often preferred was war,
whether it was motivated by religious dogmatism, by irredentism and
expansionism, or by the desire to restore or defend the independence
of the state with which the monarch and his dynasty were closely
identified."⁶ However, "losing wars in pursuit of hopeless objectives"
constitutes "unrealism,"⁷ and Ramazani's definition of a "good" foreign
policy is "a rational foreign policy directed toward good ends."⁸ It was
not until the time of Reza Shah that "a concept of national interest"
developed.⁹ The extent to which "unrealism" has been a factor in the
formulation of Iranian foreign policy, in the realms of both politics and
economics, will be discussed later. First, for assistance in identifying
the imperatives that have informed Iranian foreign policy, we shall
consider the following historical framework.

THE TRADITIONAL ISLAMIC ATTITUDE
TOWARD FOREIGN POLICY

Prior to the sixteenth century, the Islamic world, of which Iran was
and is a part, did not concern itself overmuch with foreign policy as
an important aspect of government. This attitude has its roots in the
Islamic dogma that the Islamic faith had superseded both Judaism and
Christianity and that the Islamic community (*ummah*), the only framework within which a Moslem could live his or her life to the fullest,
was "the best community that hath been raised up for mankind."¹⁰
Islam was the only path to salvation: "Whoso desires another religion
than Islam, it shall not be accepted of him; in the next world he shall
be among the losers."¹¹ These fundamental assumptions about the Islamic faith and community led logically to the formulation of the
traditional Moslem world-view, which divided the world into two blocs:

> The house of Islam (*dar al-islam*), where the true faith prevailed and the
> Muslim caliph ruled, and the house of war (*dar al-harb*), where unsub-
> jugated infidels still remained. Between the two there was a perpetual
> and inevitable state of war, which might be interrupted by a truce, but
> could never be ended by a peace. It would end only when the whole
> world was brought into the house of Islam.¹²

The great Moslem conquests of the first century of Islam confirmed, in the Moslem view, the correctness of these assumptions. When *dar al-islam* stretched from central Asia and India across the Middle East to North Africa and Spain, it seemed superfluous for Moslems to evince curiosity about the manners and customs of the infidels living beyond its borders. The Moslem *gazi* in Toledo who, in 1068, dismissed the Franks (Europeans) as "northern barbarians," merely reflected the view of the West commonly held by Moslems in medieval times. The need to have a foreign policy toward such barbarians hardly occurred to any Moslem ruler before the sixteenth century.[13]

This Islamic world-view, far from being the dead relic of a classical past, is alive and well in the thought and outlook of Imam Khomeini, the leader of the Islamic Republic of Iran. It underlies, for example, his disdain of international bodies such as the United Nations and the International Court of Justice at the Hague. Such institutions, being of Western provenance, are not only irrelevant to the world of Islam but, in Khomeini's view, constitute agencies of Western imperialism and are therefore inimical to the Moslem world and to the Third World in general. However, this has not prevented the Islamic Republic of Iran from appealing to the United Nations when it seemed to be in its interest to do so.

IRANIAN FOREIGN POLICY FROM
THE SIXTEENTH TO THE NINETEENTH CENTURIES

If "the Muslim Middle East nations . . . like other developing states, have only in recent times become acquainted with the very concept of "foreign policy,"[14] how and when did this occur? The realisation that diplomatic relations with non-Moslem powers had become imperative dawned first upon the Ottomans. This was only natural. The Ottomans, by their capture of the capital of eastern Christendom in 1453, had established themselves as the most powerful Islamic state in existence, and this status was confirmed by their decisive victory over Safavid Iran in 1514 and by their overthrow, a few years later, of the once formidible Mamluk state in Egypt and the Levant. The seventeenth century, however, radically changed this picture: It "began with a concession of equality; it ended with an admission of defeat. The second failure at Vienna in 1683 was followed by a series of military disasters; in the peace of Carlowitz, of 1699, the Ottoman Empire was compelled, for the first time, to sign a peace treaty on terms imposed by a victorious enemy."[15] Iran's case was different. At the beginning of the sixteenth century, the Safavids created a nation-state in Iran within Iran's traditional boundaries. Thus, for the first time in nine centuries,

Iran ceased to be merely a geographical entity forming part of a larger empire. The Safavids decreed that the Ithna 'Ashari form of Shi'ism should be the official religion of the new state. By so doing, they changed the whole course of subsequent Iranian history. Ithna 'Ashari tradition held that, in an Ithna 'Ashari state, the only legitimate form of governance was that of the Twelfth Imam, that of the Mahdi, or, in his continuing occultation, that of the *majtahids*, the most eminent scholars in Shi'i jurisprudence. The creation of an Ithna 'Ashari state thus institutionalized confrontation between the religious leaders and the shah, and set the stage for an eventual attempt by the religious leaders to seize political power. The religious leaders aspired to political as well as religious authority. Accordingly, as their political influence increased during the nineteenth century relative to that of the shah, Ithna 'Ashari ideology became one of the most important factors informing the internal political situation. Since one of the basic assumptions of this chapter is that the internal political situation and foreign policy go hand in hand, it follows that Ithna 'Ashari ideology increased in importance as one of the factors informing Iran's foreign policy.

When the Qajars emerged victorious from their half-century of civil war with the Zands and established a new ruling dynasty in 1796, they were obliged to acknowledge that, during Iran's preoccupation with its internal affairs, major changes had occurred in Iran's relations both with its neighbours and with European powers. During the first quarter of the eighteenth century, Tsar Peter the Great's incursions into northwestern Iran was a portent of things to come. Iran's territorial integrity had been temporarily restored by Nadir Shah, but the ill-conceived expeditions of Aqa Muhammad Shah Qajar into Georgia in 1795 and 1797 led to Russian intervention and to the eventual loss to Russia not only of Georgia but also of all former Iranian territory in the Caucasus south to the river Aras (which today forms the boundary between Iran and the Soviet Union). Iran, whether it liked it or not, was now caught in the middle of a power struggle between Russia and Great Britain—a struggle that was to continue until the end of World War II. Russia's goals were expansionist: to establish Russian control over Central Asia to the borders of Afghanistan, to ban the presence of Iranian naval vessels on the Caspian Sea, and to acquire a warmwater port on the Gulf. Britain's goals were defensive: to protect the British Empire in India from real or imaginary threats from Russia and to maintain Britain's position as "policeman" in the Gulf region. The defence of India necessarily cast both Iran and Afghanistan in the role of buffer states. Britain did not wish to go to the trouble and expense of occupying either country in order to enhance the security of India and, as a result, remained in a constant state of anxiety about the extension of Russian influence in both. Caught between Scylla and Charybdis, Iran now had an urgent need to formulate a consistent foreign policy. What were to be the imperatives of this policy?

THE POLITICAL IMPERATIVES
OF IRANIAN FOREIGN POLICY: 1800–1921

The dominant imperative of Iranian foreign policy was the need to preserve the independence of Iran as a sovereign nation in the face of political and economic pressure from Britain and Russia. In other words, it was a nationalist imperative. It seemed that a prerequisite for the preservation of this independence was the modernization of the army. When Napoleon's brief demonstration of interest in Iran came to an end with the withdrawal from Iran of the Gardane Mission in February 1809, Iran lost its best opportunity to modernize its armed forces. Two disastrous wars with Russia during the first quarter of the nineteenth century underline Iran's weakness. Devoid of military power, it adopted the only other alternative open to it: diplomacy. Mirza Taqi Khan, known as Amir Nizam or Amir Kabir, who was the chief minister (*yazir*) of Nasir al-Din Shah from 1848 to 1851, is credited with the formulation of the policy of "equilibrium." He tried to preserve Iran's independence by playing off Britain and Russia against each other, in both the political and the economic spheres. In the hands of weak shahs, however, this policy, "formulated initially to protect the interest of Iran . . . actually militated against those interests."[16] European powers imposed capitulations on Iran that represented a clear violation of Iran's status as a sovereign nation. These capitulations, extra-territorial rights for foreign nationals resident in Iran, were initially imposed on Iran by Russia, particularly by the terms of the Treaty of Turkomanchai (1828), but most other European powers followed Russia's lead.

In 1907 the policy of "equilibrium," designed to meet the need to preserve Iran's independence by playing off Russia against Britain, lay in ruins. The signing of the Anglo-Russian Convention in that year marked the first of two occasions in recent Iranian history on which this policy was vitiated by the decision of those two Great Powers to temporarily sink their differences over Iran. Iran was doubly a loser: Not only had its preferred foreign policy option been taken away from it, but the Convention left Iran at the mercy of one of the Great Powers concerned—namely, Russia. Britain had signed the Convention mainly in order to have its hands free to deal with rising German militarism; hence Britain regularly turned a blind eye to numerous and blatant violations of the terms of the Convention by the Russians, who from the outset treated the five northern provinces of Iran, which constituted the Russian zone, as an extension of Russian territory. The nationalist imperative underlying Iranian foreign relations remained the same but the policy of "equilibrium" was no longer available as a means of satisfying this imperative.

During World War I, Iran's sovereignty was again violated as its territory became the battlefield for Turkish, Russian, and British forces. The Bolshevik Revolution of 1917 and the subsequent withdrawal of Russia from the war[17] removed for a few years one of the two key players from the stage. The traditional foreign policy of Iran, the use of Britain and Russia as countervailing forces, still could not be employed; and Britain, in its turn, tried to take advantage of the situation in order to impose on Iran the Anglo-Iranian Treaty of 1919.[18] This Treaty, which was never ratified by the Majlis and was repudiated in 1921 by Reza Shah, was seen by the Iranians as a thinly disguised attempt to make Iran a British Protectorate.

As for the Russians, although the new Bolshevik Government, by the terms of the Soviet-Iranian Treaty of 26 February 1921, renounced the imperialist policies of the former Tsarist regime, it soon became clear that, as far as Iran was concerned, new Bolshevik was but old Tsarist writ large. Not only did the Bolsheviks land Red Army troops in Gilan and help to establish the Persian Socialist Soviet Republic of Gilan in 1920, but the notorious Article VI of the Treaty of Friendship between Persia and Russia (of 26 February 1921) gave Russia the right to move its troops back onto Iranian soil if Russia felt itself to be threatened by any Power operating from Iranian territory. Although this unrestricted right of sending Russian forces into Iran was subsequently restricted (in an exchange of notes between the Iranian Foreign Minister and the Soviet diplomatic representative in Tehran) to activities by "the partisans of the regime which has been overthrown" [i.e., the Tsarist regime] "or by its supporters," nevertheless Article VI remained a thorn in the flesh of Iranian governments for generations, and the Soviet Union not infrequently chose to ignore, or even to deny the existence of, the qualifying clauses.[19] The constant fear that the Soviet Union might, on the flimsiest of excuses, invoke the terms of the 1921 Treaty, henceforth became an Iranian nightmare.

If Iran were to satisfy the political imperative of maintaining its sovereignty, an alternative to the failed policy of "equilibrium" had to be found. The period between the granting of the Persian Constitution in 1906 and the coup d'etat by Reza Khan in 1921 marked the genesis of what later, under Reza Shah, became known as the "Third Power" policy. The objectives of this policy were twofold: On the political level, Iran's aim was to enlist the aid of a Third Power in the reconstruction of the Iranian economy. The criteria for selecting this Third Power were two: It should have no history of previous intervention in Iranian affairs, and it should be physically located as far as possible from Iran's borders. Iran's first choice as the Third Power was the United States, which satisfied the two criteria mentioned above. Morgan W. Shuster arrived in Tehran on 12 May 1911 as the chief of a U.S. financial mission. His service was abruptly terminated in December 1911 by direct Russian intervention.

THE ECONOMIC IMPERATIVES
OF IRANIAN FOREIGN POLICY: 1800–1921

Just as the principal imperative of Iranian foreign policy during this period was the maintenance of political independence, so the principal economic imperative was the desire to resist Western economic imperialism. The effect of Anglo-Russian rivalry on the Iranian economy during the nineteenth century was "stultifying."[20] It resulted in the "absence of railways and the smallness of the scale of the British, Russian and other enterprises in Iran."[21] Britain viewed Iran "as a glacis, to be kept denuded of any facilities which might make it easier for the Russians to advance through it to the subcontinent."[22]

As Charles Issawi points out, Iran was in a far less favourable position to resist Western economic imperialism than were other Middle Eastern countries. In countries such as Egypt and Turkey, for example, the fact that there was a multiplicity of Great Powers vying with one another "often reduced the total impact of the pressure."[23] Iran was at a disadvantage in many other respects, too. For example, its central government was weaker than that of Turkey and Egypt. Its military forces were weaker. Its administrative system was less efficient. Its fiscal system was more archaic. Its educational systems were less developed. Iran's non-Moslem minorities (Armenians, Jews, Nestorian Christians, and Zoroastrians) were few in number, "their cultural isolation was great, and their influence was too limited for them to play a major part in the economic and social development of the country."[24] In other countries of the Middle East, these non-Moslem minorities had had contact with Europe for centuries and, "as a consequence, (had) acquired a substantial amount of Western education and knowledge of Western commercial methods."[25] The unprecedented economic prosperity of Iran during the last quarter of the sixteenth century and the first quarter of the seventeenth, under Shah 'Abbas I, owed much to the commercial expertise of Jews at home and Armenians on the international scene.

Worse still, Iran's geographical location militated against its economic development in the nineteenth century. Communications overland through the Ottoman Empire, or by ship across the Caspian Sea and then by land across the Ukraine, were hazardous. Until the opening of the Suez Canal in 1869, trade by sea between Europe and Iran was not an economically sound proposition. The Gulf has been called "a most perverse and inconvenient piece of water," inasmuch as "it not only faces the wrong way; but it is on the wrong side of the Arabian peninsula. The sea mileage from anywhere in Europe to the head of the Persian Gulf is greater than to Bombay."[26] Moreover, Iran did not lie on the sea route from Britain to India.

Cumulatively, these disadvantages resulted in the "comparative neglect of Iran by European capital and enterprise and its far slower rate of development"[27] during the nineteenth century. The trade figures speak for themselves: "In 1913 Iran's total trade (imports plus exports) was estimated at $93 million, compared with $291 million for Egypt and $273 million for Turkey; on a per capita basis the figures were about $9, $24 and $15, respectively."[28]

During the second half of the nineteenth century, when the Great Powers began to involve themselves with Iran on the economic level, the nature of this involvement, because of the overriding imperative of Anglo-Russian rivalry, did not benefit Iran. Initially, Iran employed the same policy in an attempt to satisfy the economic imperative of resistance to Anglo-Russian economic imperialism—as had been used, with only moderate success, in an attempt to satisfy the political imperative of maintaining sovereignty and independence, namely, "equilibrium." Nasir al-Din Shah conceived the plan of encouraging European Powers to invest in Iran, his rather naive hope being that, once these powers had a stake in the economic prosperity of the country, they would contribute to its well-being. In practice, however, the policy of "equilibrium" meant that, whenever a concession was granted to either Britain or Russia, the other party would immediately demand a *quid pro quo*. The result was that, by the end of the nineteenth century, most of Iran's resources were being exploited or directed by foreign concessionaries who often obtained sweeping concessions in return for paltry sums of money, thus satisfying the shah's immediate needs. By 1906 the country was in debt to Russia in the amount of £7,500,000. The key concession had gone in 1901 to an Englishman, William Knox D'Arcy, in the form of an oil concession valid for sixty years and covering the whole country except the five northern provinces. Oil was first struck in 1908 and thereafter constituted the single most important source of revenue to the Iranian government. Great Britain now had a "vital interest" in Iran. In 1898 the Belgians had entered the race for concessions and, by 1901, had obtained a monopoly of all Iran's customs operations; this concession proved to be the most lucrative held by any foreign power up to that time. The concession from which Iran benefited the most during the nineteenth century was the Indo-European Telegraph Concession, granted to Britain in 1863: "The telegraph for the first time brought Persia into contact with Europe, with the result of making her a member of the comity of nations. . . . Whatever of civilisation, or reform, or regeneration has been introduced into Persia in the last quarter of a century . . . may indirectly be attributed to the influence of the telegraph."[29] No new concessions were granted to foreign powers after 1901. Although the economic benefits of the concessions had, for the most part, accrued to the country of origin of the concessionaries, and had not been integrated into a development programme, nevertheless "each of these concessions formed the basis for later sectoral advancement and general government finance which could probably not have been achieved by local entrepreneurial activity at all by means of purely domestic skills and enterprise."[30] Commercial development was hampered by the nonavailability of credit, and in 1920 Iran's total foreign debt still stood at £7 million.[31]

THE POLITICAL IMPERATIVES
OF IRANIAN FOREIGN POLICY: 1921-1979

On the night of 20 February 1921, Reza Khan, the 43-year-old commander of the Persian Cossack Brigade, and Sayyid Zia al-Din Tabataba'i entered Tehran at the head of 3,000 Cossack troops and executed a coup d'état. The alliance between the two men lasted no more than a hundred days. Reza Khan became Prime Minister in 1923 and, after having been frustrated by the opposition of the religious classes in his attempt to establish a Republic in Iran in 1924, had himself crowned in the spring of 1926 as the first ruler of the new Pahlavi dynasty.

It was obvious from the start that Reza Khan, later shah, was an uncompromising nationalist. One of his primary objectives was to free Iran from foreign domination, both political and economic. One of his first acts, in 1928, was to abolish unilaterally the hated capitulations that had constituted an infringement of Iran's sovereignty for exactly a century. Earlier, in 1922, he revived the Third Power policy, and again the United States was selected as a "distant and disinterested" party. From Iran's point of view, the United States seemed to be an even more promising ally than it had been in 1911. It had, for example, expressed its disapproval of the British action of preventing Iran from presenting a claim for reparations at the 1919 Paris Peace Conference.

It also had denounced the abortive 1919 Anglo-Iranian Treaty.[32] President Wilson seemed to be the champion of the rights of smaller nations against the Great Powers. On 18 November 1922, another U.S. financial expert, Arthur Millspaugh, arrived in Tehran and through an election was given wide powers by the Majlis to reform the financial administration. Millspaugh's personality was incompatible with that of the shah, and there was a parting of the ways in 1927. As Reza Shah put it succinctly: "There is only one Shah in Iran, and I am going to be the Shah."

The second failure of the "American option" led Reza Shah to make the (as it turned out) fatal choice of Germany as a "distant and disinterested" power. The overt German diplomatic offensive in Iran from the beginning of World War I (an offensive designed to persuade Iran to enter the war on the side of the Central Powers) and the covert operations of German agents in Iran and Afghanistan (such as Hans Wassmuss, Friedrich Zugmayer, and Hans Niedermayer) had predisposed many Iranian politicians in favour of Germany. Moreover, Germany offered Iran an opportunity to escape from economic domination by the Soviet Union. Along with Reza Shah's attempts to develop an industrial infrastructure in Iran went a policy of gradually replacing the Soviet Union with Germany as Iran's principal trading partner. Prior to World War I, two-thirds of Iran's trade had been in Russian hands. It continued to be about one-third until 1938–1939, when it fell sharply to 11.5 percent. By contrast, Germany's share of Iran's trade rose from 8 percent in 1932–1933 to 45.5 percent in 1940–1941.

When World War II broke out in 1939, Iran saw no immediate need to change its foreign policy, particularly as Germany, until at least 1942, appeared to be winning the war. Reza Shah failed, however, to react quickly enough to the dramatically changed situation brought about by the German invasion of the Soviet Union in June 1941. The refusal of Reza Shah to expel the German agents operating in Iran under the leadership of Franz Mayr was made the justification for the occupation of Iran in August 1941 by British and Soviet troops.[33] Germany's Third Power relationship with Iran came to a sudden end, and once again, as in 1907, Iran's two principal enemies, Britain and Russia, were acting in collusion with each other to the detriment of Iran, thereby once more destroying the possibility of Iran's traditional policy of "equilibrium."

During the five years of the Allied occupation (1941–1946), an independent foreign policy for Iran was out of the question, and Iran suffered great economic hardship. After U.S. noncombatant troops arrived in Iran in 1942 to assist in the shipment of supplies to the Soviet Union, Iran once more tried the "American option." Arthur Millspaugh was reappointed Financial Adviser on terms similar to those on which he was appointed in 1922. Again, the Majlis gave him wide economic and financial powers, and again his mission ended in failure. The measures he proposed (income tax, price controls, cuts in government spending, etc.) were vigorously opposed by the vested interests concerned, and Millspaugh resigned in February 1945.

The Soviet Union delayed the withdrawal of its troops long after the treaty date, but by the time they finally withdrew in 1946, a major change had occurred in the balance of power among the Allies: The United States had replaced Britain as the Western Power principally interested in Iran. For Iran, this represented merely a continuation of the "Great Game." The only difference was that one of the players had changed, and, initially, Iran continued to use the strategy of "equilibrium" in an attempt to preserve its sovereignty and independence. The United States, formerly cast in the role of Third Power, was now one of the principal players. Iran, like many other lesser powers, became increasingly constrained by the exigencies of the Cold War. If Iran was to persevere with the Third Power policy, which it had pursued for the fifty years between 1940 and 1990, it would have to find a replacement for the United States, which was no longer a "disinterested" power. In 1955 Mohammad Reza Pahlavi decided to commit Iran to a pro-Western alignment by joining the Baghdad Pact, a regional defence pact among Turkey, Iraq, Pakistan, and Great Britain.[34]

From 1949 onward, the definition of "equilibrium," as the policy intended to satisfy the political and economic imperatives of Iran's foreign policy, became the dominant issue in Iranian politics. In that year, Muhammad Mossadegh formed the National Front, an anti-Shah coalition embracing a broad spectrum of political groups including neo-Fascists, bourgeois nationalists, non–Tudeh Party leftist intellectuals, landowners, tribal leaders, members of the religious classes (including the terrorist group *fida 'iyyan-i islam*), and bazaar merchants. It was five years *before* that, however, in 1944, that Mossadegh had made his famous "negative equilibrium speech." "Positive equilibrium," he said, would mean the granting of an oil concession to the Soviet Union to balance the one already held by the Anglo-Iranian Oil Company. Instead, he advocated "negative equilibrium," which, by inference, meant the abolition of the British oil concession. In this speech, Mossadegh struck a chord that had resounded in Iranian ears for centuries, particularly since the promulgation of Ithna 'Ashari Shi'ism as the official religion of Iran in 1501. The strongly negativist and xenophobic components of Ithna 'Asharism appealed not only to the religious classes and to the traditional Moslem groups in Iranian society such as the bazaar merchants, but also to many Iranian intellectuals who, although

they did not necessarily wish to see the establishment of an Ithna
'Ashari state governed by the religious leaders, had had their xenophobia
aroused by the political and economic influence of European Powers
in Iran. For them, xenophobia was a necessary ingredient of nationalism.

To counter Mossadegh's "negative equilibrium," the shah proposed
the adoption of a policy of "positive nationalism," which he defined as
"a policy of maximum political and economic independence consistent
with the interests of one's country."[35] The National Front, however, was
not interested in compromises. It dealt only in moral absolutes, an
aspect of its ideology that permitted it to forge alliances with the
religious leaders. "The ravishment of Iran by corrupting foreign
influences"[36] was a theme common to both the intelligentsia and the
religious classes. It was a theme that Khomeini and his associates have
played *fortissimo* since the inception of the Islamic Revolutionary
Movement in the 1960s.

The depth of resentment among Iranians toward the infringement of
their national sovereignty was illustrated in 1963–1964 by their violent
reaction to the granting of certain privileges and immunities to U.S.
Embassy personnel, to which they were entitled under the 1961 Vienna
Convention. This move proved to be a major political blunder by the
shah, and it placed a powerful propaganda weapon in the hands of
Khomeini. The opposition immediately likened this concession to the
hated capitulatory rights imposed on Iran in 1828 by the Russians and
other Western Powers. This incident confirmed once again the persistent
character and durable nature of the nationalist imperative that governed
the foreign policy of Iran.

In the 1960s, the shah changed the slogan of "positive nationalism"
to one of "independent foreign policy" (*siasat-i mustaqill-i milli*), but
the essential difference between the shah and his opponents on matters
of foreign policy continued to be that between "positive" and "negative."
A clear indication of this difference may be seen in the rapprochement
between Iran and the Soviet Union during the period 1962–1967, a
rapprochement encouraged by the shah's declaration in September 1962
that Iran would not allow its territory to be used for foreign missile
bases. This rapprochement led directly to the conclusion of a number
of economic agreements with the Soviet Union and to agreements
regarding mega-projects.[37]

The National Front's interpretation of an independent foreign policy
was quite different. For the National Front, the primary criterion for
an independent foreign policy was the severing of relations with the
United States. Having achieved this, Iran should then pursue a Nehru-

style policy of "absolute neutralism" (*bi-tarafi-yi mutlaq*). In the terminology of the time, such a policy was one of "nonalignment."[38]

As noted above, the shah's "independent foreign policy" was intended to make clear to the United States, and to Western Powers generally, that he wished to continue close relations with the West but wanted these relations in the future to be on a more equal footing. In 1968, however, the sudden announcement by the British Government that Britain intended to evacuate all its bases in the Gulf region, and to withdraw all its forces from the area by 1971, created a power vacuum in the area and made it likely that the superpowers would henceforth play a greater strategic role there and thus make it more difficult for Iran to follow an independent foreign policy.[39] Not only Iran but also the Arab states in the Gulf region sought means to reassure the superpowers that they, the Gulf States, were capable of being responsible for their own security and did not need superpower intervention.[40] The Soviet Union proclaimed that "it, too, believed that all outside powers should stay out of the Persian Gulf," and a statement to this effect was included in a joint Soviet-Iranian communiqué issued on the occasion of the shah's visit to the Soviet Union in October 1972: "The Soviet Union and Iran expressed the firm conviction that questions relating to the Persian Gulf zone should be resolved, in accordance with the principles of the U.N. Charter, by the states of the region themselves without outside interference."[41] Soviet policies, however, belied this statement. The conclusion of the Soviet-Iraqi Treaty in April 1972, a treaty that was said to strengthen the front of the progressive forces opposing imperialism and to provide a long-term basis for political and possibly military cooperation between the two countries,[42] seriously alarmed Iran. So, too, did Soviet support for the so-called Popular Front for the Liberation of the Occupied Arab Gulf in the Omani province of Dhufar; increased activity by Soviet naval vessels in the Indian Ocean; and the regular passage up the Gulf of Soviet merchant ships that, the Iranians suspected, were carrying arms to Iraq.

To strengthen Iran's security position, and that of the Gulf region in general, the shah pursued two policies from 1969 onward: First, he worked hard to cultivate better relations with the nonrevolutionary Arab states in the Gulf;[43] and, second, he tried to play the "China card" and to use China as a possible countervailing force against the Soviet Union. This latter move was, in fact, a variant of the Third Power policy. The Islamic Republic of Iran has also played this card effectively, in what is yet another illustration of continuity in the fundamental political imperatives of Iranian foreign policy.

Unfortunately for Iran, and for the other countries of the Gulf region, the political imperatives of the Cold War have distorted Iran's foreign policy since World War II:

> Just as the cold war distorted Musaddiq's negative equilibrium into something anti-Western and pro-Soviet and pro-Tudeh, it portrayed the shah's positive nationalism as blindly pro-Western and anti-Soviet. . . . The strategy of positive nationalism did not amount to blind hostility with the Soviet Union, just as it did not result in uncritical friendship with the United States.[44]

From 1972 onward, three events linked Iran even more closely with the United States: greater U.S. naval activity in the Indian Ocean, the U.S. takeover from Britain of the naval base at Bahrayn, and, finally, President Nixon's announcement that the United States was now relying on the "twin pillars" of Iran and Saudi Arabia to provide local and regional security in the Gulf region.

THE ECONOMIC IMPERATIVES
OF IRANIAN FOREIGN POLICY: 1921–1979

As already noted, the dominant imperative of Reza Shah's foreign policy was nationalism. Above all, he strove to make Iran proud of its past, particularly of its pre-Islamic past, and to rid Iran of the incubus of foreign influence. This primary objective coloured the whole of his economic policy, too, and so the political and economic aspects of his foreign policy were closely interrelated. The most important elements of his economic policy—industrialization, state capitalism, and the development of a transportation system—were designed to lessen Iran's economic dependence on Britain and Russia. Unlike his predecessors, the Qajar shahs, and unlike his successor, his son Mohammad Reza, Reza Shah eschewed all foreign loans. The Trans-Iranian Railway, an impressive engineering feat, was financed entirely by means of a special tax on tea and sugar. By contrast, between 1946 and 1970, Iran received large sums in U.S. Aid grants and loans, U.K. short-term credits, and loans from the World Bank and the International Monetary Fund. These funds seemed to be a concomitant of Iran's political decision to commit itself to an alignment with the West by joining the Baghdad Pact in 1955. They also resulted from Mohammad Reza Shah's recognition that, if Iran were ever to reach the point of "take-off"[45] in economic development, injections of foreign capital were inevitable. On this policy, too, the shah and Mossadegh were in fundamental disagreement. Mossadegh "was sustained by the emotional desire on the part of the middle classes that Persia should have complete political and economic independence whatever the cost."[46] In political terms, this meant nonalignment; in economic terms, it meant the nonacceptance of economic aid from the West. When Mossadegh was in power (1951–1953), he tried to pursue such a policy but was unable to do so. The boycott of Iranian oil, organized by Britain after Mossadegh's unilateral nationalization of the Anglo-Iranian Oil Company in 1951, forced Mossadegh to accept U.S. aid in the amount of $133 million between 1951 and 1953 simply in order to balance the budget.

Reza Shah's attempts to make Iran economically independent through its own efforts were only partially successful. In the short term, if the Soviet Union's share in Iranian trade was to be reduced, Iran had to look elsewhere both for a market for its exports and for a source of indispensable imports. After the failure of the first Millspaugh Mission in 1927, Reza Shah had played the Third Power card in his quest for a replacement for the United States as a "distant and disinterested power." His choice had fallen on Germany. As a political determinant in the formulation of foreign policy, this choice ended in disaster, as already noted. As an economic determinant in the formulation of foreign policy, the choice merely meant the substitution of Germany for Russia as Iran's major trading-partner. The Soviet Union retained about one-third of Iran's total foreign trade until 1938–1939. Between 1938 and 1941, however, "Russia's share of Iran's exports fell from thirty-four percent to just over one percent, while Germany's rose from twenty percent to forty-two percent; over the same period, Iran's imports from Russia fell to 0.04 percent, while those from Germany increased to forty-seven percent."[47]

Mohammad Reza Shah, too, dreamed of making his country independent of foreign control, both politically and economically. Unlike Mossadegh, however, he also had the goal of generating an internal social and economic revolution that would finally overcome the homeostatic forces that had made the development of Iran such a slow, painful and uncertain process. The shah did not believe that political nonalignment, and rejection of foreign economic aid, was the way to achieve this revolution. The shah had staked the whole of his personal prestige, and indeed the institution of the monarchy itself, on an attempt to raise Iran from the ranks of the underdeveloped nations so as to enable it to join the ranks of the newly industrializing regions of Asia such as South Korea, Hong Kong, and Taiwan. The shah was well aware that the gap between developing and developed nations was widening rather than shrinking. If Iran was ever to have a chance of raising the standard of living of its people, time was of the essence. In 1949 Iran had been one of the first Middle Eastern countries to begin economic planning for development. Oil had been the major source of funding for this development. The nationalization of oil in 1951, and the subsequent interruption of oil revenue, had caused the First Seven-Year Plan for Economic Development to be aborted, and it had not been possible to resume economic planning until 1956. The Second (1956–1962), Third (1962–1968), and Fourth plans (the last of which was launched in 1968) had many notable achievements to their credit, but Iran had still not reached the stage of economic "take-off." The pace of development had to be accelerated if Iran was not to remain one of the countries still "grappling with the problems of the wooden pick and shovel," to use Prime Minister Amir Abbas Huvayda's graphic phrase.[48] Economic development could be accelerated only if more money were available. The key to increasing revenue was oil.

The decade from 1970 to 1979 has been called the "OPEC years" because it was during this period, and particularly after the quadrupling of the price of Middle Eastern oil in 1973, that OPEC was able to use the economic weapon of oil to its full advantage against the West. As *The Economist* put it, "Suddenly, everything was different." In 1970, it continued, there were from the Western point of view five economic postulates: First, inflation was a problem, but one that could be solved; second, reasonable economic growth seemed to be assured; third, the world economy would continue to be dominated by the U.S. dollar; fourth, Keynesian economics would cope with minor ups and downs in the economy; and, fifth, most people agreed that the world monetary system was in need of *some* sort of reform. By the end of the 1970s, the first four of these postulates had proved to be false. The economy of the Western world had suffered a number of major shocks: President Nixon's trade and currency measures of August 1971; the publication by the Club of Rome of "The Limits of Growth," which dramatically underlined the fact that the world's resources are finite; and the quadrupling of oil prices by OPEC in 1973, which caused not only a recession in those Western economies that depended heavily on Middle Eastern oil but also inflation of a degree not seen in living memory—indeed, the term *stagflation* was coined to describe it. On all sides, demands were heard for a "new economic order." New industrialized nations were springing up in the Third World. And dialogue among Western economic leaders was no longer termed "East-West" dialogue but "North-South."[49]

The shah had been the prime mover in the decision by OPEC to raise oil prices from US$3.00 to US$11.65 a barrel. As a result of this increase, the funds available to the Fifth Seven-Year Plan for Economic Development, inaugurated in 1973, multiplied tenfold. The pace of economic development accelerated at a rate that beggared description.

Per capita income, which had been a paltry $85 per annum in 1949, had risen to $815 by 1974; but it then doubled in three years to reach $1,600 in 1977, a figure that put Iran on a par with such smaller developed nations as Holland, Norway, and Belgium. Between 1962 and 1973, the average rate of growth of the GNP had been 9.2 percent per annum. According to Harold Mehner, "In the first year of the Fifth Plan, the Iranian economy grew at the rate of 35 percent and in the second year at 42 percent."[50] Predictably, the economy overheated. This development, coupled with falling world demand for crude oil, caused a downturn in the economy in 1977, which in turn led to the collapse of the Amuzegar government in August 1978.[51] What Jahangir Amuzegar termed "insatiable popular envies and expectations" could not be satisfied in the short term, and an increasing number of Iranians were demanding the millennium now. Amuzegar pointed out that "some of the dissidents' cries against the country's 'west-toxication' "[52] and their desire for a return to cultural and religious traditions were "obvious manifestations of their unfilfilled ideas and ideals." It was ironical, he added, that many of the dreams of these dissatisfied Iranians had "been created and nurtured by the recently acquired education and enlightenment to which they traditionally had limited access."[53] Because changes in traditional modes of behaviour and moral attitudes had not kept pace with economic change, feelings of psychological stress and insecurity were produced at many levels of society. Throughout history, periods of rapid social change and disruption have led people to seek the millennium. Iran was no exception. When Khomeini promised the millennium, not only the masses but also many members of the middle classes and the intelligentsia flocked to him. In these individuals, Amuzegar further noted, the drive toward modernization had produced the desire to return to the perceived safety of traditional religious and cultural norms.

The truth of the dictum that, in Iran, as in many other countries, economic policies are inseparable from political attitudes was once again demonstrated. Because the shah was the symbol of a modernization process that was clearly in opposition to the traditional religious precepts of Islam, it was easy for the mullas to mobilize opposition to him and hence to the process itself. Because U.S. personnel were the most visible manifestation of the modernization process,[54] the hostility toward economic development and modernization was focused on Americans in particular. Furthermore, the United States, as the chief purveyor of arms to Iran in the 1970s, was perceived, because of its part in the build-up of Iran's armed forces, to be the principal supporter of the shah politically. Economic and political determinants thus combined to influence foreign policy. They led to the souring of U.S.-Iran relations and, finally, to the withdrawal of U.S. support for the shah. The anti-U.S. hysteria whipped up by the mullas made it inevitable that, after the revolution, whatever new regime came into power would revert to a foreign policy of nonalignment reminiscent of the "negative equilibrium" of Mossadegh's days.

THE POLITICAL IMPERATIVES
OF IRANIAN FOREIGN POLICY: 1979–1988

The overthrow of the shah was initially hailed by many Moslems in the Middle East and elsewhere as a "victory for Islam" over a ruler who had aligned himself with the West. This initial jubilation was speedily tempered by the dawning realisation among Sunni Moslems that the ideology of the Islamic Revolutionary Movement which had brought Khomeini to power in February 1979, like the ideology of the Bolshevik Revolution in 1917, had an external as well as an internal dimension.

In the Soviet Union, the theoretical "dictatorship of the proletariat" had been rapidly converted by Lenin into the reality of the dictatorship of the Communist Party. In Iran, the theoretical expression of the "will of the people" soon became the reality of the subjection of the masses to the "Imam's line." In both cases, the ideology that was used to ensure passive acceptance of the regime internally was employed to generate political activism in foreign policy and as the basis for attempts to subvert the governments of other states.

At the Second Congress of the Moslem Communists held in Moscow in November 1919, Lenin had stressed the importance of carrying the revolutionary struggle to other countries in the East, and Iran was considered to be the Asian country "most ripe" for the application of this policy.[55] Khomeini, on the first anniversary of the Islamic Revolution in Iran, made it clear that he saw himself as the leader of a world-wide revolutionary movement. "O Muslim nations of the world who are oppressed, arise!" he declaimed. Clandestine Ithna 'Ashari cells were established in a number of Gulf countries, and between 1979 and 1981 emissaries from the Islamic Republic of Iran visited a number of Arab states on the Gulf littoral in attempts to foment trouble for the governments of those states. After Saddam Husayn assumed power in Iraq in August 1979, however, Iraq was increasingly cast in the role of "the Satan of the Great Satan" [the United States] in Khomeini's demonology. In January 1979, even before his return to Iran from France, Khomeini had issued a *fatva* calling on Iraqi Shi'is to support their religious leaders in demanding autonomy for the 5 million Shi'is living in Iraq. A virulent propaganda war developed between Iran and

Iraq, culminating in the invasion of Iran in September 1980 in what, the Iraqis seemed to have hoped, would be a preemptive strike. The Arab states in the Gulf region were sufficiently alarmed by Khomeini's claim to be the leader of *all* Moslems, not merely of Ithna 'Ashari Shi'is, that they came together to form the Gulf Co-operation Council (GCC) in 1981.[56] The six signatories were Saudi Arabia, Bahrain, Oman, Kuwait, Qatar, and the United Arab Emirates.[57] Among their objectives was the desire to prevent a possible "spill-over" of the Iran-Iraq War and to frustrate attempts by the Islamic Republic of Iran to subvert their own regimes.

Not only Iran's neighbours in the Gulf region were affected, however, by the revolutionary ideology of the Islamic Republic. The "export" version of that ideology had an impact on the superpowers as well:

> Prior to the Islamic Revolution, most analysts assumed that, if there were instability anywhere in the Middle East, the Soviet Union would be the principal beneficiary. In the long term, this may well still be true, but in the short term, the Soviet Union has run afoul of the traditional Islamic world-view described earlier. The Soviet Union had expected that the Islamic Republic of Iran, as a revolutionary state, would at once recognise the U.S.S.R. as its natural ally. Instead it has found itself, much to its chagrin, placed in the same infidel category as the United States.[58]

The Soviet invasion of Afghanistan on Christmas Eve of 1979 angered Khomeini. When the Soviet Union objected to Khomeini's support of the Afghan guerrillas and resumed its arms sales to Iraq, Khomeini vented his anger against the official Communist Party of Iran, the Tudeh Party. In February 1983, the Tudeh Party organization was virtually destroyed by the arrest of 23 members of the Party Central Committee and of some 4,000 "suspects." On 5 May 1983 the party was officially proscribed.

The impact of the Islamic Revolution in Iran on the other superpower, the United States, was even more devastating. In 1972 President Nixon had announced a policy of relying on the twin pillars of Iran and Saudi Arabia to provide local and regional security in the Gulf region. One of these pillars now lay in ruins. The Islamic Revolution had been directed against the shah, and the shah was an ally of the United States; it was therefore inevitable that the foreign policy of the Khomeini regime would be strongly anti-American. In March 1979 the Islamic Republic withdrew from CENTO, a symbolic gesture indicative of its anti-Western stance. The seizure of the U.S. Embassy in Tehran in November 1979, and the incarceration of its personnel for 444 days, made it equally inevitable that relations between the two countries would remain sour for a long time. The lack of sympathy among the American public for the victims of the Airbus tragedy in July 1988 is clear evidence that that act of state terrorism has been neither forgotten nor forgiven. The "vital" U.S. interests in the Gulf region that were enunciated in the 1980 Carter Doctrine were even then largely geopolitical rather than economic in nature. By 1983 the United States could no longer pretend that Middle East oil was a "vital" interest, inasmuch as Middle East oil imports to the United States in that year, expressed as a percentage of total U.S. oil imports, amounted to only 8 percent. In fact, in 1983 Great Britain exported more oil to the United States than did Saudi Arabia. It is true that Japan, an ally of the United States, obtains 56 percent of its oil from the Middle East, but the United States has not forced Japan to pay the military and economic costs of securing free passage of its oil tankers through the Gulf. The principal U.S. geopolitical interests in the Gulf continue to be the rendering of support to Israel; denying the Soviet Union a dominant role in the Gulf region; bolstering the security of friendly Arab states in the region; and maintaining safe passage through the Gulf for the ships of the United States and its European and Middle Eastern allies. It is, of course, this last objective that has led to a greatly enhanced U.S. naval presence in the area.

The Islamic Revolution in Iran has brought about a radical realignment of political forces in the Gulf region and the entire Middle East. What are the political imperatives upon which the foreign policy of the Islamic Republic is based? R. K. Ramazani has identified seven basic principles in the formulation of Iran's foreign policy since the revolution:

1. no dependence on East or West
2. the designation of the United States as the chief enemy
3. the struggle against the superpowers and the "Zionist power"
4. support for all "oppressed peoples" everywhere, especially "oppressed" Muslims
5. the liberation of Jerusalem
6. anti-imperialism
7. support for the *mustaz'afin,* or "oppressed masses."[59]

Khomeini's ideology is a masterly exercise in syncretism. His blend of ideas—ancient and modern, Islamic and Western, egalitarian and totalitarian, traditional and revolutionary, populist and elitist[60] has certainly produced a potent revolutionary mix offering something to people of widely differing political views. According to Ramazani, the goal of the Islamic Republic is nothing less than the "liberation of mankind" and the establishment of a "world government of the Iman

Mahdi."[61] W. G. Millward, however, sees its goal as the establishment of "an international system based on the principle of the Muslim faith."[62] This ideology and these goals have obvious implications for the foreign policy of the Islamic Republic of Iran.

The glue that has held the diverse elements of Khomeini's ideology together is, to my mind, the fundamentalist, millenarian ideology of Ithna 'Ashari Shi'ism. Without this ideology, it is highly unlikely that Khomeini would have succeeded in mobilising the masses to overthrow the shah. It is also improbable that he would have succeeded in eliminating his secularist rivals within such a short time after the February 1979 revolution. It is this millenarian ideology alone that enables the *mujtahids* to claim infallibility as the representatives on earth of the Hidden Imam and legitimacy as the only form of government in Iran until the Second Coming of the Mahdi. This millenarian ideology is the foundation on which Khomeini has built his doctrine of *vilayat-i faqih*, the "governance of the jurisprudent." This doctrine is enshrined in the Constitution of the Islamic Republic of Iran: "During the Occultation of the Lord of the Age (may God hasten his renewed manifestations!), the governance and leadership of the nation devolve upon the just and pious *faqih*."[63] This doctrine is deemed by some to be a *bid'ah*, an "innovation" tantamount to heresy;[64] but there is no doubt in my mind that it is the logical and skillful actualisation of a potential that has always existed in the Ithna 'Ashari tradition. Others have made much of the fact that there is little in the *hadith* collections or in the literature of *fiqh* to support the claim of the *mujtahids* to be the sole legitimate representatives on Earth of the Mahdi during the Greater Occultation. But it is not correct to claim, as some have, that there is nothing at all in the juristic literature on which this claim can be based.[65] At any rate, all of these arguments (both pro and con) are largely irrelevant because, in matters of ideology and propaganda, it is not what *is* but what *is believed*" that matters.

Startling as the concept of *vilayat-i faqih* may have been at the time it was propounded by Khomeini,[66] it has been carried far beyond the bounds of its original concept since the 1979 revolution. Of profound importance, not only for Iran but for the whole Moslem world, is Khomeini's declaration that his concept of *vilayat-i faqih* is not restricted to Iran but is of universal application. Spokesmen for the regime have said that there are no boundaries for the Imam and that Khomeini's form of ideology is to be exported to all other Moslem countries that refuse to accept Imam Khomeini as their leader. Moslem governments that do not accept his leadership, and therefore have "oppressive" forms of government in his view, must be overthrown; and a form of Islamic government that conforms to the ideology of the Islamic Republic of

Iran must be established in these countries. In other words, the idea of the universal nature of the concept of *vilayat-i faqih*, since it necessarily affects relations between the Islamic Rebublic of Iran and all other Moslem countries, has become an imperative in the formulation of foreign policy by the Islamic Republic.

A second major ideological development, one with profound foreign policy implications, has arisen from the creation of the Islamic Republic of Iran—namely, the development of the concept of *tawhid*. Once again, Imam Khomeini has gone above and beyond traditional Ithna 'Ashari messianism.

> In the normative Islamic tradition, the term *tawhid* (which, curiously enough, does not occur in the Qur'an),[67] means the unity or unicity of God. The ideologues of the Islamic Revolution in Iran, however, have developed the doctrine of *tawhid* into a world-view with far-reaching social and political implications.[68]

Many of these social and political implications relate to Iran's domestic politics. The doctrine of *tawhid*, as expounded, for example, by 'Ali Khamanah'i,[69] the president of the Islamic Republic of Iran, is designed primarily to reinforce (if further reinforcement be needed) the dominant position of the religious leaders in the state. According to Khomeini, sovereignty rests solely with God, and this sovereignty is exercised on earth by those appointed by God—namely, by the infallible *faqaha*, people like himself. Translated into political terms, this doctrine produces not what 'Ali Shari'ati calls "irresponsible and directionless liberalism" but, rather, "committed and revolutionary leadership."[70] Translated into an imperative of foreign policy, *tawhid* produces disdain and intolerance of all other forms of polity and, hence, of the countries espousing those polities. When international relations are metamorphosed into an apocalyptic struggle between the forces of good and evil, there is little room left for compromise. For this reason, the recent signs of a move toward a more pragmatic foreign policy are of the utmost interest and importance. Although Khomeini has never actually claimed to be the Mahdi in person, he has never been adverse to being addressed as the Imam, or at least as *nayib-i Imam* ("the deputy of the Imam"). The decision to initiate negotiations for an end to the Iran-Iraq War, a decision "more bitter than poison" to Khomeini, may in fact make the first dent in the Imam's armour of infallibility; it could also lead to a more pragmatic foreign policy and to the end of Iran's self-imposed isolation from the rest of the international community. Only time will tell. It is possible that the bazaar mentality of Rafsanjani has produced a more pragmatic outlook that may eventually triumph not only over the rigidly ideological stance of *'ulama* such as Khomeini but also over the equally rigid ideological positions of Marxist groups of various complexions and of former supporters of Mossadegh.

THE ECONOMIC IMPERATIVES
OF IRANIAN FOREIGN POLICY: 1979–1988

The self-imposed political isolation that was a by-product of the ideology of the Islamic Revolution necessarily affected Iran's economic policies, too. Iran's hostility toward foreign firms meant that little was spent on development and that most of the projects in progress at the time of the revolution came to an abrupt halt. Japan, which had not been associated with the policies of the "Great Satan" toward Iran, for a time continued work on a number of major petrochemical plants in Khuzistan; but, after some Japanese workers were killed in an Iraqi bombing raid, Japan too pulled its operatives out. Recently, the Tokyo-based conglomerate Mitsui announced that it intended to abandon its US$4.5 billion project involving the construction of thirteen petro-chemical plants at Bandar Khomeini near the Gulf.[71] The implication is that Iran, even if it has the political will to make overtures to the West, may find the major industrial power wary of immediate involve-ment in Iran's economic rehabilitation. It may be that (at least initially) Iran will be obliged to have recourse to medium-sized industrial powers such as South Korea, which completed a number of projects in Iran under the late shah.

The economic policies of the Islamic Republic of Iran, in the years following the revolution, were strongly influenced by the socialist ide-ology of President Bani-Sadr. These policies were nationalist and non-aligned, and were characterized by what the President called "Islamic socialism," which apparently meant state control of the economy. Banks, insurance companies, major industries, and many smaller industrial units were nationalized. All privately owned undeveloped urban prop-erties of more than 1,000 square metres were taken over by the gov-ernment. Industries that had thrived under the Pahlavi regime were considered "exploitative" and of doubtful value because they concen-trated on foreign-owned assembly plants. All foreign economic links, especially those with large U.S. and European companies, were eyed with suspicion. The sweeping reorganization of the Iranian economy planned by Bani-Sadr envisaged "state control of the means of pro-duction, credit and resource allocation, and foreign trade." These mea-sures, together with the commandeering of private property by the Revolutionary Guards, students, workers, and the like, produced an atmosphere of uncertainty on the part of the owners of small businesses, because they lived in constant fear of arrest by the Revolutionary Committees.[72]

Not surprisingly, these policies caused a sharp decline in productivity and a significantly reduced role for the private sector. Many members of the managerial class left Iran. By 1984 it was being calculated that more than a million Iranians, many of them professionals whose skills were vital to the economy, had emigrated. There were signs that even the bazaar merchants, who had played such an important part in financing the revolution, were being alienated by the regime's crusade against "profiteering."[73]

Since the outbreak of the war with Iraq, Iran's economic decline has accelerated. By 1984 the cost of the war had risen to $11 million a day, a sum equivalent to 30 percent of total government expenditure.[74] A high rate of inflation, shortages of basic consumer goods as well as a flourishing black market for those Iranis fortunate enough to be able to buy goods on it, widespread unemployment (only one Iranian in five was said to have regular work in 1986), and the collapse of the currency added to Iran's economic woes. By 1983 the GNP was 25 percent lower than it had been before the revolution, but worse was yet to come. The price of oil, upon which Iran (and Iraq) depended to finance the war, dropped dramatically between November 1985 and March 1986 from $28–30 per barrel to $11–13 per barrel.[75] In effect, the OPEC cartel had collapsed. Its demise had been heralded by its own action in cutting the price of oil from $34 per barrel to $29 per barrel in March 1983.[76] This cut represented the "first reduction in the official price conceded by OPEC" since its establishment in 1960.[77]

By October 1984 there were signs that the ideological reluctance of the Islamic Republic to deal with foreign nations and to have any truck with the private sector on the domestic front was beginning to give way to a more pragmatic approach. In October 1984 Imam Khomeini said it would be "unreasonable and un-Islamic" not to have relations with other governments—except, of course, those of the United States, Israel, and South Africa.[78] Early in 1985 a debate developed over the relative importance of the private and public sectors in the Iranian economy, and in January 1985 the Majlis passed a bill to encourage private business by "providing for easier access to land and credit." This was obviously a conciliation to the bazaar. By the autumn of 1986 there was increasing recognition of the fact that Iran, if it were to rehabilitate its economy, needed the professional and managerial skills of the middle classes; and the harassment of these classes eased up. The more pragmatic Rafsanjani was largely responsible for improving relations with France in November 1986 and in concluding an arms-for-oil deal with China.[79] The debate over the advisability of abandoning the policy of nonalignment as a means of achieving the political imperative of sovereignty and independence, together with its economic corollary of refusal to accept assistance from foreign, and especially Western, powers, is clearly very much alive at the highest levels of the regime. On 6 September 1988, Prime Minister Husayn Musavi was reported to have wished he could resign rather than be forced to accept foreign aid. On September 7, however, Imam Khomeini was reported to have told Musavi to "stop complaining and to get on with the job,"[80] and thus far President Khomeini has refused to accept his resignation.

CONCLUSION

It seems to me that there is one dominant theme that has shaped the foreign policy of Iran and has thus had strong influence on its economic policy since the concept of a foreign policy was first adumbrated at the beginning of the nineteenth century. This theme, or imperative, is "Iranismus," the idea of a cultural identity which is distinct from that of other races and peoples in the Middle East and which derives from a different historical and cultural tradition. It is this sense of being different from (many Iranians would doubtless say superior to!) these other races and peoples that has preserved Iranian civilization and culture throughout all the vicissitudes of Iran's long history, including its subjugation by Arabs, Turks, Mongols, and Afghans. It is this sense of distinctiveness that has bred in Iranians the passionate determination to maintain the sovereignty and territorial integrity of *Iran-zamin*, if at all possible, and, if not possible, to ensure that the Iranian cultural heritage is preserved and transmitted to future generations. The desire *not* to become a pawn of any Great Power has always been a strong current in Iranian political life. It is this strong current that the present government of the Islamic Republic of Iran has been able to channel and of which it has been able to make effective use.

Two institutions have played important roles in preserving Iran's cultural heritage: the monarchical tradition and, after the Islamicization of Iran, the mosque. Since Iranians adopted the Ithna 'Ashari form of Shi'ism, and subsequently lifted it out of its purely Islamic context and grafted it onto the Iranian historical tradition,[81] the "turban" and the "crown" have competed for the hearts and minds of Iranians. During the periods when these two powerful determinants of Iranian policies were in approximate equilibrium, the polity functioned with relative harmony. The 1979 revolution was precipitated in large part by Mohammad Reza Pahlavi's attempt to push the nation too far and too fast along the path to secularization. The reaction to this process, since the revolution, has led to the dominance of the polity by the religious leaders, to the triumph of the xenophobic and negativist ideology of Ithna 'Ashari Shi'ism. In my view, there will be no political peace in Iran until consensus is reached on the form of governance that is best suited to the nation's interests.

This predominant imperative of nationalism has been used in diametrically opposed ways as a determinant of foreign and economic policy by the supporters of the "turban" and the "crown" respectively. By the supporters of the "crown," it has been used in a pragmatic way. They have always tried to maximise Iran's political independence and to develop its economy through policies appropriate to and consonant with the political and economic realities of the moment. Thus, in the nineteenth century, the policy of "equilibrium," feeble weapon though it was, succeeded in preserving at least the nominal independence of Iran in the face of Anglo-Russian rivalry for control of the region. Almost alone among Moslem countries in Western Asia, Iran never became a colony of any European Power. As a determinant of economic policy, "equilibrium" was less successful, since a "quid" in the form of an economic concession granted to one Great Power was immediately followed by a demand for a "quo" from the other.

"Equilibrium" was succeeded by the Third Power policy, a more positive version of the same principle and one that sought to offset the power of both rival Great Powers by introducing to the Iranian stage a third player in the form of a "distant and disinterested" party. After disappointing experiments with the United States as the Third Power, Reza Shah made the fatal decision to turn to Germany. In both cases, nationalism was the primary imperative of Reza Shah's policy. When the Allied Powers finaly handed his country back to him in 1946, Reza Shah found that his options were more limited because of the exigencies of the Cold War and the polarization of politics throughout the world between the Western and the Soviet blocs. The United States had replaced Britain as the Western Power most involved in Iran and the Gulf region, and neither of the previous Third Power options was available. Germany was a nonstarter. With considerable misgivings the Shah decided in 1955 to throw in his lot with the West by joining the Baghdad Pact. Although he never became the lackey of the United States his detractors alleged him to be, a growing alliance with the United States was sufficient to cause disequilibrium in both Iranian foreign policy and the economy, again with ultimately fatal results for the regime.

With the advent to power of Imam Khomeini in 1979, the supporters of the "turban" used the predominant imperative of nationalism in an ideological, nonpragmatic, and fundamentally negative manner. This was the case with both the religious leaders themselves, who rapidly assumed supreme power in the state, and their supporters among the Iranian intelligentsia, the former supporters of Mossadegh's policy of "negative equilibrium," and members of various left-wing groups. The attitude of the religious leaders should have occasioned no surprise because the ideology of Ithna 'Ashari Shi'ism has always been xenophobic and negative. Vladimir Minorsky captured the essence of this ideology with his phrase: "Shi'ism, with its overtones and its aroma of opposition, of martyrdom, and of revolt."[82] Revolt against the late shah was seen by many Shi'is as a revolt against the "Great Satan," the United States. This ideology had its origin in the wellspring of Shi'ism. According to 'Ali Shari'ati, a leading ideologue of the Islamic Revolution in 1979, the real enemies of Islam are Jews and Christians.[83] This ideology has always tended to isolate Iran from the international community. As Ramazani has put it: "Blind adherence to Shi'i dogma narrowed the intellectual horizon of the people. Shi'i fanaticism mentally isolated Iranian rulers and their subjects alike. *Isolation from Europe proved prejudicial to the interests of Iran*" (emphasis added).[84]

The negative nationalism of the intelligentsia had its roots in emotion and the romantic unrealism to which reference was made at the beginning of this chapter. It is the antithesis of *Realpolitik*. It is a moot point whether unrealism is an actual imperative of foreign and economic policy in the ideology of the nationalist intelligentsia of the Mossadegh school, or whether it is merely a corollary of the dominant imperative of nationalism *as interpreted by them*. Whichever is the case, this "unrealism" led, on the political level, to policies that were not based on the realities of world politics and, on the economic level, to policies that were not "rational."

In 1972 I suggested that this philosophy dominated the thinking of many Iranian intellectuals, and I drew attention to the dangers inherent in applying it to the problems of the real world:

> On the political level such an attitude can at best lead to harmless romantic unrealism; at worst, it can harm the interests of one's own country by preventing one from making decisions on the basis of a rational appraisal of the facts. Moreover, people who lose touch with political reality may all too readily be swayed by unscrupulous persons who are seeking only their own ends, and are totally devoid of the idealism which may be present in the former—the classic lesson of Brutus.[85]

As Norman Jacobs has noted, "political action in Iran is personal. Iranians accommodate organizations to people rather than vice versa."[86]

As a result, he says, "political action cannot be predicted rationally, since all the determinants of action are 'non-rational.' "[87]

This same "unrealistic" or "irrational" attitude, according to Jacobs, also affects economic decisions because, "fundamentally, Iranians believe that all economic problems can be solved by political action."[88] The basis of the economy is therefore also "non-rational." Jacobs defines a "rational economic system" as one that accepts "the goal of the maximization of economic efficiency and profit as being primary in the economy." He points out that no economy is completely "rational", because "other than rational economic considerations (including political ones) are bound to enter into any economic decision."[89] Many foreign aid programmes have failed because foreign economic advisers have failed to appreciate the qualitative difference between Iranian society and other cultures.[90] Of course, "from the standpoint of the role economics is expected to play in the existing Iranian social system," the Iranian economic system *is* "rational"; Max Weber calls this "substantive rationality."[91] Jacobs's conclusion is that "a rational economic system is incompatible with the fundamental goals of each and all of the institutions of the Iranian social system."[92]

In conclusion, attention must be drawn once again to the fact, alluded to earlier, that the present regime in Iran has gone far beyond the traditional ideology of Ithna 'Ashari Shi'ism and has created a system that is activist, revolutionary, and anti-Western—a system that is not only messianic in the traditional Shi'i sense but apocalyptic as well. Khomeini claims to be the champion of the "oppressed" everywhere and sees the world within the framework of an apocalyptic struggle between the forces of good and evil. It is this distinctive feature of Khomeini's ideology that, whether one regards it as a *bid'ah* ("innovation") or not, has perhaps had the greatest impact on the formulation of foreign policy in the Islamic Republic of Iran. Now that the war with Iraq is over (for the moment, at least), Iran's decision to end its self-imposed isolation and rejoin the comity of nations depends on whether the "pragmatists" or the "romantic unrealists" hold the power in the governance of Iran. Whichever group holds the power will be in a position to interpret the predominant political and economic imperative of nationalism in the formulation of Iranian foreign policy according to its own definition of nationalism.

NOTES

1. Rouhollah K. Ramazani, *Iran's Foreign Policy 1941–1973: A Study of Foreign Policy in Modernizing Nations*, Vol. II, University Press of Virginia, Charlottesville, 1975, p. 15 (hereinafter referred to as "Ramazani II").

2. A.K.S. Lambton, "Kadjar" in *Encyclopaedia of Islam*, new edition, Vol. IV, Cambridge University Press, Cambridge, 1978, p. 396.

3. Mohammad Reza Pahlavi, *Answer to History*, Toronto, Vancouver, 1980, p. 139.

4. Rouhollah K. Ramazani, *The Foreign Policy of Iran: A Developing Nation in World Affairs 1500–1941*, Vol. I, University Press of Virginia, Charlottesville, 1966 [hereinafter referred to as "Ramazani I"]. See also Ramazani II.

5. Ramazani I, p. 32.

6. Ibid.

7. Quincy Wright, "Foreword" to Ramazani I, p. viii.

8. "Preface" to Ramazani I, pp. xi–xii.

9. Wright, op. cit., p. viii.

10. Qur'an 3:110 (Pickthall's translation).

11. Qur'an 3:79–85 (Arberry's translation). According to Qur'an commentator 'Abd Allah B. al-'Abbas, "the father of Qur'anic exegesis" (*Encyclopaedia of Islam*, new edition, Vol. I, Cambridge University Press, Cambridge, 1960, p. 40), this verse abrogated Qur'an 2:62, which seemed to offer some hope to Jews, Christians, and Sabaeans.

12. Bernard Lewis, *The Middle East and the West*, Wiedenfeld and Nicolson, London, 1963 and 1964, p. 115.

13. See, for example, Bernard Lewis, *The Muslim Discovery of Europe*, Praeger, New York and London, 1982.

14. Ramazani II, p. 4.

15. Lewis, op. cit., p. 117.

16. Ramazani I, p. 65.

17. The Soviet government signed a separate peace treaty with the Central Powers at Brest-Litovsk on 3 March 1918.

18. Iran, could, of course, have solved its dilemma by throwing in its lot with either Britain or Russia; it could also have become a colony or protectorate of one or the other. But the 2,500-year tradition of "Iranismus" militated against either option.

19. For the full text of the 1921 Treaty and of the subsequent exchange of diplomatic notes, see J. C. Hurewitz, *Diplomacy in the Near and Middle East: A Documentary Record: 1914–1956*, Vol. II, D. Van Nostrand Co., Princeton, N.J., 1956, pp. 90–94.

20. Charles Issawi, *The Economic History of Iran 1800-1914*, University of Chicago Press, Chicago, 1971, p. 15.

21. Issawi, op. cit., p. 16.

22. Ibid.

23. Ibid.

24. Ibid.

25. Ibid.

26. Sir Roger Stevens, *The Land of the Great Sophy*, Michael Joseph, London, 1962, p. 4.

27. Issawi, op. cit., p. 16.

28. Issawi, op. cit., pp. 16–17; figures taken from *League of Nations Statistical Yearbook, 1928*, UN Publications, Geneva, 1929.

29. George N. Curzon, *Persia and the Persian Question*, Vol. II, Her Majesty's Stationery, London, 1966, pp. 614–615.

30. Julian Bharier, *Economic Development in Iran 1900-1970*, Oxford University Press, London, 1971, p. 84.

31. Bharier, op. cit., p. 118.

32. Ramazani I, p. 203.

33. The validity of this reason for the joint Anglo-Soviet occupation was impaired to some degree by conflicting British estimates (ranging from 1,000 to 5,000) of the number of German nationals residing in Iran. The more important reason for the occupation was the urgent need to open up a supply route through Iran for war material for the beleaguered Soviet defenders at Stalingrad. According to Roger Savory, "The only other available route, the Arctic route round the north of Scandinavia, was fraught with extreme climatic difficulties, and was also within range of German submarines and aircraft . . . with Vladivostok threatened by the Japanese, and Murmansk icebound for part of the year" ("Modern Persia," in *Cambridge History of Islam*, Vol. I, Cambridge University Press, Cambridge, 1970, p. 612). And according to Winston Churchill, the arguments for opening a supply-route to Russia through Iran were "compulsive" ("The Second World War," Vol. III, in *The Grand Alliance*, Her Majesty's Stationery, London, 1950, p. 482). The late Shah of Iran, Mohammad Reza Pahlavi, has asserted that the *strategic* case for a supply route was never made to his father, and the available evidence supports this contention.

34. In 1958 the monarchy in Iraq was overthrown by a military coup, and in 1959 Iraq withdrew from the Baghdad Pact, which was then renamed the Central Treaty Organization (CENTO). The Shah became totally disillusioned about the value of CENTO in the aftermath of the two wars between India and Pakistan in 1965 and 1971—wars in which the United States sided with India against Pakistan.

35. Mohammad Reza Shah Pahlavi, *Mission for My Country*, McGraw-Hill, London, 1961, p. 125.

36. Peter Avery, *Modern Iran*, Michael Joseph, London, 1965, p. 468.

37. These mega-projects include construction of Iran's first steel mill (completed in 1973); construction of a natural gas pipeline from Iran's southern oilfields to the Soviet border (completed in 1970); construction of a machine-tools plant at Arak employing 2,000-3,000 workers (completed in 1972); and a major hydro electric and irrigation project utilising the waters of the Aras river.

38. Ramazani II, pp. 323–324.

39. The Arab states of the southern littoral of the Gulf decided to sink their differences in the face of the threat of superpower intervention in the region, and the formulation in 1971 of the group calling itself the United Arab Emirates was a direct result of their concern.

40. The late Shah made a number of statements indicating that Iran did not want any of the Great Powers to replace Britain as "policeman in the Gulf." See Ramazani II, p. 348.

41. This and the preceding quotation were taken from Ramazani II, p. 349.

42. Ibid.

43. For example, Bahrayn, a perpetual irritant to Irano-Arab relations, was removed from the political agenda by Mohammad Reza Pahlavi in January 1969. Iran signed continental shelf agreements with Qatar and Kuwait in 1969 and 1970, respectively. Diplomatic relations between Iran and Egypt were resumed in August 1970. This policy bore fruit in December 1971, when the Arab League chose not to support Iraq's call for the severance of diplomatic relations with Iran by all Arab states following Iran's occupation of three small but strategically important islands at the mouth of the Persian Gulf: Abu Musa and the Greater and Lesser Tunb.

44. Ramazani II, p. 447.

45. "Take-off" is W. W. Rostow's term.

46. R. M. Savory, "Persia Since the Constitution" *University of Toronto Quarterly*, January 1960, p. 256.

47. Savory, op. cit., p. 606.

48. Prime Minister Amir 'Abbas Huvayda, in an interview with Amir Taheri, published in *Kayhan International,* 24 December 1972, under the title "The Silhouette of the Future."

49. *The Economist*, 29 December 1979, p. 39.

50. Harold Mehner, "Development and Planning in Iran After World War II" in George Lenczowski (ed.), *Iran Under the Pahlavis*, Hoover Institution Press, Stanford, 1980, p. 197.

51. Jahangir Amuzegar, "Middle East Problem Paper No. 18," *Growth Without Pain: The New Iranian Development Strategy*, Middle East Institute, Washington, D.C., 1978, p. 8.

52. "West-toxication" is one translation of the term *gharbzadagi*. For the origin of the term, popularised by Jalal Al-i Ahmad, see Yann Richard, "Modern Iranian Political Thought," in Nikki R. Keddie, *Roots of Revolution*, Yale University Press, New Haven and London, 1981, p. 203, and p. 293, note 19.

53. Amuzegar, op. cit., p. 10.

54. Some 24,000 Americans are said to have been working in Iran by 1976, "with their number increasing at a remarkable rate." See Barry Rubin, *Paved with Good Intentions: The American Experience and Iran*, Oxford University Press, Oxford, 1980, p. 137.

55. Sepehr Zabih, *The Communist Movement in Iran*, University of California Press, Berkeley and Los Angeles, 1966, pp. 6–7.

56. Impetus to the establishment of the Gulf Co-operation Council was given by the enunciation of the "Carter Doctrine" of January 1980: "[A]n attempt by any outside force to gain control of the Persian Gulf region will be regarded as an assault on the vital interest of the U.S.A., and such assault will be repelled by any means necessary, including military force."

57. The United Arab Emirates, consisting of Abu Dhabi, Dubai, Sharjah, Ajman, Fujayrah, and Umm al-Qaywayn, was formed in 1971; Ra's al-Khaymah joined later.

58. Roger Savory, "'The Added Touch': Ithna 'Ashari Shi'ism as a Factor in the Foreign Policy of Iran," *International Journal*, Volume XLI, No. 2, Spring 1986, p. 416.

59. R. K. Ramazani, "Khumayni's Islam in Iran's Foreign Policy," in Adeed Dawisha (ed.), *Islam in Foreign Policy*, Cambridge University Press, Cambridge, 1983, p. 21 [hereinafter referred to as "Ramazani III"]. In regard to item 7, it should be noted that the occasions on which derivatives from the Arabic root *z'f* appear in the Qur'an in no way support the interpretation given to the word *mustaz'afin* by the Khomeini regime. See Roger Savory, "Ex Oriente Nebula: An Inquiry into the Nature of Khomeini's Ideology," in Peter J. Chelkowski and Robert J. Pranger (eds.), *Ideology and Power in the Middle East: Studies in Honor of George Lenczowski*, Duke University Press, Durham and London, 1988, pp. 358–359.

60. See Nikki R. Keddie, "Introduction" pp. 9–12, in Nikki R. Keddie and Eric Hooglund (eds.), *The Iranian Revolution and the Islamic Republic*, Proceedings of a conference held at the Woodrow Wilson International Center for Scholars, Middle East Institute, 21–22 May 1982, in cooperation with the Woodrow Wilson International Center for Scholars, 1982; see also Savory, op. cit., 1988, pp. 339–362.

61. Ramazani III, p. 17.

62. W. G. Millward, "The Principles of Foreign Policy and the Vision of World Order Expounded by Imam Khomeini and the Islamic Republic of Iran," in Nikki R. Keddie and Eric Hooglund (eds.), *The Iranian Revolution and the Islamic Republic*, Proceedings of a conference held at the Woodrow Wilson International Center for Scholars, Middle East Institute, 21–22 May 1982, in cooperation with the Woodrow Wilson International Center for Scholars, 1982, p. 189.

63. This passage was translated from the Persian by Hamid Algar. See *Constitution of the Islamic Republic of Iran*, Article 5, Mizan Press, Berkeley, 1980, p. 29.

64. See the discussion of various legal objections to the doctrine in Said Amir Arjomand, *The Turban and the Crown*, Oxford University Press, Oxford, 1988, pp. 177-83.

65. Said Amir Arjomand, "The Shadow of God and the Hidden Imam: Religion, Political Order and Societal Change in Shi'ite Iran from the Beginning to 1890," *Publications of the Center for Middle East Studies*, No. 17, University of Chicago Press, Chicago, 1984, p. 185. Arjomand's statement that there was an "absence of any jurisprudential theory of viceregency" in Shi'i doctrine is an overstatement. As A. A. Sachedina notes in *The Just Ruler in Shi'ite Islam*, forthcoming. "The concept of 'guardianship' (*wilaya*) in general, and the 'guardianship' of a jurist (*wilayat al-faqih*) in particular, has its genesis in the early history of Imamite jurisprudence."

66. This concept was particularly startling to the liberal and leftist Iranian intelligentsia, who naively hoped that the overthrow of the shah would be followed by the establishment of some form of secular regime.

67. See D. B. Macdonald, "Tawhid," in *Encyclopaedia of Islam*, old edition, Cambridge University Press, Cambridge, 1906, p. 704.

68. See Roger M. Savory, "Islam and Democracy: the Case of the Islamic Republic of Iran," in C. E. Bosworth et al. (eds.), *Historian of the Middle East: Essays in Honor of Bernard Lewis*, forthcoming.

69. See Sayyid 'Ali Khamanah'i, "Al-Tawhid (Qur'anic monotheism) and Its Social Implications," *Al-Tawhid*, Vol. I, No. 3, Islamic Propaganda Organization, International Relations Department, Islamic Republic of Iran, Tehran, Rajab A.H.1404, April 1984, pp. 55–77.

70. 'Ali Shari'ati, "The Ideal Society—The Umma," in Hamid Algar (trans.), *On the Sociology of Islam*, Mizan Press, Berkeley, 1979, pp. 119–120.

71. *Globe and Mail*, (Toronto), 1 September 1988.

72. *The Economist*, 2 February 1980, p. 48; 23 February 1980, p. 32.

73. *The Economist*, 28 April 1984, p. 13.

74. *The Economist*, 25 August 1984, p. 28.

75. *The Economist*, 29 March 1986, p. 54.

76. *The Economist*, 19 March 1983, p. 89.

77. Ibid.

78. *The Economist*, 22 November 1986, p. 41.

79. *The Economist*, 15 February 1985, p. 43, and 11 October 1986, p. 39.

80. *The Economist*, 15 February 1985, p. 43; 11 October 1986, p. 39.

81. The Iranians performed this grafting unsuccessfully, in the view of Sir Hamilton Gibb, for whom the Sasanian tradition "introduced into Islamic society a kernel of derangement, never wholly assimilated yet never wholly rejected." See Stanford J. Shaw and William R. Polk (eds.), *Studies on the Civilization of Islam*, Cambridge University Press, New York, 1962, p. 72.

82. V. Minorsky, "Opposition: Martyrdom and Revolt," in G.E. von Grunebaum (ed.), *Unity and Variety in Muslim Civilization*, Indiana University Press, Bloomington, 1967, p. 201.

83. 'Ali Shari'ati, *Tashayyu'-i 'alavi va tashayyu'-i safavi*, Tehran, 1352/1973, p. 307.

84. Ramazani I, p. 28.

85. Roger M. Savory, "The Principle of Homeostasis Considered in Relation to Political Events in Iran in the 1960s," *International Journal of Middle East Studies*, Vol. III, 1972, pp. 294–295.

86. Norman Jacobs, *The Sociology of Development: Iran as a Case Study*, Praeger, New York, 1966, p. 29.

87. Jacobs, op. cit., p. 30.

88. Jacobs, op. cit., p. 371.

89. Jacobs, op. cit., p. 314.

90. Jacobs, op. cit., p. 336.

91. Jacobs, op. cit., p. 418.

92. Jacobs, op. cit., p. 416.

PART TWO

Iran and Its Non-Arab Neighbors

3

Relations with Pakistan and India

Ashok Kapur

INTRODUCTION

I plan in this chapter to assess the main elements in Iran's relationship with Pakistan and India. No attempt is made here to provide data in the form of trade statistics, military balances, and so on, as such information is readily available. Rather, the effort is to search out for each country the diplomatic and political circumstances and the domestic and external imperatives (compulsions and opportunities) in which its relations have evolved and continue to do so. At present, there are elements of both strain and cooperation in the two sets of relations. The relations are neither one of hot war (peace or death) nor of cold war (neither peace nor honour). The relationship between Iran and Pakistan was a special one between two Moslem neighbours in the days of the Shah. But, significantly, there has been a sharp divergence between the strategic outlooks of Ayatollah Khomeini's Iran and Zia-ul-Haq's Pakistan. The attitudes and policies concerning regional and international affairs have sharply differed in the 1980s. Many of the divergent elements are likely to persist in the relations between Khomeini's (or post-Khomeini's) Iran and Benazir Bhutto's Pakistan unless the two regimes change radically from their present forms. Between Iran and India the relationship is one of increasing dialogue that is driven by a common strategic outlook on Gulf and South Asian affairs as well as matters concerning the United States and Pakistan. Overall, the Pakistan-Iran relationship has evolved from special relations (1950s–1979) to strained and competitive relations (1980–1988). The Iran-India relationship has evolved from strained relations (up to mid-1970s) to relations of competitive co-existence (1975–1979) and strategic convergence as well as strained religious relations (1980 to present). The two sets of relations are driven by imperatives of religion (Shia versus Sunni, Moslem versus Hindu), diplomatic and military strategy (regional and superpower politics), economic development, regional cooperation, and Arab politics.

It is widely held that foreign relations are governed by domestic and external imperatives as well as by the mental outlook of a country's political leadership, and that revolutions have foreign inputs. In Iran's case it is necessary to look closely into the Khomeini revolution (1979) and discover the undercurrents that have shaped American and Iranian thinking. The Khomeini revolution was inspired by an unlikely combination of Iranian communists, oil workers, bazaris, the middle classes, intellectuals (including leftist and rightist students), mullahs, and the United States. But the revolution was given a religious coloring. Despite the modernisation during the Shah's time, religion provided a strong undercurrent in Iranian political and social thinking. Soviet-style communism was anathema to most Iranians, and the leftists knew this well. A number of Iranian social, economic, and political forces came together for different reasons, but with a common contempt for the Shah and a shared hope to bring down his regime in 1978–1979.[1] But there was no single driving force behind the Shah's fall.

Khomeini's opposition to the Shah and his conception of an Islamic state in Iran was articulated in 1944 and again in his 1971 and 1977 publications.[2] Thus, Khomeini had an audience in Iran even during his exile (1963–1979). However, the ideological basis of the 1979 Iranian revolution was not simply centered on Khomeini. Different centres of political gravity were at play in Iran in the 1970s. In his 1978–1979 article James Bill did not see Khomeini as the driving element in the Iranian opposition, which had gained momentum from the early 1970s and crystallised by 1978.[3] But Khomeini certainly emerged as the main symbol of the Iranian revolution, even though he was not its sole author. Behind the revolution lies the history of an extended power struggle. Pierre Salinger shows that this power struggle affected not only the events leading to the Shah's ouster but the U.S. Embassy takeover as well.[4]

The anti-U.S. orientation of the Iranian public got out of control after the U.S. Embassy takeover. It was orchestrated by rightist student militants and communists and was joined by other Iranians, but it did not have the support of A. Bani-Sadr, S. Ghotbzadeh, and Iranian moderates who were anti-Shah but wanted a new Iran-U.S. relationship. To them the U.S. Embassy takeover isolated Iran in the international community. Khomeini's turn against the "Great Satan" was the result of a ground swell. A comparison of Iran and Pakistan is relevant in this context. President Zia's Sunni Islamic revolution was by nature a status quo, feudalistic, anti-democratic exercise. The Khomeini revolution has been anti status quo and, despite its excesses, continues to possess a democratic potential so long as internal debates also continue. Despite the intense sloganeering and mass rallies, the devotion to Shia Islam has not precluded internal debate in Iran. There is freedom of discussion (unlike Iraq) and Iranians remain willing to learn about the intellectual and cultural traditions of their Persian ancestors.

IRAN AND PAKISTAN

It may be tempting to describe Iran and Pakistan as partners in security, but to do so would be misleading. Shah's Iran and Pakistan had a network of agreements. (Research is needed to determine how many of these were repudiated, modified, or continued after the 1979 revolution.) For instance, a sign of intimacy between Iran and Pakistan in the security sphere was given in the 1965 Indo-Pakistan war when Pakistani planes, as a protective measure, were shifted to Iranian sanctuary. On the economic level, during the Iran-Iraq war, Pakistan and USSR served as a conduit for land trade with Iran. This had a favourable political effect on the Iran-Pakistan relations. But Zia's poor treatment of Pakistan's Shia population, his support of the Saudis ("an attack on Saudi Arabia is an attack on Pakistan"), and the extensive involvement of Pakistani soldiers in the Gulf region were seen in Tehran as aiding the Iraqi cause and were resented by the Khomeini government.

Thus, the record of Iran-Pakistan relations and the current agenda is mixed and complicated, and defies neat labelling. To capture some of the nuances we must explore the themes and issues in Iran-Pakistan relations against the background of Iran-India relations. The main elements in the two sets of relations will be outlined below.

On the religious plane, the Saudis and Iranians have been engaged in a bitter struggle, the prize being the hearts and minds of 130 million Moslems. The Saudis are going after the Sunni constituency; the Iranians are developing a Shia one. With its 80 percent Sunni majority, Zia's Pakistan aided the Saudi cause. The Iran-Iraq cease-fire is likely to increase Iranian opportunities and incentives to engage in economically and diplomatically cheaper interventions in support of the Shia cause, especially in Pakistan with its 20 percent Shia population. Iran used Pakistan's Shias to demonstrate against both Zia and the United States.

Many in the Middle East and South Asia believe that a Khomeini-inspired Islamic radicalism is desirable to effect a real transformation of political, social, and regional as well as international relations, thus curbing the interventionist impulses of the superpowers and their local clients. This represents a sea-change in the mental attitudes of several

Third World constituencies—attitudes unlikely to be changed by international conventions against terrorism. The Shia-Sunni controversy is an erosive element in the Iran-Pakistan relationship.

Thus, the establishment of sectarian/ethnic conflict as an element of contemporary power relations in the critical Gulf/South Asian region is undeniable. Today, as the Soviet Union becomes more interested in détente, arms control and regional conflict management through concerted superpower actions rather than revolution, the Iranian mullahs and intellectuals increasingly see themselves as the movers of revolutionary forces. Iranian fundamentalism is anti–status quo, unlike the Zia-type fundamentalism in Pakistan, which rested on a status quo, feudal orientation.

The U.S. encouragement of anti-Soviet fundamentalism in Iran, Afghanistan, and Pakistan has also affected Iran-U.S. relations. Given the broader U.S. strategy to foster anti-Soviet fundamentalism in the Soviet periphery, it made sense for the United States to encourage the build-up of Khomeinism, even though a rampant and out-of-control Iranian radicalism has damaged U.S. interests.

Since the 1950s, Pakistan (with its five nationalities—Punjabi, Baluch, Pathan, Sindhi, and Mohajirs) has been predicated on Islam, foreign aid, overseas remittances, a clever military-civil bureaucracy, and close links between the Pakistani oligarchy and the U.S. government.[5] It cannot function without these five pillars. For the first and the second Pakistan needs Saudi help. The third one depends on the good will of overseas Pakistanis. Pakistan depends also on the United States for aid. Zia's Pakistan sensibly extricated itself from the vague nonaligned, socialist, Islamic, democratic agenda of Zulfikar Bhutto by embracing the Americans and their strategic consensus in 1979. In this connection, Islam and geopolitics worked favourably to give Pakistani diplomacy an anti-Soviet, anti-Kabul, and anti-Indian focus and to a lesser extent, an anti-Iranian focus.

What Iran and Pakistan share is a belief in a radical type of Islam: The governments in both countries believe that such radical measures are necessary to restore Islam. In Pakistan's case, this attitude is revealed by the country's militarisation, nuclearisation, and Islamisation programmes as well as by its support for the Afghan mujahedeen and Sikh terrorism, and by the Pakistani authorities' tolerance of gun-running and drug trade in the region. In Iran's case, it is revealed by the export of Islamic radicalism, especially into Lebanon. In the Middle East there is a Shia/Sunni divide, but in South Asia there is a potentially bigger and more explosive Hindu/Moslem divide. The first divide has created problems in Iran-Pakistan relations, but the second is a unifying element: Both the Iranian and Pakistani press and the respec-

tive governments criticise the Rajiv Gandhi government for the poor
conditions of the Indian Moslems.

At the level of higher strategy there is a polarity between the Iranian
and Pakistani approaches and, conversely, a commonality of approach
and interest between Iran and India. Pakistan is a part of the U.S.
strategy in the region, whereas Iran explicitly rejects the United States.
The big difference between Iran and Pakistan is that the Khomeini
regime rejects both superpowers with equal force, whereas the Pakistani
approach under Zia and the new Benazir Bhutto government has been
to embrace the United States while keeping the Soviet option alive.
Iran's stance is that the great powers' presence in the Gulf aggravates
tensions, whereas Pakistan's stance is that the United States is a positive
force in the region against Soviet expansionism. Iran's aim is to eliminate the U.S. naval presence in the Gulf, but this clearly has not been
Pakistan's objective. India sympathises with Iran over this matter in
accordance with its Indian Ocean diplomacy, which is now more specifically focussed on the Gulf and Sri Lankan affairs; but its naval
policy is to concentrate on the Indian Ocean sea-lanes (in both the
Arabian Sea and the Bay of Bengal). The quest for a zone of peace in
the Indian Ocean is no longer plausible in India's thinking.

During the Shah's time the Indo-Iranian relationship was driven by
a desire for economic accommodation and competition in the naval
sphere. Today, the economic content of the Indo-Iranian relationship is
limited to trade in oil and sulphur. Iran's emergence as an independent
centre of diplomatic thinking appeals to India's government, and Iran
claims that in diplomatic and military affairs Pakistan is totally sub-
servient to the U.S. government. Iran objects to the nature of the
Pakistani relationship with the United States. The controversy concerns
Afghan policy as well. In this connection, Iran's main point has been
that the Afghan problem should be solved through discussion between
the USSR, Pakistan, Iran, and the mujahedeen as directly involved
parties, and that the United States has little to do with Afghanistan.
The issue is a regional, not East-West one. In Iranian thinking, Pakistan
was a U.S. tool in Afghanistan. India was seen as a legitimate regional
power and as having a (still undefined) role to play in Afghanistan. In
this regard, note the convergence in the Iran-India outlook on Afghanistan and the nature of the U.S.-Pakistan relationship; conversely, note
the sharp divergence in approach toward regional issues between Iran
and Pakistan. The convergence in Iran-India thinking is not total,
however. In Iranian thinking Afghanistan should not be an U.S. outpost.
India's concern is not necessarily anti-U.S., but it reflects Zia's policy
of seeking to set up a client regime in Afghanistan. Such a regime
would institutionalise the fundamentalist forces in Afghanistan and

strengthen the vision of an Islamic order in Iran, Afghanistan, Pakistan, and Bangladesh.

REGIONAL COOPERATION AND CONFLICT

The idea of a regional link-up among Turkey, Iran, and Pakistan crystallised in the early 1950s as a result of U.S. cold war strategic planning.[6] This arrangement had both an economic and a military content. In recent years the basis of this arrangement was that Turkey was an integral part of NATO and, potentially, a part of the European Economic Community (EEC); Pakistan was an integral part of the Western alliance system (CENTO, SEATO, and now CENTCOM); and Iran was the linchpin of Western security planning in the Gulf area. Consequently the military-economic cooperation among the three moderate Moslem states made sense in terms of both the U.S. containment of the USSR and the cooperation among the moderate Moslem states. The arrangement did not constitute a formal bloc, but the network of relations formed by the arrangement has continued to work despite ideological and policy differences among these states and changing regimes. For example, in the critical area of nuclear cooperation, envoys went to Pakistan via Turkey, and recently Iran-Pakistan nuclear contacts were reported in the press. In this respect Turkey, Iran and Pakistan are good neighbours.

What is the impact of both the Iran-Iraq conflict and the cease-fire on the Arab-Iran power equation and on the Iran-Pakistan relationship? My contention is that the cease-fire affects the lineup of the Gulf states in relation to Iran and could also affect Pakistan's place in U.S. strategic planning and its diplomatic and military weight in the region.

After the fall of the Shah, the Gulf States were divided in their approach to Khomeini's Iran. On the one hand, Saudi Arabia, Bahrain, and Kuwait were wary of Iran; on the other hand, Oman, Qatar, and the United Arab Emirates felt the need to live in understanding with Iran. As long as the Iran-Iraq war continued, there was no dialogue between Iran and the latter group. Now there is speculation about the dismantling of the Gulf Cooperation Council (GCC). This may not come about, but in any case the GCC may not bankroll Iraq as before and the GCC members may begin to worry about Iraqi intentions. Meanwhile, India is quietly trying to strengthen the nonalignment in the region and to develop Iran–Gulf Arab security arrangements that respect existing territorial boundaries. India has been building its diplomatic strategy on the basis of its apprehension over Pakistani-U.S. ties and was acutely worried about the Zia brand of Islam.

U.S. policy in the Gulf is governed by two main concerns: to contain the USSR, and to secure oil supplies. Iran was always considered a country to be coveted. Pakistan became the centrepiece in U.S. strategic planning in the Gulf region after the Shah's fall and as a result of the Soviet invasion of Afghanistan in 1979. As the United States chases the bigger Iranian prize, following the Soviet decision to withdraw its invasion forces from Afghanistan and after the Iran-Iraq cease-fire, Pakistan may lose the central place it has gained for itself since 1979. These developments in the region can be expected to reduce Pakistan's importance as a military and diplomatic extension of the United States.

SUMMING UP

The Iran-Iraq cease-fire represents a sea-change in the Gulf situation, but inherent hostilities remain on the diplomatic and strategic planes between Iran and Iraq, Iran and Saudi Arabia, Iran and Pakistan. The question of potential Iraqi aggression is still an unsettled issue, as is the future of U.S. ties with its Gulf clients.

It is difficult to say whether Iran will ever be moderated. It has emerged as an independent decision-maker in the Gulf and, as such, is a pole of attraction to many states in the region. It is both feared and respected by the Arab states. The Iran-Iraq cease-fire has increased Iran's diplomatic and economic opportunities with respect to oil trade, arms trade, and contracts for foreign companies to rebuild Iran.

The defusion of the Afghanistan and Iran-Iraq crises have diminished Pakistan's diplomatic opportunities because Zia's Pakistan thrived on these crises. Iran and Pakistan are likely to remain uneasy neighbours because their strategic outlooks, domestic and external compulsions, diplomatic opportunities, religious imperatives, and political systems are significantly different and competitive. The new Bhutto government is not driven by the late President Zia-ul-Haq's commitment to fundamentalism in Afghanistan and Pakistan. (Nor is Bhutto sympathetic to the Saudis, whose intervention with Zia could have saved her father from execution.) Hence the Shia-Sunni divide may be less of a divisive factor in Iran-Pakistan relations. However, Bhutto is dependent on the Pakistani Army and the U.S. government for political support, and the matrix of competing strategic interests that affect Iran and Pakistan is likely to persist unless the United States changes its attitude about regional clients and regional affairs. As such an attitude change is unlikely, the U.S.-Pakistan relationship will probably act as a divisive element in Iran-Pakistan affairs and work as a cohesive element in as Iran-India affairs (see Table 3.1).

TABLE 3.1: OVERVIEW OF THE DRIVING FORCES IN IRAN'S
RELATIONS WITH PAKISTAN AND INDIA

Period	Cooperative Elements	Competitive/Conflictual Elements
I. IRAN AND PAKISTAN A. 1950s to 1979	1. Both maintained a self-image as moderate Moslem states with cultured heritage and shared strategic interests. 2. Both were key players in the U.S. struggle against Soviet expansion through development of the "northern tier." 3. Through the regional cooperation program, both were partners in search of economic security. 4. Both were partners in border security concerning Baluchistan. 5. Both were aware that Pakistan was a geostrategic buffer between India and Iran that needed to be maintained. 6. Iran served as a sanctuary to Pakistan's Air Force in a military crisis (e.g., in the 1965 war) and as a source of material and diplomatic support in Pakistan's fight with India.	Not important
B. 1980 to 1988	1. There is economic cooperation (e.g., land trade) between China and Iran via Pakistan. 2. Pre-1979 Iran-Pakistan agreements have not been repudiated by Iran. 3. There is nuclear cooperation between the two countries. 4. There is continued awareness that Pakistan is a buffer between Iran and India. 5. Border security in the sensitive Baluchistan province is maintained by both countries.	1. The Shia-Sunni divide affects political and cultural relations between the two. 2. Both countries fundamentally about Gulf policy, Afghanistan policy, and their roles in relation to U.S. policies concerning regional and international affairs.

Period	Cooperative Elements	Competitive/Conflictual Elements
II. IRAN AND INDIA		
A. 1950s to 1971	Not important	Iran-India relations unfavourable because of Iran-Pakistan cooperation and India-Pakistan hostility
B. Early 1970s to 1979	1. The Shah of Iran has pushed the proposal to develop a regional economic common market encompassing Iran, Pakistan, and India. India likes the idea; Pakistan does not. 2. The Shah seeks a bilateral economic relationship with India.	1. Iran-Pakistan military cooperation is a divisive issue in Iran-India relations. 2. The Shah's push to develop Iran's role as a regional policeman and an Indian Ocean naval power threatens India naval and diplomatic interests. 3. Religious differences divide the two countries.
C. 1980 to present	1. Economic cooperation is marginal. 2. There is a convergence in the strategic outlook of Iran and India concerning Gulf and Afghan affairs as well as U.S./Pakistan factors in the Gulf/South Asia regions.	1. The Hindu-Moslem divide has had a negative effect on Iran-India political and cultural relations.

NOTES

1. In *The United States and Iran*, Praeger, New York, pp. 82–90, R. K. Ramazani outlines the multiple sources of opposition to the Shah and the United States.

2. Ramazani, *op. cit.*, pp. 78–86.

3. James A. Bill, "Iran and the Crisis of '78," *Foreign Affairs*, Winter 1978-1979, Vol. 57, No. 2, pp. 323–342.

4. In *America Held Hostage*, Doubleday, New York, 1981, pp. 247–248, Pierre Salinger argues convincingly that the students, not Ayatollah Khomeini, caused the downfall of the Shah, and that the Ayatollah was aware of the need to act according to popular views for fear of losing his position.

5. The origins and the history of this relationship are revealed in detail in M. S. Venkataramani, *The American Role in Pakistan, 1947–1958*, Radiant Publishers, New Delhi, 1982. Venkataramani's analysis is based on U.S. government documents.

6. This idea originated in October 1951 and crystallised in policy form in 1953. See ibid., pages 181, 219, and 222.

4

Iran and Turkey:
Permanent Revolution
or Islamism in One Country?

Fuat Borovali

There are some who view the Iranian Revolution as belonging, in terms of its political scope and philosophical impact, to that category of world-shaking events comparable to the French, Russian, and Chinese revolutions. Others have drawn parallels between the Napoleonic expansionism that was sparked by the unleashed energies of 1789 and the intransigence displayed by the Islamic regime in Iran. Whatever the characterization, the ripple effects of the revolution were unquestionably felt in varying degrees across the globe.

The impact of the Iranian Revolution was different in the West than in the Soviet Union; it was different in the Gulf than in Muslim North Africa. Even the term *Western* would have to be qualified by the distinction between what we know as Western Europe and the United States. It was the Arab world that felt the ostracism of Ayatollah Khomeini's regime—an ostracism directed primarily against the entrenched Arab monarchies in addition to Iraq. Syria and Libya did not fall into that category, however.

As one of the five countries sharing borders with Iran on land, Turkey was not expected to be totally immune from the political, diplomatic, and ideological ramifications of the Iranian Revolution. The period leading to that Revolution and the actual change of regime coincided with a particularly turbulent period in the history of Turkey. During 1978–1979 Turkey passed through a period of intense turmoil bordering on civil war. Indeed, as mass demonstrations against the Shah gained momentum, Turkey was heading for chaos and the escalating political violence claimed many casualties every day. In Turkey the era ended with a military takeover on 12 September 1980—ten days before the start of the Iran-Iraq War.

HISTORICAL PARALLELS

Thus, both Iran and Turkey emerged from the 1970s with changes of regime. The very nature of these regime changes can tell us something about these countries from a comparative perspective. In Turkey power was seized by the armed forces, the traditional custodians of the Kemalist state, which intervened for the third time in two decades (previous interventions occurred in 1960 and 1971); in Iran, it was the Shi'ite clergy that seized total power.

Considering the structural similarities between the two countries, going back to the Ottomans and the Safavids, how did this drastic parting of ways come about? Reflection on this point may tell us something about the relationship between these two countries, particularly in the post-revolution era.

During the nineteenth century both Ottoman Turkey and Persia were driven by two imperatives: westernization and the desire to stem the Russian threat from the north. Indeed, as Edward Mortimer points out, there was a dialectical relationship between the two elements: "In 1828, when the Russians occupied Tabriz and demanded reparations as specified by the Treaty of Turkmenchai, the Persians had to turn to the West to borrow the money. . . . And, as in the Ottoman Empire, borrowing money from the West went along with attempts to strengthen the state through Westernizing reforms and technical innovations."[1]

What led to the Ottoman Empire's westernization drive was a string of military defeats at the hands of the Russians. Iran likewise underwent a process of westernizing reforms during the long reign of Shah Nasir al-Din (1848–1896). By the end of the nineteenth century, there was a proliferation of groups and movements opposed to the increasing economic and cultural penetration by the West—an opposition reflected in the Great Tobacco Boycott of 1891–1892 in Iran.

There are other similarities between Turkey and Iran. The Iranian Constitutional Revolution of 1906 was followed by the Young Turk Revolution of 1908 (also a constitutional revolution). But the most striking parallel occurred during the period between the two wars, when Turkey experienced the Kemalist reforms and Reza Shah was engaged in similar secular changes in Iranian society.

By the late 1950s, both countries had been integrated into the Western alliance systems—that is, Turkey into NATO and CENTO, and Iran into CENTO. Both were also following Western, essentially U.S., economic guidelines. As developing economies, both were experiencing the vagaries of Third World development—inflation, the widening gap between rich and poor, corruption, and social instability. But, in Turkey's case there was at least a genuine attempt at parliamentary democracy and a home-grown system of "checks-and-balances" in the form of military interventions when matters got out of hand. A periodic house-cleaning of the government (as in 1960–1961 and 1971–1973), which acted as a type of deterrence, not only prevented the political and economic corruption from reaching the excesses of the Shah's regime but kept the reaction in check as well. Iran never had such a system. The resources available for corruption were much more plentiful, particularly after the OPEC price hikes of 1973–1974, but the military was an integral part of the system. If the Iranian military had been able to develop an autonomous system of values akin to the Kemalist tradition upheld by the Turkish military, the outcome might have been very different indeed.

CHANGING RELATIONS IN THE 1970s

The impact of the 1973–1974 OPEC price rises on the two countries was as different as can be imagined. Whereas Iran became awash with petrodollars, Turkey, an oil-importing country, was thrown into severe balance-of-payments problems and rampant inflation (at one point, in 1980, inflation reached 120 percent). But the oil money was not a blessing for Iran either. As the two countries started dealing with the instabilities of the OPEC era, the ensuing situation also affected the relationship between them.

Until 1973, Iran and Turkey had a fairly stable and predictable relationship, mostly within the confines of CENTO and Regional Cooperation and Development (RCD). There was even a sense of *camaraderie*—of being in the same boat in terms of development and ties to the West. But when Turkey started experiencing economic difficulties, in large part due to its heavy oil import bill, and requested easier payment conditions from fellow Muslim countries in OPEC including Iran, the Shah reportedly gave a curt reply. In Turkish diplomatic circles this response created the image of a Shah flaunting his country's wealth in "parvenu" fashion.[2] A certain resentment was felt among Turkey's bureaucrats, who were not enamored with the excesses of the Shah's bourgeoisie to begin with, and this resentment turned into cold indifference when the Shah's troubles began in earnest in 1978.

Meanwhile, Iran was engaged in an unprecedented buying spree of defence equipment worth billions of dollars, as would befit the "gendarme of the Gulf," and Turkey was not favorably impressed by these developments. Since the founding of the Baghdad Pact, particularly during the Nasser era, numerous Arab countries had been painting Turkey as an extension of the United States, and Turkish diplomacy was reluctant to reinforce that impression.

The signing of the Algiers Accord in 1975, in which the Shah agreed to withdraw his support from insurgent Iraqi Kurds in exchange for concessions on the Shatt al-Arab, was closely monitored in Turkey as to what it might portend for Turkey's own Kurdish problem. It should be recalled that internal instability, somewhat quelled during the 1971–1973 military regime, had returned by 1975. The next five years, until yet another military intervention in 1980, turned out to be the most unstable period in the entire history of the Republic; indeed, polarization and political violence reached unprecedented levels. During this time, it was not always easy to distinguish between Kurdish insurgent activity and the broader Leftist dissidence. Many Kurdish groups, rather than portraying themselves as narrow ethnicists, chose to operate under the wide umbrella of the Turkish Left.

In this environment, the Shah's manipulation of the Kurdish groups in Iraq—notably the Barzani clan under Mulla Mustafa—had serious implications for Turkey. Needless to say, Turkish authorities closely watched the Shah's regional power plays involving the Iraqi Kurds. So, when he finally pulled the rug from under Barzani after the Algiers Accord, there was some relief in Turkey. But there was also the realization that Iran would not shrink from playing the dangerous Kurdish card if it meant gaining leverage against Iraq, even if that move had consequences for Turkey.[3]

In the 1970s, there was also a growing Islamic movement in Turkey, as reflected in the political fortunes of the National Salvation Party (NSP). Although it received around 10 percent of the popular vote, NSP managed to take part in a series of coalition governments starting with the "Ecevit-Erbakan" coalition of 1974. It should be pointed out, however, that even during the height of the turmoil in the 1970s, NSP was never seriously associated with the political violence sweeping the country at the time. Nevertheless, the very presence of NSP leaders in prominent cabinet positions, along with their appointees in the state bureaucracy, was a source of irritation for the generals and the secularist bureaucrats.

In the days leading to the 12 September 1980 army takeover, a mass demonstration was held in Konya, a traditionalist bastion in central Anatolia, during which posters bearing Arabic inscriptions (legally banned in Turkey) were displayed and slogans were chanted demanding restoration of the Shari'a. The meeting, attended by the top leadership of the NSP, has been cited as the last straw, forcing the generals to intervene a few days later.[4] It would be misleading, however, to suggest that the Konya incident figured prominently in the generals' decision to seize power. The decision had been made much earlier, and the incident might have been nothing more than a pretext to justify the intervention.

THE WAR AND THE REVOLUTIONARY DECADE

Following the second wave of OPEC price shocks in 1979 and the worsening of its balance-of-payments situation, Turkey sought to establish closer trading relations with the Muslim countries of OPEC—particularly Iraq, Libya, and Saudi Arabia. Turkish construction companies started getting big contracts in these countries. Easier payment arrangements and credit facilities were sought to help meet the oil bill. In this environment, the Iran-Iraq War, which broke out on 22 September 1980 (barely ten days after the 12 September takeover in Turkey), signalled a new opportunity.

By that time, a Western trade embargo had been placed on Iran because of the "hostage crisis." Turkey decided not to go along with the embargo and, as a result, the two-way trade with Iran soared to an annual $2 billion by 1985. In a short time, Turkey had become a major supplier of agricultural commodities and light manufactures to *both* Iran and Iraq. Turkey also emerged as an honest broker between the two countries, undertaking diplomatic initiatives to end the war, but with no substantial results. Instead, the war came closer to Turkey as the belligerents started playing off each other's Kurds against one another.

As noted earlier, Turkey had already experienced Kurdish insurgent activity during the 1970s. The crackdown by the military during the 12 September regime had brought a temporary respite in Kurdish activism. But it started to intensify in 1983 as the military prepared to hand back power. After the November 1983 elections there was a gradual escalation in Kurdish guerilla activity, conducted from the border areas in northern Iraq. This activity prompted Ankara and Baghdad to conclude an agreement allowing "hot pursuit" operations to be carried out by either side in each other's territory. From 1984 onward, the Turkish Air Force (TAF) conducted several bombing raids against guerilla camps and hide-outs in northern Iraq, often in joint operations with ground troops.

The Kurdish involvement in the Gulf War reached a new plateau in 1986. During that year the two major Kurdish factions that had been feuding since 1975—the Patriotic Union of Kurdistan (PUK) led by Jalal Talabani and Masoud Barzani's Kurdish Democratic Party (KDP)—formed an alliance with the Iranians. By November 1986 they were receiving large quantities of arms and assistance from Iran as the Iranians intensified their military campaign along the northern front. Several offensives in the Haj Umran area were undertaken with substantial KDP and PUK involvement. Some observers have noted that the alliance bore some resemblance to the "disastrous agreement" made between Mulla Mustafa and the Shah a decade earlier.[5]

The upsurge in military activity following the KDP-PUK-Iranian alliance in November 1986 was accompanied by low-intensity guerilla attacks by the Workers Party of Kurdistan (PKK) in Turkey.[6] The activities of the PKK, on the rise since 1984, prompted another round of air raids by the TAF in northern Iraq in August 1986. Extensive casualties reportedly resulted.[7] By March 1987, PKK attacks targeting Kurdish villages in Turkey's southeastern region had become more and more audacious, leading to yet another retaliatory raid in which thirty TAF jets bombed Kurdish camps inside Iraq.[8] Yet a few days later, the PKK, this time conducting its operations from Syria, attacked another village.[9]

This sequence of events further strained the already tense relations between Turkey and Iran. The Iranians were bitterly critical of the bombing raids on the Iraqi-based Kurds, whom they regarded as their allies in the Gulf War.[10] It was particularly galling that the raids had come at a time when Iran was launching a new offensive in the Haj Umran area.[11]

Following the 1986 incidents, headlines appearing in *Kayhan* (which reflects the Iranian government's views) announced that Turkey had been "advised to maintain neutrality."[12] Allegations of Turkish "irredentism" concerning the Mosul-Kirkuk region were made in full candor. *Kayhan* quoted a Kurdish deputy in the Iranian Majlis who said that the Turkish government should not covet the oil-rich Kirkuk province, and that "Iraq's natural resources should belong to the Muslim Iraqi nation."[13]

Throughout 1986, Iran's fortunes on the war front were on the rise— from the gates of Basra to the border areas of the north. Meanwhile, there was some concern reflected in the Turkish press about the possible consequences of an Iraqi collapse.[14] On the Iranian side, Prime Minister Hossein Musawi, in an unmistakable jibe at Turkey, stated that the shakiness of the Saddam regime should not give rise to territorial ambitions against Iraq or its resources.[15] A similar note was struck by President Ali Khamenei, speaking to a gathering of Iraqi dissident groups in Tehran in December 1986, to the effect that Iran was fully committed to an independent and free Iraq within its recognized international boundaries, and that Iran would not hesitate to challenge any intervention in Iraq's affairs by other countries.[16]

All these developments seemed to indicate that Turkey and Iran were being polarized over the Kurdish issue. Although Iran had its problems with its own Kurds (notably the Kurdish Democratic Party of Iran led by Abdurrahman Ghassemlou), its alliance with Barzani and Talabani provided considerable leverage in the Gulf War, with KDP and PUK pinning down an estimated 160,000 Iraqi troops.[17] Therefore, any action weakening the Iraqi Kurds was seen as detrimental to the Iranian war effort. For its part, Turkey had reason to be worried about the possible formation of an autonomous Kurdistan in northern Iraq beholden to the Islamic Republic of Iran, thus raising the double specter of a Kurdish insurgence buttressed by an Islamic resurgence. How seriously that scenario was taken by the Turkish General Staff may be difficult to establish in precise terms, but the relocation of an unprecedented 60 percent of the country's land forces along the length of Turkey's Syria-Iraq-Iran border should give some indication.[18]

Although developments involving the Kurds were the immediate point of contention between Turkey and Iran, the ideological challenge posed by the Iranian Revolution had more far-reaching implications, given the latent ideological incongruity between Khomeini's vision of an Islamic order and Kemalist westernism upheld by the Turkish state. Khomeini's brand of Shi'a Islam was not going to attract many followers in overwhelmingly Sunni Turkey, but the establishment of a Fundamentalist regime next door was bound to have repercussions. As noted earlier, the initial years of the Iranian Revolution coincided with the military regime in Turkey (1980–1983), during which there was a heavy crackdown on all kinds of political activity. So it is not surprising that manifestations of Islamic resurgence in Turkey were unseen before the November 1983 elections, which brought the Motherland Party (ANAP) led by Turgut Ozal into power. Ozal has since adhered to an eclectic mix of economic liberalism and cultural conservatism. And in ANAP itself, there has been a sizeable representation of the religious Right led by the former mayor of Konya, who had organized the mass rally in September 1980, days before the military takeover.

As with the Kurdish issue, 1986 was the year in which Islamic activity reached a new level of intensity in Turkey. Although observers disagree on the seriousness of the Islamic challenge, no one could ignore such visible changes occurring in Turkish society as the proliferation of the Quran courses (particularly for girls), increased wearing of the *charshaf* (chador), stricter observance of the Ramadan, and the controversy created by the wearing of headscarves by female students at university campuses.[19]

Such developments did not fail to produce the predictable reaction from the military. "On the domestic front, the Islamic ferment has put the delicate modus operandi between Ozal and the military under severe strain," noted one observer.[20] In January 1987, President Kenan Evren delivered a televised speech in which he branded Islamic resurgence as a subversive threat comparable to communism. The Islamic extremists, he said, had infiltrated the armed forces, resulting in the expulsion of nearly 100 cadets from military academies.[21] The generals, too, were worried about the prevalence of Islamic sect members in government departments. Many leading officials of the ruling ANAP were said to belong to such "Islamic freemasonries" as the Nakshibendis.[22]

The growing strains between the generals and the government came to a head when Ozal did the unthinkable and sacked the incoming chief of general staff, General Necdet Oztorun, in June 1987. The ostensible reason was the alleged failure of Oztorun, then commander of the land forces, to inform the prime minister of a PKK massacre that had occurred a few days earlier. But the general was also known to be a vocal critic of Ozal's lenient policies regarding *irtica* (a blanket term signifying the backing away from Kemalist reforms as well as a retrogressive yearning for a return to an Islamic past). "At the root of the estrangement, now a feud, between the prime minister and the top generals," concluded one observer, was the resurgence of Islamic activity since Ozal came to power.[23]

The Oztorun affair has an intimate bearing on Turkish-Iranian relations, thus demonstrating, once again, how intricately interwoven domestic and foreign policies can be. During a visit to Ankara a month before the Oztorun incident, Prime Minister Musawi had publicly criticized the westernizing reforms of Kemal Ataturk and refused to pay homage at Ataturk's mausoleum—a protocol requirement for visiting dignitaries. (He also made it clear that he would rather be visiting the Maulana shrine in Konya.) For General Oztorun and his colleagues this was nothing short of a personal insult. They were particularly outraged by the deferential treatment shown by Ozal toward the Iranian prime minister.[24] But it can be said that Musawi was being consistent with the clerical tradition in Iran. However undiplomatic his actions may have been, he was merely fleshing out the existing ideological divide between the two countries. And in so doing, he was drawing attention to the fact that Turkey's elected governments do not always see eye to eye with the custodians of Kemalism, particularly in matters relating to the dichotomy between religion and state.

By 1987, Turkish intelligence services had collected sufficient evidence linking the Iranian government to instances of Islamic radicalism in Turkey, and to propaganda efforts among Turkish workers in West

Germany. The question of Iranian involvement in Turkey's internal affairs was given prominence in the Turkish press, through commentaries urging the public to recognize that Turkey has an "Iranian problem" on its hands—a problem compounded by the presence (mostly in Istanbul) of an estimated half-million Iranian refugees.[25]

Yet, despite the tensions at the diplomatic level, the Ozal government exercised remarkable restraint in avoiding a confrontation. In fact, Ozal added new impetus to his peacemaking efforts, revisiting both Tehran and Baghdad in early 1988 and consistently maintaining a stance of "active neutrality." But even as his peace efforts continued, several Turkish divisions were massed along Turkey's southern borders.[26]

Such concentration of troops, however, was not solely due to developments relating to northern Iraq. An increasingly worrisome problem has been the worsening relations with Syria over the PKK terrorism evidently launched from that country. The emergence of Damascus as the nerve-centre of PKK operations (given the easy access from that city to PKK training camps in the Bekaa Valley) and the fact that the Syrian border has become the primary conduit for transport of men and weapons to be used during PKK massacres have strained relations between Syria and Turkey to the breaking point. After a particularly brutal PKK massacre in March 1987, crowds in Ankara demanded military action against Syria.[27] The government, however, decided to apply nonmilitary forms of pressure, using Turkey's ability to regulate the flow of the Euphrates as leverage against the Syrians, who are heavily dependent on that water.[28]

THE CEASE-FIRE AND BEYOND

The Iranian declaration on 18 July 1988 of a readiness to comply with U.N. Resolution 598 prompted a rethinking of the entire complex of relations revolving around Iran. A series of Iranian reverses on the battlefield during the early half of 1988 meant that the prospect of an Iraqi collapse, with all its consequences for the region, subsided for the time being. And the establishment of an Iranian-sponsored autonomous Kurdish entity in northern Iraq has since lost much of its plausibility.

Relieved of the Iranian pressure, the Iraqi army took immediate steps to reestablish control in the northern areas which were conceded to Kurdish rebel forces during the war. Baghdad wasted little time in bringing a heavy clampdown on Kurdish areas, reminiscent of the period following the Algiers Accord back in 1975. Part retribution, part restoration of control, the Iraqi army's drive into the northern border areas resulted in the fleeing of about 70,000 Kurds into Turkey. Offered "temporary refuge" by the government, they were settled in makeshift

camps. In subsequent days, it was reported that about 1,700 of them
went back to Iraq and 13,000 were transferred to Iran.[29] Subsequently,
the refugee question became a matter of some controversy between Iran
and Turkey, prompting a visit by the Iranian deputy premier to Ankara.
The Iranian government complained that too many Kurdish refugees
were being transferred to Iran from Turkey.[30]

There were other sources of irritation between the two countries.
About 100 Pasdaran (Iranian Revolutionary Guards) had previously
been arrested by the Turkish authorities in border areas and, conversely,
a number of Turkish soldiers were being held by the Iranians.[31] Moreover, there was the expulsion of two Iranian diplomats, along with four
others, after the kidnapping of a Mujahidin-i Khalq member in Turkey
in an attempt to smuggle him into Iran.[32] Iran retaliated by asking two
Turkish diplomats to leave the country.[33]

Such developments have been causing concern in Turkish diplomatic
circles for some time. But there have also been reports of increased
resentment in Turkish military circles. In October 1988, a Turkish daily
published a circular, sent by the former commander of the navy to his
units in August 1985, alerting them to Islamic propaganda activities
"masterminded by Iran."[34] The circular also drew attention to a number
of publications viewed as part of the propaganda campaign. But some
of these publications (*Yeni Asya, Yeni Nesil, Kopru*) are generally known
as "Nurcu" publications. Prominent Nurcus have been on record dis-
counting links with the Iranian regime and pointing to philosophical
and doctrinal differences between their movement and the revolutionary
regime in Iran.[35]

In any case, the experience of the revolutionary decade in Iran,
coupled with the outcome of the Iran-Iraq War, had a dampening effect
on Islamic movements in Turkey, if the tone of the Islamic press is
any indication.[36] With the surge of excitement generated in the initial
years of the revolution on the wane, the Islamic movements in Turkey
can be expected to lower their expectations. That does not mean,
however, that the impact of the Iranian Revolution is about to disappear
from the Turkish political scene altogether.

The Turkish government has been on the "right side" of the Salman
Rushdie affair—not only banning the book in Turkey but publicly
criticizing the author of *The Satanic Verses* for trampling upon genuine
feelings of Muslims around the world. That was done despite the
unmistakable stance taken by the EEC, and some have suggested that
the Rushdie episode has, amongst other things, revived the whole
question of Turkey's credentials to become a bona fide member of the
European *cultural* community.

It has also been suggested that the Rushdie affair may give Turkey a chance to win Iranian business, in view of the strained diplomatic and trade relations between the EEC and Iran.[37] This author thinks that too much has been made of the Rushdie affair, and although it is something more than a blip in the chequered history of the West's relations with Iran, its impact on established trade routines is not likely to be significant. The cessation of the Gulf War may well end up having the paradoxical effect of undermining Turkey's trading advantages, not only in Iran but in Iraq as well, as trade embargoes are lifted and the Gulf is opened to safe navigation once again.[38] As trading nations, from Japan to Brazil, scramble to take advantage of the long-heralded "postwar reconstruction," Turkey may find that the going will get tougher.[39]

EPILOGUE

The revolutionary decade in Iran has done much to crystallize Turkey's own unresolved problems, bringing into sharp focus the old debates about the proper role of Islam in the political context. But it has also given rise to fears that a populist Islamic movement, deriving encouragement from the model already established in Iran, might pose a challenge to the Kemalist state. This fear has been prevalent particularly within the military and among the secularist judiciary in Turkey.

Now that the perceived threat has subsided, Turkey is likely to channel its energies toward getting its proper share of the "reconstruction boom," if and when it comes, while monitoring the seismic counts along the faultlines of Islam.

As for Iran, its external relations can be expected to fluctuate according to the dynamics of its internal politics. And its relations with Turkey are likely to be conditioned, in large part, by the ongoing struggle between the champions of permanent revolution and those espousing Islamism in one country.

NOTES

1. See Edward Mortimer, *Faith and Power* (New York: Vintage Books, 1982), p. 111.

2. The conclusion is based on the author's interviews with Turkish government officials in the late 1970s.

3. For an extensive review of the Kurdish issue in the overall context of Turkish-Iranian relations, Fuat Borovali, "Kurdish Insurgencies, the Gulf War, and Turkey's Changing Role," *Conflict Quarterly*, Fall 1987.

4. This is the official narrative of events published (in English) by the military regime (1980–1983) entitled *12 September in Turkey: Before and After*, National Security Council Publications Office, Ankara, July 1982.

5. *Middle East International (MEI)*, December 5, 1987, p. 718.

6. Ibid., p. 17.

7. *South*, October 1986, p. 18.

8. *Globe and Mail*, March 5, 1987.

9. PKK's operations have been masterminded by Abdullah Ocalan ('Apo') who is known to have moved the headquarters of the PKK from northern Iraq to Damascus.

10. *MEI*, March 20, 1987, p. 12.

11. *Globe and Mail*, March 5 1987; see also *The Economist*, March 14, 1987.

12. "Turkey Advised to Maintain Neutrality," *Kayhan*, November 1, 1987, p. 1.

13. Ibid.

14. Fahir Armaoglu, "Iran Konusu (On Iran)," *Tercuman*, November 5, 1986, p. 4; Talat Halman, "Seytan in Sisesi" (Satan's Bottle), *Milliyet*, November 17, 1986, p. 10.

15. *Kayhan*, November 8, 1987, p. 10.

16. *Afkar-Inquiry*, February 1987, p. 9.

17. *South*, October 1986, p. 18.

18. *MEI*, December 5, 1987, p. 17.

19. *MEI*, February 6, 1987, pp. 15–16. See also Coskun Kirca, "Irtica Tartismasi" (The Debate over Retrogression), *Hurriyet*, July 11, 1987.

20. *MEI*, February 6, 1987, p. 15.

21. Ibid.; see also *The Economist*, January 17, 1987, p. 54.

22. *MEI*, February 6, 1987, p. 15.

23. *MEI*, July 11, 1987, p. 13.

24. Ibid.; see also *The Economist*, July 4, 1987, p. 47. In my interview with Oztorun, I found his criticisms to be directed at Ozal rather than the Iranians.

25. See Armaoglu, *op. cit.*, p. 10.

26. *MEI*, April 25, 1987, p. 11.

27. *The Economist*, March 14, 1987.

28. *MEI*, December 5, 1986.

29. *Cumhuriyet*, 15 October 1988, pp. 1, 11.

30. *Milliyet*, 15 October 1988, p. 13.

31. M. Ali Kislasi, "Iran Gucluk Cikariyor" (Iran Causing Difficulties)," *Tercuman*, 15 October 1988, p. 6.

32. *Washington Post*, 28 October 1988.

33. *Foreign Broadcast Information Service (FBIS)*, 22 November 1988.

34. *Hurriyet*, 17 October 1988, pp. 1, 18.

35. *Nurculuk* is a term used to denote the movement propagated by Said-i Nursi (1873–1960), said to have close to 2 million followers in Turkey today. Traditionally active in Turkish politics, the Nurcus are said to have been supporters of the Democrat Party, Justice Party, and, more recently, the True Path Party led by Suleyman Demirel; see *Nokta*, 3 May 1987, pp. 12–21.

36. I am referring in particular to the September-October 1988 issues of *Milli Gazete* and to the editorials by Abdurrahman Dilipak.

37. See *The Economist*, 18 March 1989.

38. This is the view taken by *The Economist*, 15 October 1988.

39. A useful account of what can and should not be expected of the post-war reconstruction can be found in the *South*, September 1988, pp. 47–52.

PART THREE

Iran and the Middle East Situation

5

Iran and the Arab World

Shireen T. Hunter

Since the advent of the Iranian revolution in February 1979, Iran's relations with the Arab world have undergone considerable change. At the interstate level, Iran's pattern of alliances and enmities has been completely reversed. Thus, unlike the past, when Iran had close relations with most of the moderate Arab states, revolutionary Iran has been at odds with these countries; at the same time, it has developed better relations, and sometimes tactical alliances, with the so-called radical Arab states such as Syria and Libya.

At the mass level, Iran for the first time has become a force to be reckoned with in the Arab world. The Iranian revolution, despite later disappointments, did inspire many Arabs, as did Iran's defiance of the two superpowers. Indeed, this aspect of the Iranian revolution, more than Iran's alleged, or actual, subversion, was the cause of Arab fears of the so-called Iranian challenge.

Yet beneath these seemingly drastic changes, the underlying pattern of Arab-Iranian interaction has remained remarkably constant, and subject to the influence of a number of forces that also influenced Arab-Iranian relations during the pre-revolution period. Thus, before surveying the evolution of Arab-Iranian relations in the post-revolution period, we shall consider those fundamental factors which have always determined the shape of Arab-Iranian relations, and continue to do so now.

ETHNO-RELIGIOUS DIFFERENCES

Since the Arab defeat of Iran in the seventh century A.D., ethnic and religious differences have not only created a background of tension in Arab-Iranian relations, but have also exacerbated the divisive impact of other differences. This is so because Iran, despite Islamicization, has retained its ethnic and cultural distinctiveness.[1]

Indeed, Islam, rather than unifying the Arabs and the Iranians, has further divided them. The prophet of Islam had brought a universalist message to humankind, transcending ethnic and racial barriers. But after his death, the Arabs forgot the universalist and egalitarian dimensions of Islam, viewed the revelation of Islam to Mohammad as proof of their racial superiority, and embarked on racially discriminatory policies toward the conquered peoples.[2]

One result of this policy in Iran was the tendency of the Iranians to dissociate themselves from the religious beliefs of their rulers—hence their attraction to Shi'ism.[3] Iran's Shi'atization enhanced the Iranians' sense of distinctiveness and deepened the Arab-Iranian chasm. Iran's Islamization also gave rise to a cultural competition between the Arabs and the Iranians, as well as to a bone of contention between them in terms of their respective contributions to the development of Islamic culture.[4]

Since the revolution, the Iranian government has systematically tried to downplay the national factor and to emphasize Islam as the core of Iran's national identity. Yet the evolution of the post-revolution Arab-Iranian relations has illustrated the continuing influence of these factors. For example, faced with Iran's ideological challenge, conservative Arab states have effectively argued that the Iranian experience is irrelevant to the Arab world because it is a purely Persian Shi phenomenon and thus alien to the Arab-Sunni world.[5] Iraq has successfully used Arab nationalism and racially charged symbols to harness support of its war against Iran.[6] The result of this Arab attitude has been an upsurge of nationalist feelings in Iran and the emergence of anti-Arab sentiments, despite the government policy of downplaying Persian nationalism.[7]

COMPETING NATIONALISMS

The rise of modern nationalism in Iran and in the Arab world in the twentieth century has added political dimensions to Arab-Iranian ethno-religious differences and their cultural competition. Two characteristics of Arab nationalist thinking have been particularly ominous from the Iranian perspective. These are what Majid Khaduri has called the "irredentist" and "romantic" dimensions of Arab nationalism.[8] Iran has been a prime target of Arab irredentist ambition in the form of an Arab claim to Khusistan and Bahrain.

In the Gulf region, the Arab nationalist challenge to Iran has been manifested in the form of Arab efforts to change the name to Arabian Gulf and to challenge the legitimacy of the Iranian presence.[9] Mean-

while, in the last several decades Iranian nationalism has been preoccupied with the reassertion of Iran's position in the Gulf, thus bringing
it into completion and conflict with Arab nationalism. The Islamic
regime rejects Iranian nationalism as anti-Islamic. Yet its perceptions
of Iran's interests in the Gulf and its regional role are remarkably
similar to those of Iranian nationalists.[10] Thus, in the post-revolution
period, too, Arab and Iranian nationalist goals have continued to clash.

SYSTEMIC FACTORS

In the last several decades, factors related to the nature of international and regional political systems have deeply affected Arab-Iranian
relations. For example, during the immediate post–World War II period,
the polarization of the international system along the East-West divide
affected Arab-Iranian relations in the following way.

Iran, preoccupied with the Soviet threat, chose the Western camp
and joined the U.S.-sponsored Baghdad Pact. Many Arab states, such
as Egypt, viewed Israel as their primary security concern. Since the
United States was Israel's principal supporter, they turned to the Soviet
Union for help and against the Baghdad Pact. These diverging positions
on the East-West conflict between Iran and such Arab countries as
Egypt, Syria, and later Libya became a principal cause of discord in
their relations. By the late 1960s, the rigid bipolarity of the international
system had begun to erode, a process that would accelerate in the
coming two decades. The East-West dichotomy also began to lose some
of its importance as the dominant paradigm in international relations.

As a result, regional factors acquired greater importance in deter-
mining the state of Arab-Iranian relations, although the Arabs' and
Iranians' superpower connections would continue to affect their ties. At
the regional level, the most important systemic factor has been the
gradual, but complete, integration of the Arab side of the Gulf into the
Arab world. This development has brought Iran into closer interaction
with the Arab world and has meant that the Iranians' and the Arabs'
respective positions on regional and international issues have become
of increasing significance for the other party. Thus, during the 1960s
and the 1970s, when Iran was part of a Western-sponsored security
pact and was actively involved in combating radical forces in the region,
it became a prime target of Arab radical subversion while maintaining
reasonably good ties with the moderate Arabs.[11]

Since the Islamic revolution, the process of intraregional linkage
between Iran and the Arab world has intensified and acquired a new
popular dimension. The anti-imperialist, anti-Zionist, and anti-Israel
rhetoric of the new regime, as well as its emphasis on Islamic unity

and its downplaying of Persian nationalism, have enhanced its ability to reach the Arab masses. This newfound ability has been one of the reasons for the moderate Arabs' anxiety regarding the impact of the Iranian revolution and Iran's so-called subversive activities.

This dimension of Arab-Iranian relations, however, has essentially remained one of intrinsic competition between the forces of change and those of status quo. In the pre-revolution period, Iran represented the status quo in the region and was attacked by those seeking to change it. After the revolution, Iran has been the primary force for change, which the status quo powers have tried to control and contain.

INTRA-ARAB POLITICS

The growing integration of the different parts of the Middle East regional subsystem, as well as increased Arab-Iranian interaction, has made Arab-Iranian relations vulnerable to the developments in intra-Arab politics and to the shifting pattern of intra-Arab alliances. As noted earlier, one aspect of intra-Arab politics with significant consequences for Arab-Iranian relations has been the influence of the Arab nationalist ethos. The other important aspect has been intra-Arab ideological as well as political divisions and rivalry for power and prestige. Thus, Arab states have often used Iran to affect the intra-Arab balance of power in their own favor. Iran, for its part, has forged tactical alliances with Arab countries to create a regional environment congenial to its interests.

During the 1950s, Iraq's cooperation with Iran within the framework of the Baghdad Pact was due partly to Egyptian-Iraqi rivalry. In the 1960s and 1970s, Iran and Saudi Arabia cooperated to combat Egypt's Arab socialism and other radical forces.[12] In the post-revolution period, Syria's alignment with Iran has resulted from its rivalry with Iraq. Moreover, following the 1982 Israeli invasion of Lebanon, Syria has been relying on Iran to check the influence of Israel and the PLO in Lebanon and to extend its own control. Meanwhile, Iran has likewise been banking on Syria to improve Iran's position in its war with Iraq and to gain a foothold in Lebanon. Libya and Syria have used Iranian policy to strengthen the so-called Arab rejectionist front on the Arab-Israeli issue. Meanwhile, Egypt and conservative Arab regimes have used the Iranian threat to facilitate the readmission of Egypt into the Arab fold, arguing that the Arab world needed Egypt as a counterweight to Iran.[13]

TERRITORIAL DISPUTES

Several long-standing territorial disputes have affected Arab-Iranian relations in the last several decades, including the years of the revolution itself. The most important of these disputes have been those pertaining to the Arab claim to Khusistan and Iran's historical claim to Bahrain.

The Bahrain dispute was settled in 1970, when Iran gave up its claim. However, as illustrated by Iran's alleged support for a coup attempt in Bahrain in 1981, many Iranians still feel bitter about this issue. This feeling is further intensified by the fact that Bahrain has gradually become a Saudi appendage in all but name. The Khusistan issue, however, has never been quite settled. Of course, Arab governments have legally recognized Iran (and, by implication, have recognized its borders as well), but they have also kept alive their claim to Khusistan.[14] Other territorial disputes include the Arab claim to the three Gulf islands of Abu Musa and the Greater and Lesser Tumbs, and Iraq's claims of total sovereignty over Shat-al-Arab (Arvand Rud).

The most dramatic impact of the territorial disputes was Iraq's invasion of Iran on 22 September 1980. Iraq's desire to vindicate the Arab claim to Khusistan was one of the war's more powerful causes. In the final analysis, however, these disputes—though clearly an underlying irritant—have not shaped Arab-Iranian relations. Whether or not they have been used actively by individual Arab states, or have been conveniently ignored, has depended on other factors, including the state of their relations with Iran.[15]

THE IMPACT OF IDEOLOGY

In the last three decades, Arab-Iranian relations have been shaped primarily by ideological affinity, or the lack of it; by the respective positions of Iran and the Arab countries on the East-West conflict; and by the nature of their respective relations with the superpowers. Of course, ideological affinity has not always guaranteed fully cooperative relations, and other divisive factors have continued to affect relations between Iran and the like-minded Arab states. But ideological affinity has certainly enabled them to gloss over their differences.

Under the Shah, Iranians and moderate Arabs cooperated; and since the revolution, Iran has had better ties with the so-called radical Arabs. However, there are certain differences between the pre- and post-revolution periods. In the past, Iran and moderate Arabs cooperated because, in addition to common friendship with the United States and common animosity toward the USSR, they shared more or less similar views on the structure of their respective societies. During the post-revolution period, by contrast, only a common animosity toward the United States as well as a similarity of position on the Arab-Israeli conflict has been responsible for Iran's cooperation with radical Arab states.[16]

THE ISRAELI FACTOR

Many Arabs have often cited Iran's close relations with the state of Israel during the rule of the Shah as the primary cause of Arab-Iranian tensions. Without a doubt, Iran-Israel ties under the Shah were a principal cause of radical Arab animosity and subversion toward Iran, as well as an irritant in Iran's relations with other Arab states. In the final analysis, however, Iran's attitude toward the Arab-Israeli conflict and its ties with the state of Israel have not determined the state of Arab-Iranian relations; other divisive factors have been more important.

Some of these other factors, such as the anti-Iranian dimensions of Arab nationalism, have indeed colored the Arabs' view of Iran-Israel ties. For example, although Turkey has recognized Israel de jure, it has not become the subject of Arab animosity in the way Iran has.[17] It is for this reason that, in the past, Iran's ties with Israel were not an insurmountable barrier for Arab-Iranian cooperation when other factors brought the two together.

The experience of the Islamic regime has illustrated that the same principle still applies. Thus, Iran's new virulent anti-Israel posture and its total support for the Palestinian cause have not ensured the amity of the Arabs, including the Palestinians, toward it. Indeed, it is ironic that while Iran has paid a heavy price for its hard-line position on the Palestinian issue, and because of its anti-Israel posture, the PLO and most Palestinians supported Iraq in its war against Iran.

Similarly, when Iran, out of necessity, bought arms from Israel, the Arabs used this fact as evidence of Iran's duplicity and its inherently anti-Arab nature. What was forgotten was that Iran was forced to buy arms from Israel because Iraq, an Arab country, had invaded it.

THE IRAN-IRAQ WAR

Nothing illustrates the impact of these factors on Arab-Iranian relations better than the Iran-Iraq war and the response of the Gulf Arab states to it. (As detailed study of the Iran-Iraq war is beyond the scope of this chapter,[18] only certain aspects of the conflict and the responses of the Gulf Arab states, best illustrative of the impact of the above factors, will be discussed here.) The general consensus (with only a few dissenting opinions) is that Iraq started the war by escalating what were essentially minor border skirmishes into a full-scale military invasion of Iran.[19] It is also generally agreed that several factors contributed to the outbreak of hostilities. But opinion is divided as to the primary impulse behind Iraq's action. Some believe that Iraq's principal motive was fear of the contagious impact of the Islamic revolution and its impact on the survival of the Ba'athist regime. Others, by contrast, put more emphasis on the factor of Iraqi ambitions and on the systemic changes that made invasion a tempting possibility. The weight of evidence supports the latter interpretation. No doubt the success of Islamic forces in Iran was disturbing to Iraq, as was the Iranian propaganda urging the Irani Shi'as to follow suit. However, by the time of the invasion, Iraq's Shi'a movement was in disarray as a result of the Ba'athist regime's execution of its charismatic leader, Imam Mumammad Baqir as-Sadr, and it was thus in no position to seriously threaten its survival. Moreover, with $30 billion in foreign reserves and its regional rivals—Iran and Egypt—either in turmoil or politically isolated, Iraq was at the pinnacle of its power.

Meanwhile, Iran was in a weak and chaotic state. Its military forces—especially its army and air force—all but disintegrated. And because of the American hostage crisis, it was internationally isolated. Even if it is assumed that Iran had intended to impose its ideology on its neighbors by force of arms, in September 1980 it was in no position to do so.

The following statement by the Iraqi Minister of Culture illustrates that Iraq had arrived at the same assessment, despite its conscious exaggerations of the Iranian threat:

> Khomeini is a madman, a lunatic, and therefore he is not dangerous. Iran cannot threaten Iraq. A dangerous enemy means a strong country with a strong government, a strong army and a clear plan. In Iran there is only chaos. . . . Iraq has a ruling party, a strong government, a sound economy, no unemployment, a people willing to follow its leaders, *and we have a strong army.*[20]

Thus, it was the change in the regional balance of power that prompted Iraq to invade Iran and achieve such long-held Arab goals as the liberation of Khusistan. This invasion, if successful, not only would have served Iraq's more narrow power interests, but it would have consolidated Hussein's position as the true inheritor of the Arab nationalist mantle.[21] It would have also established Arab superiority over the Persians. After all, Saddam Hussein on many occasions had said that he wanted to repeat the historic Arab victory over the Persian

Empire in Qadisiya in the seventh century A.D. In sum, all the factors discussed earlier constituted Iraq's motivation, while the change in the regional balance of power offered it the opportunity to try to achieve its goals.

IRAN-GULF RELATIONS

The reaction of the Gulf Arab states to the Iranian revolution, the Iran-Iraq war, and the general course of the evolution of their relations in the post-revolution period also reflect the impact of these underlying factors. Moreover, the pattern of Iran-Gulf interaction reveals certain continuities with the past. As with other aspects of Iran's foreign policy, Iran-Gulf relations have also been affected by Iran's domestic political conditions, especially ideological divisions within its leadership, the shifting balance of power between principal internal adversaries, and the parallel and often contradictory activities of nongovernmental revolutionary groups and certain individuals.

This last aspect of Iranian policy in the Gulf region was particularly troublesome during the early days of the revolution and of the premiership of Mehdi Bazargan, when Iran's official policy of good neighborly relations with the Gulf states was overshadowed by the activities of revolutionary clerics.[22] The activities of nongovernmental groups and individuals have been curbed. After the consolidation of power in the hands of religious factions, the uncertainty as to which tendency and which personalities really represent the Islamic regime has continued to vex the Gulf Arabs.[23]

The Gulf Arabs' initial reaction to the Iranian revolution was a mixture of apprehension and expectation. The Gulf Arab states had benefited from Iran's stabilizing role under the Shah, but they had also resented Iran's tendency to act as the regional great power. Thus, the declaration by the transitional government of Mehdi Bazargan that Iran would no longer play the role of the regional gendarme was appealing to them, as was Iran's new anti-Israel and pro-Palestinian stand. In their most optimistic moments, they hoped that Iran would return to Arab sovereignty the three disputed islands.[24]

Meanwhile, they were concerned about the contagion effect of the Iranian revolution, inasmuch as they realized it was just one manifestation of a deep-rooted Islamic movement. Events such as the seizure of the Grand Mosque in Mecca in November 1979 and the Shi'a riots in Saudi Arabia, Kuwait, and Bahrain in 1980 and 1981 brought the threat of Islamic revolution dangerously close to the Arab side of the Gulf.

Iranian propaganda further exacerbated these fears. Thus, the fear of Islamic revolution and efforts to contain it would become a guiding principle of the Gulf Arabs' regional policy and their approach toward Iran. Until the outbreak of the Iran-Iraq war, the Gulf Arabs' approach to this problem would be a mixture of firmness and efforts to continue dealing with Iran as normally as possible. Thus, in 1979 the Kuwaiti and Bahraini governments expelled two Iranian revolutionary clerics, Hodjat-al-Islam Hadi Mudarisi and Abbas Muhri, who were agitating among their Shi'a populations and enticing them to establish Islamic republics. Later, this pattern of expulsion would continue and Kuwait, in particular, would expel large numbers of Kuwaitis of Iranian origin, charging them with subversion.[25] Meanwhile, however, they kept the channels of communication to Iran open.

The Iran-Iraq war also presented the Gulf states with a dilemma. On the one hand, Arab nationalists hoped that Iraq would succeed in dislodging the Islamic regime; they also welcomed the prospect of the so-called liberation of Khusistan.[26] On the other hand, they were concerned that Iraq might become too powerful. However, the combined effect of fear and Arab nationalism led them to support Iraq. But the Gulf states that supported Iraq to a lesser degree risked confrontation with Iran. Rather, a number of Gulf states—such as Oman, the United Arab Emirates (UAE), and even Qatar—maintained good relations with Iran, even at some risk to their ties with Iraq. For example, the Iraqis accused Dubai of being a traitor to the Arab nation because it maintained extensive trade links with Iran. This, in turn, reflected not only the differences in the Gulf states' perceptions regarding their security needs, but also their political divisions and rivalries, as well as aspects of their domestic political conditions.

In the case of Kuwait, for example, the Iranian challenge was exacerbated by the existence of large numbers of Shi'as, including those of Iranian origin; fear of Iraqi intentions and reactions played a vital role in its assistance to Iraq. Moreover, the existence of a large and influential Palestinian community with extreme Arab nationalist, and to some extent pro-Iraqi, tendencies contributed to Kuwait's decision to provide all-out support for Iraq.

In the case of Saudi Arabia, intensive anti-Shi'a and anti-Persian feelings (partly a function of Wahabism), as well as Saudi Arabia's own regional power ambitions, played important roles. Indeed, these factors had affected Iran's relations with the above countries under the Shah, putting limits on the extent of their cooperation despite their common security interests. Similarly, under the Shah, too, Iran had cordial relations with the UAE and Oman. In the case of Bahrain, in addition to its Shi'a problems and the legacy of Iran's historic claim, Saudi

Arabia's overwhelming influence over the island's policies determined their stand *vis-à-vis* Iran and the war.

By contrast, Oman and the UAE, which had always had good relations with Iran, continued to pursue a more even-handed policy. It is interesting that, in the case of the UAE, the existence of a large Iranian community and a significant number of Shi'as helped rather than hindered the goal of keeping some measure of normalcy in relations with Iran.

It was the Gulf Arabs' position regarding the Iran-Iraq war, in turn, that, more than anything else, determined Iran's attitude toward them. Thus, Iran maintained reasonably good relations with the UAE, Oman, and Qatar, while its relations with Kuwait and Saudi Arabia suffered. Saudi and Kuwaiti assistance to Iraq went beyond financial help. Saudi Arabia provided Iraq with intelligence information and made its AWACs available. Both Kuwait and Saudi Arabia allowed their territory to be used for the transfer of war materials to Iraq and by the Iraqi air force for strikes against Iranian targets. In 1986, Saudi Arabia and Kuwait, by forcing oil prices down, in fact waged economic warfare against Iran. Under such circumstances, these countries could hardly be considered "neutral" in the war.

Much has been made of Iranian subversion in Kuwait and Saudi Arabia, including the use of the Hadj ceremonies to make propaganda against the Saudi regime. Yet, given the extensive involvement of these two countries in the war, the Iranian response was not as strong as might have been expected. For example, there were no suicide attacks against vital energy and economic sectors of either country. Iranian subversion, at best, had only a nuisance value.

This situation derived both from Iran's limitations in trying to penetrate the Gulf Arab societies and from its fear of Western intervention. The events that followed the U.S. reflagging of Kuwaiti tankers in the summer of 1987, especially the U.S. military strike on Iran in April 1988, illustrated that Iranian apprehensions about Western reactions were well founded.

What has not received enough attention has been Iran's efforts at conciliation with the Gulf states, as well as its attempts to persuade them to adopt a more even-handed policy toward the Iran-Iraq war. Yet on several occasions, Iran did try to separate the issue of war with Iraq from the border issue of Gulf security, and offered to reach mutually acceptable arrangements. In response, it expected the Gulf Arabs to halt their assistance to Iraq.

The Gulf states responded positively to Iranian overtures. Indeed, in 1985 Iran-Gulf relations seemed to be rapidly improving. On 18 May, the Saudi Foreign Minister, Prince Saud-al-Faisal, visited Tehran.

There was also talk of Hodjat-al-Islam Hashemi-Rafsanjani visiting Saudi Arabia on the occasion of the Hadj.[27] During November 1985, the Gulf Cooperation Council (GCC) Summit communique struck the most balanced chord ever on the Iran-Iraq conflict, indicating a possible movement toward a more even-handed posture.[28]

However, neither Saudi Arabia nor Kuwait was willing to end its support for Iraq unless and until Iran accepted a negotiated peace. The reason is that they could not be confident that Iran would not try to subvert them more vigorously once it had defeated Iraq. This was quite an understandable fear—a fear intensified by the Iranian capture of the Fao Peninsula in February 1986 and the siege of Basra later in the same year. Nevertheless, the fact remains that the Gulf states never seriously tested Iran's intentions.

The course of events in 1987–1988 may yet lead to even more direct confrontations with Kuwait and Saudi Arabia. The Kuwaiti reflagging strategy succeeded in internationalizing the Gulf war by bringing Western navies to the region—something that Iraqi efforts, including its tanker war, since 1984 had failed to achieve. The Western, especially U.S., naval presence, in turn, contributed to Saudi and Kuwaiti determination to remain uncompromising on the issue of the war. This new determination was graphically illustrated during the Hadj ceremonies of 1987, when the Saudi police, for the first time, opened fire on protesting Iranian pilgrims—an incident that resulted in the death of 400 Iranians.[29]

IRANIAN VIEW OF
THE GULF COOPERATION COUNCIL

One of the significant events of the last several years has been the formation of the Gulf Cooperation Council in 1981. Efforts to develop a regional security framework for the Gulf date back to the late 1960s. But all along, competition for power between Iran and Iraq, as well as a variety of territorial and other disputes among the Gulf Arabs, prevented its realization. The absence of a compelling reason, such as a serious and identifiable common threat, also contributed to this failure. By 1981, the preoccupation of Iran and Iraq with their war had eliminated that obstacle. The Gulf Arabs had also resolved many of their disputes, though by no means all of them. More important, the Islamic revolution had presented all the Gulf states with a serious, identifiable, and common threat.

The creation of the GCC was viewed with apprehension by Tehran for the following reasons. First, it was viewed as an anti-Iranian military pact. The following commentary by IRNA (Iran's official news agency) sums up Iran's fear. After posing the question as to which threat the GCC countries are organizing against, and after rejecting the idea that the GCC is designed to meet the Israeli and U.S. challenge, it concludes:

> The reactionary groups which believe the Islamic government and the Islamic Republic of Iran constitute a danger threatening the region must be told the following: The Iranian Islamic Revolution regards the question of establishing peace and security in the world, and particularly in the Persian Gulf, as one of the most important basic issues. . . . In the event other countries in the region favor tranquility and peace, the Iranian Islamic Republic—as the strongest and the largest country in the region, particularly in the Persian Gulf—is prepared to cooperate with them in the direction of this objective. However, if a number of small regimes in the region wish to make decisions concerning the waters of the Persian Gulf without attaching any importance to the Islamic Republic of Iran, *their initiative will undoubtedly be regarded as a conspiracy against the interests of the Muslim Iranian people.*[30] (emphasis added)

Second, Iran was concerned about the exclusive nature of the GCC and viewed the organization as a ploy to further Arabize the Gulf and keep Iran out. Iranian anxieties were exacerbated by occasional calls for the inclusion of Iraq in the GCC, as the following comment illustrates: "If the Gulf states do not consider seriously the inclusion of Iraq in the Council and the formation of a unified Arab army to be deployed along the Gulf shores to confront the Islamic revolution, then any talk about Arab security is without avail."[31]

Third, Iran viewed the GCC as a cover for the expansion of Saudi influence. This perception, while not totally justified, is nevertheless shared by others in the Gulf states.[32] Fourth, Iran viewed the GCC as an instrument of U.S. policy in the Gulf region, ironically much in the same way as radical Arabs had viewed the Shah's regime as a Western surrogate.[33]

However, as the GCC failed to develop into a tightly knit security organization, as Saudi Arabia failed to completely dominate the organization and dictate its policy, and as individual Gulf states adopted their own independent approach toward Iran, Iran's fears regarding the GCC were reduced. Indeed, what was more worrisome to Iran were international issues, including the Arab-Israeli conflict, and U.S. policies in the Middle East.[34]

The common challenge of Iraq has been another impetus behind the Syrian-Iranian alliance. Developments in 1979 and 1980 in the intra-Arab balance of power had led to a weakening of the Syrian position and to the country's isolation. Cooperation with Iran was one way to help Syria reverse this negative shift. But Syria has been careful to prevent Iran from becoming too powerful, either in the Gulf region by defeating Iraq, or in Lebanon through the manipulation of the Shi'as.

The Syrian-Iranian alliance has been a very unequal relationship favoring Syria. No doubt Syria did close the pipeline carrying Iraqi oil through its territory in April 1982, and some weapons reached Iran through a Syrian intermediary. These, however, had marginal impact on the course of the war. Moreover, Syria never favored an Iranian victory, and it favored even less the creation of an Islamic republic there. Rather, Syria's goal was to topple Saddam Hussein by using Iran's policies and then to install a pro-Syrian Ba'athist regime in Iraq.

Syria also used its ties with Iran to increase its influence with the Gulf Arab states by acting as an intermediary between the two. In Lebanon, Syria used Iranian policies to counter the Israeli-Maronite challenge. When Iran began to develop a significant foothold in Lebanon, and when pro-Iranian Shi'a groups, including the Hizb-ul-Allah, gained more influence at the expense of the pro-Syrian Shi'a movement, AMAL, Syria used its 30,000-strong military force in Lebanon to subdue pro-Iranian forces and check Iranian influence. In this way, Syria made clear that it considered Lebanon as belonging to its special sphere of influence and would neither share it with Iran nor allow Iran to supplant it as the dominant power in Lebanon. Syria also received financial benefits from Iran in the form of free oil and other economic assistance.

The question thus arises as to why Iran persisted in this unequal relationship. The answer lies principally in Iran's desire both to show that the Iran-Iraq war was not an Arab-Persian war and to thwart the attempts of those who tried very hard to portray it as such. Iran's hope of spreading its revolution rested largely in its ability to demonstrate that it was not a Shi'a-Persian phenomenon. Alliance with Syria and, to some extent, relations with Libya and Algeria were to prove this point.[35]

IRAN AND THE PALESTINIANS

The Palestinians viewed Iran under the Shah as one of their principal enemies. Thus the PLO was actively involved in subversion against it. When the Islamic revolution succeeded, the PLO viewed this success as a major victory for itself. Yasser Arafat was the first visitor to post-revolution Iran.[36] PLO-Iran relations, however, suffered after the outbreak of the Iran-Iraq war, ultimately resulting in a total breach between Iran and the mainstream Palestinians represented by Arafat.

The strength of Arab nationalist feelings and the PLO's financial dependence on the Gulf Arab states led them to support Iraq. Iran, however, has made a conscious distinction between Arafat and his supporters and the Palestinians in general. Thus it had condemned Arafat. But it has continued to support factions opposed to it, and the Palestinian cause. In fact, the PLO has an embassy in Tehran.

IRAN AND THE REST OF THE ARAB WORLD

In the post-revolution period, with few exceptions, notably Libya, Algeria, and the People's Democratic Republic of Yemen (PDRY), Iran's relations with the rest of the Arab world have contracted and deteriorated. For example, Iran has either broken diplomatic relations with Arab states such as Jordan and Morocco, or others such as Tunisia and Mauritania have broken ties with Iran. While there are additional specific reasons for the deterioration in Iran's relations with individual Arab countries, the primary reasons have been Iran's efforts to export its revolution and its actual or alleged ties with radical Muslim groups in these countries.[37]

Yet, while there has been considerable sympathy for Iran's revolution in the Arab world, Iran has not been able to transform it into active political support, even among the Shi'as of Iraq and the Gulf region (Lebanon is an exception). Ethno-linguistic and sectarian barriers have limited Iran's ability to penetrate the Arab masses. Nationalism has also proven a strong force, and many Arab governments have effectively manipulated Arab nationalist feelings to check the appeal and influence of Iran's revolutionary ideas.[38]

Iran's cooperation even with countries such as Libya has remained limited, partly because of deep philosophical differences and despite common views on such issues as the Arab-Israeli conflict and the U.S. role in the Middle East. This outcome has, in turn, disabused Iran of its earlier visions of its relations with the Arab world and of its ability to transcend barriers of ethnic and sectarian divisions through the application of its universalist Islamic message. The result has been a reemergence of nationalist tendencies in Iran and a greater appreciation of the limits of Iran's ability to influence the Arab world.

CONCLUSION

In sum, the evolution of Arab-Iranian relations in the post-revolution period has confirmed the continued importance of certain underlying factors in shaping these relations. It has demonstrated the limits on Iran's ability to influence the Arab world. Despite the Islamic regime's denigration of Iranian nationalism and exaltation of Islamic brotherhood and unity, paradoxically the revolution and, more important, the Iran-

Iraq war have deepened the ethno-religious Arab-Iranian chasm. Iraq's characterization of the Iranians as the "fire-worshipping Persians" and the Arabs' appeal to nationalism as a counter to Iran's Islamic universalism have enhanced the divisive impact of these factors. The revolution and the Iran-Iraq war have also rekindled territorial disputes that seemed more or less settled after the Algiers agreement of 1975.

Yet in the meantime, the underlying pattern of Arab-Iranian relations has, in its essential features, remained constant. As in the past, this pattern has remained a mixture of deeply rooted divisions, potential conflicts, and tactical limited cooperation. Barring drastic change in Iran, in the Arab world, or in the nature of the regional system, this pattern is likely to continue in the future.

NOTES

1. In fact, in the third century after the Arab invasion there was a Persian literary and linguistic renaissance accompanied by the emergence of local Persian dynasties. Some of these dynasties—such as the Shi'a dynasty of Al-Buyeh (The Buyids)—became strong enough to challenge the authority of the Khalif in Baghdad. See *The Cambridge History of Iran*, Vol. 4, Cambridge: Cambridge University Press, 1975.

2. For example, the third Khalif, Omar, prohibited marriage between the Arabs and the Iranians. See Hamid Enayat, *Modern Islamic Political Thought*, Austin: University of Texas Press, 1984, p. 33.

3. For example, according to Hamid Enayat, one of the reasons for the Iranians' attachment to the house of Ali was that, unlike Omar, the Iranians were treated with kindness and respect by Ali and his followers. See Ibid.

4. The Iranians have been particularly resentful of the Arab practice of equating Islamic culture with Arab culture and ignoring Iran's contribution. As Edward Brown, the famous British Iran scholar, has said, "Take of what is wrongly known as Arabian sciences . . . what has been contributed by the Persians and the best is gone." Quoted in A. J. Arberry (ed.), *The Legacy of Persia*, London: Oxford University Press, 1953, p. 204.

5. See, for example, King Fahd's statement that Iran should stop imposing its alien ideas on the Arab world. *Washington Post*, 28 December 1987.

6. See Adeed Dawisha, "Invoking the Spirit of Arabism," in Adeed Dawisha (ed.), *Islam in Foreign Policy*, Cambridge: Cambridge University Press, 1983, pp. 112–127. See also the editorial *Al-Oabas*, "In a Confrontation Between Arabs and Persians, the Arab Is True to Himself," reprinted in *Foreign Broadcasting Information Service (FBIS), Middle East and North Africa (ME and NA)*, 11 April 1980.

7. Indeed, these statements had become so obvious that Hodjat-al-Islam Rafsanjani had to deny that there were any anti-Arab sentiments in Iran. See *FBIS, South America (SA)*, 6 May 1985.

8. See Majid Khaduri, *Political Trends in the Arab World: The Role of Ideas and Ideals in Politics*, Baltimore: Johns Hopkins University Press, 1970, pp. 194–195, 205–207.

9. For details, see R. K. Ramazani, *The Persian Gulf: Iran's Role*, Charlottesville: University of Virginia Press, 1973.

10. See, for example, the comments by Ali-Akbar Hashemi Rafsanjani and the commander of the Iranian navy in *FBIS/ME and NA*, 29 December 1982, and *FBIS/SA*, 24 October 1984.

11. For example, the PLO and AMAL trained Iranians for urban guerrilla warfare and other subversive tactics. Radical Arab regimes from Nasser's Egypt to Qadhafi's Libya rendered all forms of assistance to anti-Shah forces in Iran. See Amir Taheri, *Holy Terror: Inside the World of Islamic Terrorism*, Bethesda, Maryland: Adler & Adler, 1987. See also, Michael Ledeen and William Lewis, *The Debacle: The American Failure in Iran*, New York: Alfred A. Knopf, Inc., 1981.

12. However, in many other areas, from the Gulf region to Pakistan and Africa, Saudi Arabia and Iran competed for influence. See, for example, Judith Perera, "Together Against the Red Peril: Iran and Saudi Arabia Rivals for Super Power Rule," *Middle East Journal*, No. 43, May 1978, pp. 16–25.

13. There is a certain irony here given that, in the 1960s, Iran was called in to be a counterweight to Nasser's Egypt.

14. For example, under the Shah, despite Jordan's close ties to Iran, Jordanian maps and schoolbooks showed Khusistan as part of the Arab world. Since the revolution, Syria and Libya's tactical alliance with Iran has not changed their views on this issue. On the Bahrain issue, the Iranian media has characterized the linking of Bahrain with Saudi Arabia through a causeway as its "annexation." See *FBIS/SA*, 28 January 1982.

15. Thus, under the Shah, Iran's military occupation of the two Tumbs did not generate active opposition, whereas Libya and Iraq mounted a major campaign. In the post-revolution period, moderate Arabs have raised the issue of the islands, whereas Syria and Libya have remained silent.

16. Indeed, Iran's Islamic ideology is diametrically opposed to the secular, nationalist, and semi-socialist ideology of Ba'athist Syria. Qadhafi's Islamic socialism is also vastly different. Moreover, while Libya and Syria have close Soviet ties, Iran has adhered to strict nonalignment and has challenged Soviet supremacy in the region.

17. Indeed, Iran's recognition of Israel was only *de facto*. Moreover, Iran's ties with Israel were in part a function of Arab cooperation with the Soviet Union and the irredentist Arab nationalist claims toward Iran. Even so, Iran's position on the Arab-Israeli conflict since 1967 has been supportive of the Arabs. See R. K. Ramazani, "Iran and the Arab-Israeli Conflict," *Middle East Journal*, Vol. 32, No. 4, Autumn 1979.

18. For a detailed study of the war and its evolution, see Anthony H. Cordesman, "The First Round: Lessons of the Iran-Iraq War," *Armed Forces Journal International*, April 1982; "The Iran-Iraq War: Attrition Now, Chaos Later," *Armed Forces Journal International*, May 1983; and Shahram Chubin and Zalish, *op. cit.*

19. See Nita M. Renfrew, "Who Started the War," *Foreign Policy*, No. 66, Spring 1987, pp. 98–108.

20. See *FBIS/ME and NA*, 1 August 1980.

21. Immediately after the revolution, Saddam Hussein had begun agitating the Arabic-speaking population of Khusistan with propaganda and delivery of arms. However, Iraq's subversion of Khusistan goes well back into the 1970s, when Iraq established the so-called Front for the Liberation of Ahwaz, which is still active in Baghdad.

Iraq also hoped that the separation of Khusistan would be a prelude to Iran's disintegration. On many occasions, Tariq Aziz had said that "five small Irans are better than one big Iran." Saddam Hussein has also warned Iran that any revolution that calls itself Islamic should be friendly to the Arab revolution, betraying Arab nationalist's belief in Arab supremacy and their tendency to subordinate Arabism to Islam. For more discussion of these issues, see R. K. Ramazani, *Revolutionary Iran: Challenge and Response in the Middle East*, Baltimore: Johns Hopkins University Press, 1986.

22. A good example of these activities was the statement by a fairly obscure cleric, Sadez Ruhani, that Iran would annex Bahrain if the latter did not establish an Islamic republic. This statement was rebuked by the Iranian government, which sent a delegation to Bahrain to ease its citizens' fears and anger. See Ramazani, *op. cit.*, p. 49.

23. An official from the area told me that the Gulf Arabs did not know which one of the Iranian officials they should believe regarding Iran's intentions.

24. This hope, however, was more representative of Arab wishful thinking than of Iranian realities. The Gulf Arabs soon realized that opposition in Iran to aspects of the Shah's policy derived not from doubt about the legitimacy and rightfulness of Iran's claim or its regional role. Rather, it derived from opposition to the performance by Iran of this regional role as a Western surrogate.

25. For details, see Ramazani, *op. cit.*, pp. 118–119.

26. A Pakistani diplomat who was in Bahrain at the time told me that the mood in Bahrain was "jubilant." According to Dilip Hiro, King Khalid telephoned Saddam Hussein and congratulated him on his invasion of Iran. See Dilip Hiro, *Iran Under the Ayatollahs*, Bloomington, Indiana University Press, 1985, p. 355.

27. See *FBIS/SA*, 17 July 1984; and *Middle East Economic Digest*.

28. See Ramazani, *op. cit.*, p. 99.

29. See "Iran Vows to Avenge Pilgrim Deaths in Saudi Arabia," *Washington Post*, 3 August 1987.

30. See *FBIS/ME and SA*, 29 January 1982.

31. See *Financial Times*, 19 March 1984.

32. Note, for example, the statement of a Kuwaiti member of Parliament made after the closure of Parliament (in part, as a result of Saudi pressure): "Now we are really part of the GCC." See *Middle East Economic Digest*, Vol. 30, No. 28, 12 July 1986.

33. The radical Tehran daily, *Jomhuri-e-Islam*, stated that "[t]he setting up of the GCC is the brainchild of the Arabs of the area and the product of the

propaganda machinery and power network of the West." See *FBIS/ME*, 29 January 1982.

34. Syria, at least initially, thought that the change in Iran's attitude was a major strategic gain for the Arabs in their struggle against Israel.

35. The following statement by Rafsanjani illustrates this point: "The enemies of Islam are raising the issue of the Arabs and non-Arabs. *Fortunately such Arab countries as Libya and Syria which are alongside us have thwarted this propaganda of the enemies. If this issue existed at all, Syria and Libya would not side with us particularly that most of them are Sunnis*" (emphasis added). See "Majlis Speaker: No Anti-Arab Sentiment in Iran," *FBIS/SA*, 6 May 1985.

36. See *FBIS/ME and NA*, 21 February 1979.

37. For example, Tunisia broke ties with Iran, alleging that the Iranian Embassy was engaged in subversive activities within its revolutionary movement.

38. For a detailed study of this issue, see Shireen T. Hunter, "Iran and the Spread of Revolutionary Islam," *Third World Quarterly*, Vol. 10, No. 2, 1988, pp. 730–749.

6

Iran's Relations with Israel, Syria, and Lebanon

Shaul Bakhash

INTRODUCTION

The Iranian revolution of 1979 brought about significant changes and sometimes dramatic reversals in Iran's foreign policy. True, there have been continuities in foreign policy across the watershed of the revolution, and these continuities have been in greater evidence during the last two or three years. However, in the immediate aftermath and in the early years of the revolution, the shifts in foreign policy were far more pronounced than the continuities; the effects of these shifts are still with us today. Consider the following:

Virtually all economic, military, security and diplomatic relations with the United States were severed; indeed, the United States, which under the Shah had been Iran's closest ally, came to be depicted as "the great satan" and as Iran's principal enemy. Iran, considered a source of stability in the Gulf region, became a source of instability and an exporter of a revolutionary ideology. Despite rivalries, relations with the Arab states of the Gulf, including Saudi Arabia and Kuwait, were generally quite good under the Shah, but they grew strained and hostile after 1979. On the Arab-Israeli question, Iran, once a decided moderate, joined the camp of the radical, rejectionist states.

These shifts were a product of revolutionary ideology and revolutionary turmoil, the influence of key individuals, and an almost instinctive determination to reverse and overturn the foreign policies of the former regime. They also derived from unforeseen events, such as the war with Iraq and the opportunity for intervention created for Iran and other outside states by the breakdown of central authority in Lebanon. These shifts were also reflected in Iran's policies toward Israel, Syria, and Lebanon. Policies toward these three countries are, moreover, still evolving. These shifts and their evolution are the subject of this chapter. I will adopt the somewhat artificial but convenient approach of examining, in turn, Iran's policies and dealings with each of these countries. I will then draw some general conclusions in light of the cease-fire with Iraq and related internal developments in Iran.

RELATIONS WITH ISRAEL UNDER THE SHAH

The Iranian revolution of 1979 had serious and adverse implications for the state of Israel. It replaced a regime in Tehran that was highly favorable to Israel with a regime implacably hostile to it.

Under the Shah, Israel had enjoyed excellent relations with Iran. By 1950, Iran had accorded *de facto* recognition to the new Jewish state. Between 1948 and 1952, tens of thousands of Jews fleeing Iraq were allowed to use Iran as a transit point on their way to Israel. In the 1950s, and more intensively in the 1960s, a multifaceted relationship developed between the two governments. Iran drew on Israeli expertise for military training and intelligence gathering. Iran bought arms from Israel and shared intelligence with it. It drew on Israeli expertise in both the private and public sectors in agriculture and other technical fields. During the Arab oil boycott of 1973, Israel did not want for oil because Iran was willing to meet its crude oil requirements. Iran, in fact, became Israel's principal oil supplier. By the mid-1970s, Israeli firms were involved in a variety of enterprises in Iran, particularly in agriculture, construction, and the import-export trade.

For Iran, this relationship was based on a number of considerations. There was the traditional hostility, or at least rivalry, between Iran and certain Arab states. In the Cold War atmosphere of the early 1950s, Iran was careful to align itself closely, both diplomatically and militarily, with positions adopted by England and the United States. The rise of radical regimes—in Egypt under Nasser, in neighboring Iraq after the overthrow of the monarchy, and in Syria and Yemen—reinforced the Shah's inclination to seek insurance elsewhere. The relationship with Israel appeared to offer such insurance.

The nature of this relationship changed in the 1970s. Shifts in Iran's military and security capabilities, and improvements in its relations with Arab states, made the Shah less dependent than in the past on ties to Israel. Iran grew rich on the explosion of oil prices and revenues after 1973. The Shah turned Iran into a militarily powerful state and assumed a major regional role in maintaining Gulf security. He repaired relations with Nasser in Egypt after the 1967 war and developed close relations with Nasser's successor, Anwar Sadat. By 1975, rivalries with Saudi Arabia had been muted, major differences with Iraq had been settled, and the Shah had entered into intelligence-sharing arrangements with both of these countries.

On the Palestinian question, even if his heart was not in it, the Shah formally adopted a "correct" position from the Arab point of view, calling for Israeli withdrawal from the occupied territories and for self-determination for the Palestinian people. If by the mid-1970s relations between Iran and Israel remained close, it is because the Shah, feeling more self-confident and stronger both at home and abroad, and becoming a major player on regional issues, felt less dependent than in the past on the Israeli relationship. He also found himself in a position to treat questions of importance to Israel or the Arab states with considerable suppleness and flexibility.

We should also note that Iran's relationship with Israel remained one that the government publicly acknowledged only with reluctance. Visits by Israeli officials to Iran under the old regime—and there were many— were never reported in the Iranian press. Israeli firms operating in Iran were generally expected to maintain a low profile. The Shah remained sensitive to Arab and domestic opinion. In Iran, the Israeli connection had support in the military and in senior official circles; but the Shah was pursuing a policy that had little support among various other politically aware constituencies such as the left-wing intelligentsia, the religious community, traditional elements of the bazaar, and radical opposition.

By the mid-1970s the Shah felt confident enough to speak more openly to foreign journalists about Iran's relations with Israel; but he remained reluctant to speak as openly to his own countrymen. The tie to Israel remained a politically exploitable issue. Particularly after the 1967 war and the occupation of the West Bank, there was potentially a much larger constituency that could be aroused over the issue of Israel, its occupation of Islamic holy sites, and its treatment of fellow Muslims. As opposition elements piled up grievances against the Shah in the 1960s and 1970s, they increasingly began to hold against him his special relationship with both the United States and Israel; they also held against these two countries the support they believed Washington and Jerusalem were extending to an unpopular and autocratic ruler.

ATTITUDES OF THE ISLAMIC REPUBLIC
TOWARD ISRAEL AND THE ARAB STATES

The Iranian revolution in 1979 not only brought about an upheaval in Iran's domestic politics and power structure. It also brought to power a coalition of forces that were inherently hostile to Israel and the conservative Arab states, and thus creating conditions for a potentially radical reversal of Iran's foreign policies. The revolutionaries were in any case committed to undoing much of what the Shah had accomplished, abroad as well as at home.

Neither Syria, with whom the Islamic Republic eventually formed a close alliance, nor Lebanon, where Iran eventually established a significant presence, was initially a focus of Iranian attention. In the Arab Middle East, attention in the immediate aftermath of the revolution was directed primarily at the Gulf states, which became a target of hostility and revolutionary energy. In many of these states there were large Shi'ite populations and communities of merchants and workers of Iranian origin. The Islamic Republic sought to exploit these assets as well as the excitement Khomeini and the Iranian revolution had aroused in the Gulf states. Iranian leaders directly and indirectly called on their Muslim co-religionists on the other side of the Gulf to follow the example set by revolutionary Iran. Propagandists from Iran toured the Gulf, spreading Khomeini's message of Islamic militancy and revolution. The Constitution of the Islamic Republic committed Iran to the support of oppressed Muslims and liberation movements everywhere, and to the creation of a single, unified Islamic *umma* transcending national frontiers.

Abol-Hasan Bani-Sadr, who became the first president of the Islamic Republic, asserted soon after the overthrow of the monarchy that the Iranian revolution would not be secure against Great Power interference unless similar revolutionary and anti-imperialist regimes were established in neighboring states. Later, as president, he spoke contemptuously of Saudi Arabia and the Gulf emirates as U.S. "client states" that were afraid of the Iranian revolution and their own people. "We do not consider them to be independent governments," he said, "and therefore do not wish to cooperate with them." He predicted that if the people in the Arab states that were opposed to Iran adopted the techniques developed by the Iranian revolutionaries, "not one of these regimes would remain in existence, and they know it. . . . All these overlords would be like dust in the wind." Iran, he said, would help other people to liberate themselves, not so much by material or military assistance as by the example of the Islamic government it had established. If an Islamic popular movement asked for Iran's help, he affirmed, "we would definitely help such a movement."[1]

The informal alliance with Israel suffered in the same way as did the formal alliance with the United States. The reasons are fairly obvious. Hostility to Israel and support for the PLO were prevalent sentiments among left-wing groups. The left had played a significant role in bringing about the overthrow of the monarchy and had exercised influence on the shaping of post-revolution foreign policy. Some radical elements in the revolutionary coalition had trained in PLO camps. Within the clerical leadership and among their young followers in the urban centers the hostility to Israel took on a religious coloring: Israel had occupied the lands of Muslims; Jews were ruling over their co-religionists; and the Jewish state was in control of Jerusalem and of one of the holiest shrines in Islam.

Moreover, there was the Ayatollah Khomeini himself. Khomeini first threw down the gauntlet to the Shah in 1962; and he remained an impassioned and implacable opponent of the Shah, both in Iran and, after 1964, from exile, over the next decade and a half. In these years, he pressed his case against the Iranian regime in a seemingly endless barrage of sermons, declarations, and teachings. In this struggle, he consistently employed anti-Jewish, anti-Israeli rhetoric to arouse and manipulate public passions. He linked the United States and Israel with the Shah's repressive policies; he aroused fears that Israelis, or Jews, were taking over the country; he depicted Israel as the foe of Islam and the Muslims. "In the interests of the Jews, America and Israel," he said after clashes between seminary students and government troops at the Fayziyyeh Seminary in Qum in March 1963, "we must be jailed and killed; we must be sacrificed to the evil intentions of foreigners." In June of that year, in the highly explosive sermon that led to his arrest and to three days of widespread rioting, he linked together the Shah's and Israel's alleged designs against Islam and against the country: "Israel," he said, "does not want the Koran to survive in this country. Israel through its black agents crushed the Fayziyyeh seminary. It crushes us. It crushes you, the nation. It desires to take over the economy. It desires to destroy our commerce and agriculture. It desires to seize the country's wealth."[2]

In exile, after 1965, he persisted in these themes; and after 1967, he harped on the usurpation by Israel of Muslim lands and took up, more forcefully, the Palestinian cause. He spoke of the "gang of Jews" who ran the Jewish state, of the need to "uproot this germ of corruption" from the Islamic world. Israel was "that cancerous growth in the Middle East" that must be uprooted from the Islamic world. It was "the universally recognized enemy" of Islam and the "usurper of the rights of Muslims."[3]

Khomeini blamed Israel for helping to dream up and organize the highly unpopular celebrations that marked the 2,500th anniversary of Iranian monarchy. He repeated the oft-heard canard that Jews, and Israel, had tampered with the text of the Koran. He castigated the Shah for selling oil to Israel. And he depicted Islam as the unifying force and ideology that would permit Muslims to get rid of their own autocratic rulers, end imperialist influence in their countries, and permit the defeat of Israel.

Against this background, it was hardly to be expected that, following the victory of the revolution, the new regime would leave relations with Israel undisturbed. Even the Shah's last prime minister, Shapour Bakhtiar, found it necessary to ban any further oil deliveries to Israel. Within a week of the seizure of power, the Khomeini regime broke all relations with Israel. The same day, the PLO leader, Yasir Arafat, was given a hero's welcome in Tehran. He met with leading government officials and leading clerics. He was granted the rare privilege of an audience with Khomeini. All national papers the next day carried pictures of Arafat planting a fulsome kiss on Khomeini's cheek, and for months afterward this picture was placarded in prominent public places. To drive home the point of Iranian support for the Palestinian cause and the reversal of the policy pursued by the Shah, the PLO was allowed to establish its representative office in the very building that had housed the Israeli diplomatic mission.

For his part, Arafat spoke with becoming modesty (and gross exaggeration) of the assistance the Palestinians had provided the Iranian revolution; he called Iran his second home; he declared the Iranian revolution to be the beginning of a reversal of the tide in the Middle East. Clearly he expected considerable assistance for the Palestinian movement from the Islamic Republic. Indeed, to Arafat, the Iranian revolution and prospective Iranian support for the PLO must have seemed an extraordinary windfall.

We should note, however, that the honeymoon between Islamic Iran and the PLO did not endure. The government soon refused the PLO permission to establish a second representative office in Ahwaz, Khuzestan, the center of Iran's Arab-speaking population. It discouraged prominence for the declarations of the PLO representative in Tehran in the press and mass media. By 1983, relations between Khomeini's regime and the PLO were so deeply strained that one of Arafat's chief lieutenants met in Paris with Rajavi, the leader of the outlawed Mujahedin, which still constitutes the major radical exile opposition group and one deeply hostile to Khomeini.

The reasons for this dramatic turnabout are not far to seek. The new government, much like the Shah's, feared the radicalising effects of the PLO presence on Iranian youth, particularly those of Arab extraction in the south. The PLO's secular style did not sit well with Iran's Islamic elements. The Iranians, it is said, were nonplussed to discover that members of Arafat's delegation were less than punctilious in performing their five daily prayers. Perhaps Arafat's presumption and overly familiar style was more than Khomeini could bear. One may, after all, be permitted respectfully to kiss the Ayatollah's hand; but one does not presume to plant a kiss on the Ayatollah's cheek.

More important, when the Iran-Iraq war broke out, Arafat refused to condemn the Iraqi aggression, as Khomeini demanded of all Arab and Islamic leaders, and, instead, offered his good offices as mediator. To Khomeini, who in general had little use for neutrals and believed that the Iraqi attack on Iran was a clear case of aggression, Arafat's position was tantamount to betrayal. When, in May 1989, Rafsanjani actually called upon Palestinians to go ahead and kill Westerners for every Palestinian killed by Israelis, Arafat repudiated the Islamic Republic altogether.

Iran-PLO relations also suffered due to tensions and rivalries in Lebanon. There were, of course, clerics and others in the ruling coalition with strong pro-PLO sympathies. But even before the Israeli invasion of Lebanon, links with the Shi'ite population in that country tugged more powerfully at the loyalties of many in the ruling coalition than did sympathies for the PLO. There was little love lost between the Lebanese Shi'ites and the Palestinians; and as relations between the Shi'ites and the Palestinians deteriorated in 1981–1982, this tension was reflected in Iranian-PLO relations. The opportunity offered Iran following the Israeli invasion to establish a military presence and to support its own informal militia network among Lebanese Shi'ites created new sources of tension between Iran and the Palestinian organization. Finally, the increasingly close alliance between Iran and Syria placed the Islamic Republic on the side of factions hostile to Arafat and the mainline PLO.

The cooling of relations with the PLO did not, however, imply a diminution of hostility toward Israel. If anything, after an initial period when the attention of the Khomeini regime was taken up with internal upheavals and problems, Iranian hostility toward Israel came to be articulated in more specific, more uncompromising terms. At least at the rhetorical level, the men of the Islamic Republic developed themes and positions that placed Iran among Israel's most implacable enemies. Some Arab states, even elements in the PLO, have suggested that they might be willing to accept the existence of the Jewish state as part of an overall settlement of the Palestinian question. The Islamic Republic took the position that Israel has no right to exist and must be eradicated. Some Arab states may look to a negotiated settlement of the Palestinian question. Iran took the view that the conflict can only be settled through war. Iran has opposed every peace initiative in the Middle East over the past eight years, including the Camp David accords, the Reagan Plan, and the abortive agreement between King Hussein of Jordan and Yasir Arafat on a common negotiating posture toward Israel.

Moreover, the Islamic Republic, more than any other country, has given another dimension or at least emphasized one particular aspect of the Palestinian-Israeli conflict by depicting it as a war of Islam against Islam's enemies. It is not fanciful to argue that in using Islam as a vehicle for mass mobilization and opposition, some of the leaders of the *intifada*, or uprising, on the West Bank have learned from the Iranian example and from the techniques and rhetoric redefined by Khomeini and his followers.

Iran's dramatic victories over Iraq in June 1982 also influenced Iranian perceptions of the potential role of the Islamic Republic in the Palestinian-Israeli conflict. The victories led to the belief that Iran, powerful and triumphant under the banner of Islam, could lead the battle against Israel. It was precisely at the height of Iran's successful counter-offensive that a slogan, which until recently was such an integral part of the propaganda ideology of the Islamic Republic, first gained wide circulation: "The road to Jerusalem lies through Baghdad." The slogan implied, of course, that Iran would concentrate on defeating Iraq before taking up the cudgels against Israel. At the same time, however, the slogan suggested that the Iran-Iraq war was just a way-station, a transit route to the real battle for the conquest of Jerusalem and the restoration of Palestine to its rightful owners.

However, the militancy of the Iranian position toward Israel must be qualified in a number of ways. So far, Iranian hostility toward Israel has been expressed primarily in rhetorical terms. Aside from Lebanon, where it has operated quite effectively, Iran has not committed significant material resources to the struggle against Israel. It has been able to be uncompromising at the rhetorical level precisely because it is not a front-line state and geographically lies far from the center of the conflict. In this sense, the slogan, "The road to Jerusalem lies through Baghdad," even before Iran accepted a cease-fire with Iraq, was as much a way of postponing the ultimate battle with Israel as an articulation of realistic and achieveable long-term goals. With the cease-fire, the slogan itself has had to be abandoned.

Moreover, despite the radical rhetoric, Iran has not been above dealing with Israel, if only indirectly. Some Israeli food products have continued to find their way into Iran, although they may be routed through third countries. Iran, hard-pressed in the war with Iraq, purchased arms from Israel and through Israeli intermediaries as early as 1981. It is possible to argue that during the "Irangate" arms-for-hostages negotiations, Iran did not realize that one of the members of the American "team" was in fact an Israeli adviser to then Prime Minister Shimon Peres. But the Iranians certainly knew that the initial intermediary, Manuchehr Ghorbanifar, an Iranian national, was also an informal Israeli agent, and that the arms supplied by the United States were either coming from or being routed through Israel. In fact, one shipment of missiles was returned because it bore Israeli markings.

IRAN AND SYRIA

The close if informal alliance that has developed between Iran and Syria since the revolution is rooted both in revolutionary ideology and in the conditions created by the Iran-Iraq war. The general radicalization of the revolution, marked by the seizure of the U.S. Embassy in November 1979 and the elimination of moderate elements from the revolutionary coalition two years later, reinforced trends already evident in the Islamic Republic's foreign policy—trends that favored an alliance with "radical" regimes in the Middle East.

The Iran-Iraq conflict geared up the whole society for war. It led to the rapid expansion of the Revolutionary Guard and strengthened those elements in Iran most hostile to Israel and the Arab moderates and most sympathetic to the radical Arab states. Moreover, the war left Iran isolated in the Gulf. The sympathies of the Gulf Arab states lay with Iraq. Saudi Arabia and Kuwait, along with Jordan, extended material support to Baghdad. Iran, already tempermentally inclined in this direction, was forced to turn to the "radical" Arab states, Syria and Libya. Both these countries gave Iran diplomatic and material assistance, but it was the Iran-Syrian connection that has proven to be the more important of the two.

The Iranian-Syrian alliance was not based on religious affinities. The Alawites who rule Syria, though nominally Shi'ites, have generally been regarded by the majority of Iran's leading clerics as lying outside the pale of Shi'ite orthodoxy. Moreover, the Asad regime has repressed the Islamic movement in Syria and treated its adherents with great harshness. The two countries have been drawn together, rather, by a shared hostility to Iraq, the material incentives they have been able to offer to one another, and a certain affinity of attitudes toward such countries as Israel and the United States.

Syria clearly welcomed a war that would preoccupy Iraq, drain its resources, and even threaten the stability of its Ba'ath government. It helped Iran by providing general diplomatic support in Arab councils and by supplying Iran with some arms, including Scud missiles and technical assistance in their use. The alliance provided some material benefits for Syria as well. Under an agreement reached in March 1982, Iran undertook to meet Syria's oil requirements in exchange for Syrian goods. Thus assured of secure oil supplies, in April 1982, Syria shut down the pipeline through which Iraq exported some 400,000 to 500,000 barrels of oil a day across Syrian territory to Mediterranean ports. Iran provided Syria with some oil at preferential prices as well as with loans at below-market interest rates.

The Iran-Syrian alliance was not without its frictions. The Syrians may have had a hand, or may at least have acquiesced, in the spectacular and deadly suicide bombings, attributed to Iran's proteges in Lebanon, that in 1982–1983 took the lives of hundreds of U.S. marines and French military personnel. But in time, Syria desired to distance itself from identification with such terrorist activities and had difficulty in restraining the Iranians and their Lebanese proteges. Iran's Shi'ite proteges in Lebanon, operating under the umbrella of Islamic Amal and the shadowy Hezballah, competed with Syria's Lebanese protege for power and influence in the country and threatened Syria's bid for dominance in Lebanon.

Iranian-sponsored and Iranian-encouraged resistance to the Israeli occupation and presence in South Lebanon threatened to involve the Syrians or their proteges in unwanted confrontations with Israel. The Iranians and their clients chafed at the control that Syria attempted to exercise over their activities in Lebanon, and at their dependence on Syrian goodwill for communications and movement between Iran and Lebanon. And Syria of course earned the opprobium of other Arab states for supporting a non-Arab country in conflict with an Arab "brother." An indication of Syrian discomfiture here was evident at the last Arab summit, when Syria joined other Arab states in condemning Iran for not accepting the UN cease-fire proposal.

Nevertheless, for both Iran and Syria, a common enmity toward Iraq generally overrode these other considerations. Syria did not wish a conclusion to the war that would leave Iraq militarily or diplomatically in an advantageous position (although in fact the cease-fire left Iraq in precisely such a position). Iran, whatever its ambitions in Lebanon, could not afford to pose an excessive threat to Syrian interests. The alliance thus held despite frictions. But the Iran-Iraq cease-fire and the possibility that hostilities will end even if a peace treaty is not signed weaken the primary foundation on which the Iran-Syrian alliance is based. Both countries will need to rethink the basis of this alliance.

IRAN AND LEBANON

The event that in retrospect permitted the marked expansion of Iranian influence in Lebanon was the Israeli invasion, its galvanising effect on the Lebanese Shi'ites, and the opportunity that the breakdown of central authority in Lebanon provided for intervention by outside players. However, links between Iranian and Lebanese Shi'ite clerics go back much further. In the 1950s and 1960s, many prominent Lebanese Shi'ite clerics trained in Najaf under the same Shi'ite teachers who were training their Iranian counterparts. Some trained at the Iranian holy city in Qum. In both places, they formed personal links and a shared universe of ideas about the proper role of a revived Islam in shaping society, caring for the underprivileged, giving an Islamic character to the state, and limiting external, non-Muslim influence over Islamic societies. There are family links between some leading Lebanese and Iranian Shi'ite clerical families as well. The outstanding example is Musa Sadr, an Iranian cleric who could claim both Lebanese and Iranian ancestry, and who played a profound role in awakening Shi'ites in Lebanon to a sense of their common identity and in encouraging them to organize for social and political action.

When Israel invaded Lebanon, moreover, Iran sent a small contingent of Revolutionary Guards to that country, presumably to help fight Israel. This small contingent was stationed, with Syrian acquiescence, at Baalbak, in the Bekaa Valley. The Iranians used this small base, their armed contingent, the powerful pull of Khomeini's revolutionary message, and Iranian money to considerably expand Iranian influence. They spread the message of the Islamic revolution among Lebanon's Shi'ites. In 1982, they encouraged and supported a young, nonclerical Shi'ite leader, Hussain Musavi, to split with the mainline Shi'ite organization, Amal, and to establish a rival, more radical group, Islamic Amal. They became the main promoters of Hezballah, the umbrella organization of which Islamic Amal is a constituent part and whose leaders are primarily clerics with Iranian links. Iranian proteges have been linked to the 1983 bombing of the U.S. marine barracks and French military barracks in Beirut, attacks on Israeli positions in Lebanon, and the taking of numerous hostages.

The Iranians have also energetically built up a network of clerics and mosques sympathetic to Iran and Iranian causes. They established mini-seminaries to train clerics in compressed courses, who then went out to preach the message of revolutionary Islam. They urged Shi'ites to resist Israeli occupation, using the method of mass protest that the Iranians had perfected in their own movement against the Shah. They gave guerrilla training to young Shi'ite volunteers and encouraged them to attack Israeli positions in southern Lebanon. The emergence of Hezballah and cleric-led Shi'ite activism in Lebanon was not, of course, all Iran's doing; both stemmed primarily from Lebanese energies and conditions. Moreover, while many leaders of Hezballah pay homage to the leadership of Khomeini, not all share Iran's vision of a Lebanese state organized along the same principles as the Islamic Republic.

Nevertheless, by 1985, the Iranians and their proteges had become major players in the Lebanese game.

For Iran, the involvement in Lebanon has served a number of goals. Iran was thwarted in its effort to export the Islamic revolution to the Gulf sheikdoms. Lebanon appeared to be the most promising country in which the next Islamic Republic would be established. The involvement in Lebanon provided a means for confronting the United States and other great powers by violent means if necessary. It served as a living proof of the Islamic Republic's commitment to the cause of the disinherited and oppressed classes. Khomeini and many of his lieutenants attach importance to the image of Iran as a preeminent revolutionary Islamic state; one of the titles by which Khomeini was addressed is "the hope of the world's disinherited."

The taking of hostages, even if not instigated by Tehran, placed in the hands of groups friendly to Iran coin that could be exchanged for concessions or materials desired by Iran. This proved to be the case in the "Irangate" arms-for-hostages exchange and the agreements that led to the release of French hostages in exchange for diplomatic concessions and the release of Iranian assets held by the French government.

Iran nevertheless has had to weigh real and potential gains in Lebanon against real and potential losses. The friction with Syria has already been alluded to. By 1984, elements in the ruling coalition in Iran, eager to end its diplomatic isolation, sought to avoid the identification of Iran with hostage-taking and terrorist activities. But the government could not always control its Lebanese proteges and allies. The negotiations that took place during Robert McFarlane's trip to Iran in May 1986 indicated, for example, that in the matter of hostage release, the Khomeini regime could not always pressure its Lebanese allies to do its bidding. The Lebanese operations thus interfered with Iran's other foreign policy interests.

In addition, the Lebanese operations proved a source of difficulties at home. Mehdi Hashemi, the head of the organization in the Revolutionary Guards charged with supporting liberation movements abroad and Iran's liaison with Hezballah in Lebanon, often seemed to be pursuing his own agenda in that country. Hashemi, well connected, well funded, and well armed, appeared not to be subject to control by the central government. He used the resources at his disposal to maintain armed retainers in Iran, to interfere in the affairs of the provincial government in the Isfahan area, and, it was later alleged, to plan to seize power in the name of Ayatollah Montazeri after the death of Khomeini. It was probably his followers who leaked the story of the Iran-U.S. arms-for-hostages negotiations late in 1986 and thus effectively brought an end to the exchanges between the two countries.

THE CEASE-FIRE AND ITS IMPLICATIONS

The cease-fire and the end to hostilities in the Iran-Iraq war is certain to affect Iran's relations with each of the three countries we have been considering. Iran and Syria have developed a close working relationship and will continue to need one another. However, the cease-fire allows Iraq to direct its energies and hostility at Syria; already the Baghdad regime is attempting to frustrate Syrian aims in Lebanon by supporting elements in that country hostile to the Syrian presence. As Syria seeks to overcome its isolation in the Arab world and to cultivate new allies against a well-armed, war-tired, and hostile Iraq, it could well edge away from Iran. By the same token, the end of war reduces Iranian dependence on Syria; and Iran's current campaign to normalize relations with countries in Western Europe and, even, perhaps, the United States means that Iran's foreign policy will be dictated by other priorities.

Insofar as Israel is concerned, the experience of the last ten years suggests a number of tentative conclusions. The Islamic Republic, by example and revolutionary rhetoric, has no doubt helped inspire Muslims as far away as the West Bank to utilise Islam as a vehicle of social protest; it has given credence to clerics as leaders of such protest movements. In Lebanon, of course, it has been able to buttress its role as exemplary model with material assistance and to direct contact with clerical and lay leaders and with their rank-and-file followers.

Iran was always geographically too distant to be a direct player in the Palestinian-Israeli conflict. The slogan, "The road to Jerusalem lies through Baghdad," was never very credible; in the wake of the cease-fire it appears even less realistic a program for action. Moreover, despite the anti-Israeli rhetoric, it is clear that Iran, when in dire need, may even buy arms from Israel, although it will always deny it is doing so.

But this hardly means that the hope, entertained by some Israelis, of a resumption of a working relationship with Iran is realistic. Since the overthrow of the monarchy, Israeli assessment of the Iranian revolution has wavered between two views. On the one hand, there has been concern in Israel lest the Iranian message of revolutionary Islam will sweep the region and infect Arab states closer to Israel. For a time, Iranian encouragement of armed resistance to Israel in Lebanon was a cause for Israeli anxiety. Some in Israel have recently argued that Iran is a greater threat to Israel than Iraq, and have even discerned a new-found "moderation" in Baghdad on the question of Israel and other regional issues.

On the other hand, however, some Israeli officials have held to the traditional view that Iran is a major power in the region and must be cultivated; that Iran and Israel have many interests in common, including a common hostility to the Arab states; that these common interests will prevail no matter what the regime in Tehran; and that the close working relationship that existed between Iran and Israel under the Shah can be revived. Israeli arms sales to Iran and the Israeli promotion of the "Irangate" initiative was based on this traditional view.

This point of view was succinctly expressed last year by Israeli Defense Minister Yitzhak Rabin. In remarks on the question of relations with Iran, Rabin emphasized once again the importance for the West and the United States of maintaining a dialogue with Iran. Looking to the post-Khomeini period, he also considered the possibility of rekindling an old Iran-Israeli relationship: "[F]or 28 of 37 years," he remarked, "Iran was a friend of Israel. If it could work for 28 years . . . why couldn't it once this crazy idea of Shiite fundamentalism is gone?"[4] This optimism, however, overlooks the immense hostility to Israel articulated year after year at all levels of the Iranian leadership and the immense difficulty any Iranian government would have with its own important constituencies if it elected openly to deal with Israel.

The cease-fire may also affect Iranian activity in Lebanon. If Iran and Syria feel a less urgent need to work together in other areas, their different agendas in Lebanon could lead to increased friction. Iran's strength among the Hezballah militants derives to a large extent from its reputation for Islamic militancy and its uncompromising defense of Islamic values against the great powers. An Iran that fails to pursue the war with Iraq, deals with the United States, urges the release of hostages, and stands for moderation and compromise is an Iran that risks losing credibility among its followers. Moreover, internal faction and division, absorption in the tasks of post-war reconstruction, straitened economic circumstances, and the removal by death or disability of the charismatic figure of Khomeini could also curtail Iranian capabilities in Lebanon. At the same time, the concepts of social justice, support for the cause of the disinherited, and the assertion of Islamic identity with which the Iranian revolution has always been associated retain a powerful appeal and could serve as the basis by which Iran retains the loyalty of its Lebanese adherents.

NOTES

1. Based on author's own interviews.
2. Based on author's own interviews.
3. Based on author's own interviews.
4. Based on author's own interviews.

PART FOUR

Focus on the Iran-Iraq War

7

Iran and the War: From Stalemate to Cease-fire

Shahram Chubin

Among conflicts in the Third World, the Iran-Iraq war is unusual in several respects. Most commonly cited are its costs in human life and economic resources, and its inordinate length. Less often remarked about is the genre of conflict it represents—a conflict untypical of the prevailing pattern in nonindustrial areas, where the tendency has been internal or civil wars. In contrast, this war was a relatively rare case of interstate conflict. It also represented not simply a dispute over territory but, rather, a contest over power and ideas.

The war, which ended one month short of its eighth anniversary, had become part of the political and strategic landscape of the Middle East throughout the decade, establishing or accelerating new alignments and forcing new priorities. Because of its durability, its bouts of intense clashes alternating with seasonal lulls, and the impenetrability of the Iranian revolution, it had by the middle of the decade given rise to a host of assumptions, *bon mots*, and clichés among observers that substituted for informed analysis. The Islamic republic, which challenged the prevailing international system and seemed bent on reversing it, appeared implacable in purpose and insensitive to pressures, threats, and punishment. No part of the war, I believe, came as a greater surprise to that class of spectator (as well as to others) than the way it ended. It is upon this phase in particular that the present chapter is concentrated.

The onset of the war, at least, should not have come as a surprise. The relationship between revolution and war is a close one often noted in history. In this as in other cases, the advent of a cataclysmic change in a major state and its replacement by a revolutionary order that makes claims on its neighbours were bound to cause instability. The revolution in Iran upset the balance in two ways: militarily, by replacing the Shah's army with what looked like a revolutionary rabble, and politically, by making a conservative and satisfied Iran into a revolutionary power intent on the quasi-universal mission of spreading its version of true Islam and hence destabilising its neighbours. What made war likely—even inevitable—was not simply Iran's provocations but also its neglect of, and disdain for, the traditional military balance that obtained between the two countries. (It had been this balance—in Iran's favour—that had secured the 1975 Algiers agreement and sustained the new relationship of respect and reciprocity that followed it.)

Iran's rhetorical excesses and claims, as well as its inattention to the military balance, were matched on the Iraqi side by a compound of fear and ambition—fear about Iran's goals if the revolution were to become entrenched, and ambition to achieve a position of regional supremacy while Iran was preoccupied and Iraq was in a relative position of unmatched military/economic strength. From Iraq's perspective, the time to strike (preventively perhaps) was unlikely to be better than in 1980, before the revolution put down its roots, while its forces were in disarray, and while its relationship with both superpowers and most regional states was at best strained.[1]

Iraq's miscalculation was nearly total in that the country overestimated its own capabilities while misconstruing the nature of its adversary and the sources of power at *its* disposal. For while revolutionary Iran was deficient in the traditional or quantitative indices of military power, it made up for this, to a certain extent, by relying on the superior commitment of its populace to the regime and hence the war. Indeed, so eagerly did the revolutionary regime embrace the war as a "blessing," labelling it as a struggle between "Islam and blasphemy" and defining its war aims as the overthrow of the Ba'athist regime in Baghdad, and using the war to suppress its enemies at home, that Iraq's leaders might well have wondered what Iran would have done in the absence of such an external diversion.

Iraq's inability to capitalise on military surprise in the early weeks of the war was not as serious as its failure to fashion a clear political objective. It seems to have expected either a quick collapse of the regime or a willingness to sue for peace, based on limited losses. In so doing, it completely misjudged the nature of revolutionary systems, which do not traditionally understand or wage limited wars (let alone a revolution based on the Shi'i emphasis on the positive value of martyrdom and sacrifice). Martin Wight noted this phenomenon common to most revolutions:

> International revolution . . . transforms the character of war. It blurs the
> distinction between war and peace, international war and civil war, war
> and revolution. . . . International revolutions generate revolutionary wars,
> in the sense that their wars are tinged with a doctrinal ferocity, and have
> unlimited aims. They tend to be not wars for defined objectives but
> crusades or wars for righteousness. They aim not at a negotiated peace
> but at a "Carthiginian peace" or unconditional surrender.[2]

Iran stumbled into a war that it did much to provoke and little to
prepare for. Once embarked upon the "imposed war," which it embraced
with characteristic ardour and militancy, Iran used it to harness the
energies of the mobilised revolutionary rank and file, settle domestic
scores, consolidate power, and focus on the revolution's mission abroad.
The latter was less controversial than the content of the revolution at
home, which remained contentious. The war thus came to represent a
test not only of the revolution and its capacity for commitment and
sacrifice but also of its ingenuity and self-reliance. It came gradually
to epitomise all the themes of suffering and martyrdom that the leadership seemed determined to cultivate. In time, it simply displaced any
other item on the revolution's agenda. The war and the revolution had
merged; support for the two had become so intertwined that they
became virtually indistinguishable.

If Iran's revolution and its claims helped to precipitate the conflict,
its definition of the absolute stakes that the war represented (which
brooked no compromise) helped fuel it long after it made any sense.
Iran's expulsion of Iraqi forces from its territory had been effected by
mid-1982, yet the momentum of war and the drive to extend the sway
of the Iranian revolution throughout the region prevailed over a more
sober assessment of Iran's military capabilities. A series of costly offensives led by revolutionary guards and volunteers (Basijis) failed. In
the next two years the war settled into a pattern of reckless Iranian
attacks on Iraqi forces dug in behind water and earth obstacles and
defended by a network of mines, artillery, and automatic weapons.
Iran's attacks at Majnoon and Howeizah in the spring of 1984 and
1985, respectively, demonstrated Iran's ingenuity and tolerance for punishment but also its inability to hold the territory it captured.

Iraq seemed unwilling to resort to counteroffensives or to take
casualties; consequently, it let Iran dictate the tempo of the war. Iraq
also relied on superior weapons systems because of its continued access
to friendly governments (i.e., the USSR and France, especially after
1982) but otherwise resorted to universal conscription. The morale of
its forces appeared suspect if only because it had lost three times as
many pow's to Iran as its adversary.

Iran, by contrast, relied heavily on the superior commitment of its forces. It constantly affirmed and came to believe the slogan articulated by Rafsanjani in 1984 that "the faith of the Islamic troops is stronger than Iraq's superior firepower." As a consequence, Iran's leaders really believed that they could demonstrate the vitality of the revolution and affirm its message and validity by confronting and overcoming adversity through self-reliance. They were in no mood for lessons from the West or the professional military; their war, like their revolution, was to be an experience unique in the annals of war, unsullied by practical considerations or constraints.

If Iran's military successes between 1982 and 1986 were ephemeral and costly, with long gaps between major offensives in 1984–1986, the problem stemmed as much from deficiencies in strategy as from logistics. Alternating between frontal offensives and attrition along the length of the frontier ("defensive Jihad"), between enthusiasm for the derring-do of the revolutionary guard and the more sober appraisals of the professional military, Iran's leaders were unable to frame a strategy that tied their war aims—the overthrow of the enemy—to their military capabilities, which in terms of equipment dwindled with each offensive. To achieve their war aims, which were total in Clausewitzian terms, Iran needed either to defeat the enemy's forces decisively or to capture a major strategic asset, thereby precipitating its surrender (e.g., the southern port city of Basra, which was predominantly Shi'i). The problem was that Iraq's forces would not venture out into the field to fight (or be defeated), while the capture of Basra or Baghdad remained difficult (and even became more so) because of their redundant defence lines.[3] This gap between aims and capabilities was to widen (as we shall see) and eventually precipitated the process that led to the end of the war.

Iran fought the war with both hands tied: without dependable or rich allies, without access to weapons systems compatible with those in its inventory, and without the benefit of its own best-trained minds. Iran's leadership revelled in this arrangement, insisting, as Khomeini said in 1984, that "those who think that the Koran does not say 'war until victory' are mistaken." If self-sufficiency was the goal, improvisation, self-reliance and a refusal to be bound by conventional approaches had to be the means. At times, the war appeared to be merely a vehicle for consciousness-raising, rather than a deadly serious business. It was "a continuation of politics with the admixture of other means," but in a sense that Clausewitz had surely not meant or intended. Even so, Iran seemed to be winning the war. The breakthrough at Fao in February 1986 seemed to confirm that an Iranian victory was only a matter of time. Jeffrey Record's analysis (to name one) was typical of this conventional wisdom:

> The longer the war lasts, the greater the prospects for a decisive Iranian victory. Iran has three times the population of Iraq, and Iranian forces, though less well equipped, appear to be much more highly motivated than those of Iraq. In February 1986 Iran launched a series of offensives that succeeded in gaining firm control of the Shatt-al Arab waterway. Iraqi counterattacks, which deliberately sought to avoid high casualty rates for fear of undermining already tepid popular support for the war, relied primarily upon artillery fire and failed to dislodge Iranian forces. According to some Western observers of the conflict, Iraqi military leadership borders on the incompetent, and Iraqi troops, especially infantry, have little motivation.[4]

By February 1986 a number of cliches had achieved wide currency. One was that "peace was only possible with the removal or disappearance of one or both of the two leaders, Saddam Hussein and Ayatollah Khomeini," the implication being that compromise short of victory (for Iran) would be unimaginable and tantamount to political suicide. Another was that "Iran could not lose the war nor Iraq win it," meaning that time was on Iran's side. For the Iranian leadership the lesson drawn from Fao had been that a military solution to the war was now indeed possible, contrary to the cautious (and possibly faint-hearted) advice of the professional military. In this view, one Fao followed by several others could wrap up the war quickly. What was lacking was not material for the war effort but commitment and faith. Iran's political leaders began to unlearn what had been painfully learned on the battlefield—namely, that incremental success was an inadequate basis on which to achieve the total victory required to attain Iran's ambitious war aims, and that only a smashing, devastating defeat of the enemy could possibly achieve this end in any case. But victory was unattainable as well. After Fao, it looked somewhat more attainable, and the Iranian leadership sought to capitalise on this success to proclaim "a year of decision." Naturally it again reverted to the style of war most suited to its forces, the frontal offensive.

In fact, it was in one of those paradoxes where strategy abounds[5] that Fao was to be the culminating point of Iran's success—the point at which it both overreached itself and misled itself as to the implications. Why was the prevailing wisdom so wrong regarding the likely outcome of the war if it continued? In war the relative positions of the two sides is in constant flux, and the longer the war the more fluid the picture and the more delicate the assessment of the relative balances on various levels between the two adversaries. Consider but one element in relative strengths, Iran's superior commitment: Its principal asset was neither indefinitely sustainable nor by itself an adequate substitute for access to weapons systems, spares, training, and so on. While "final offensives" gave at least a semblance of momentum to Iran's war effort, a momentum so necessary to stimulate the "bandwagon effect" on the popular forces of the revolution, they also chewed up trained manpower and hard-to-replace equipment. And the prospect of breakthrough seemed to recede with each effort. At the same time, however, recourse to a strategy of attrition held obvious drawbacks: It could not deliver the decisive victory essential for the achievement of Iran's war aims; it was uncongenial to the revolutionary spirit nurtured on elan; and it was a two-edged sword in that it could wear down Iran's will to fight as much as Iraq's, and (because of the importance of commitment in Iran's limited inventory of assets) with quite devastating consequences. A casualty of attrition, or a strategy that relied on incremental progress without the dynamic momentum of battlefield success, could be the superior commitment of Iran's troops and of its will to continue the war.

Yet the instruments for prosecuting the war were dwindling; Iraqi air attacks and the sharp drop in the price of oil in 1986 made the replacement of weapons more onerous economically. At the same time, the inventory of arms inherited from the Shah's day was a finite resource; at some point it could no longer be cannibalised and had to be replaced. Furthermore, Operation Staunch, in place since 1984, was being taken more seriously by the United States which appeared in a vengeful mood after the revelations of "Irangate". European governments also began to take the issue more seriously. In addition, there is reason to suppose that Iran's suppliers from the east, China and North Korea (though perhaps for different reasons) began to limit their supplies to Iran. Thus Iran's access to arms was being curtailed at precisely the time when its strategy called for more resources, and existing stocks could no longer be raided to serve as improvised replacements.

The gap between Iran's military needs and its political aims had widened as the war went on. On every quantitative index of power, Iraq's position, compared to that of Iran, improved year by year. In terms of arms purchases, for instance, Iraq spent more than Iran during every year between 1981 and 1985, in ratios varying between 6 and 3 to 1.[6] In military expenditures, Iraq consistently outspent Iran and maintained a constant rate of between \$12 and \$14 billion in 1984–1987, whereas Iran's plunged and dipped from \$14 billion in 1985–1986 to \$5.89 billion in the next year and to between \$6 and \$8 billion in the succeeding years. As the war dragged on, Iraq gained increasing access to superior sources of arms. In 1984, it managed a 2.5:1 superiority in tanks and a 4:1 superiority in aircraft and armoured personnel carriers (APCs). (In artillery, however, it had a 3:4 inferiority.)[7] These ratios widened by 1988 to a 4:1 superiority in tanks, 10:1 in aircraft, and 3:1 in artillery. The Commander of the Revolutionary Guards, Mohsen Reza'i, was to say after the war:

> They had armour and we did not. If our circumstances in the war are not taken into account when comparisons are made with classical warfare, it will be a major error on the part of the analysts. We were unarmed infantrymen against the enemy's cavalry. There are few instances in the history of Islam of such a war.[8]

Even Iran's much-vaunted demographic advantage of 3:1 was not much in evidence at the battlefield toward the end of the war. Whereas between 1986 and 1988 Iraq was able to increase its manpower by some 150,000 men and expand and reorganise its forces from 30 to 39 infantry divisions, Iran's manpower fell in the same period by 100,000 men.[9]

In addition to a declining pool of volunteers necessitating greater reliance on conscripts who could not match the former in zeal, Iran's war effort was clearly hampered by logistic difficulties. These stemmed partly from political decisions such as the fielding of two sets of armed forces, the regular military, and the Revolutionary Guards, who duplicated each other and did not always work harmoniously. They were compounded, no doubt, by the difficulty of supplying troops with an astonishing variety of ammunition and spare parts, partly of Western origin, partly Soviet bloc (bought and captured), partly from third sources, and partly of indigenous manufacture. It would have been surprising if under these conditions Iran could have obtained a "teeth-to-tail" ratio anywhere near that of Iraq.

As Iran launched what were to be the last major offensives of the war at Basra and in the central sector between December 24 and mid-March 1986–1987, the attacks took on the aspect of a last gasp, a make-or-break attempt to force a military decision. Even the limited advance toward Basra was revealing for it demonstrated not an unstoppable, dynamic force but a strenuous and costly effort barely adequate to sustain itself. Hence Iran could scarcely count on Iraq's collapse, even in the unlikely event of the capture of Basra.

If the war was becoming harder for Iran to prosecute militarily, by demanding greater resources, it was also becoming politically more onerous, in two ways. Iraq's strategy of internationalising the conflict, begun in 1984, was beginning to bear fruit. In 1986 the Tanker war had expanded, with more ships hit and more casualties than the cumulative totals of the preceding years. Iraq's aircraft, with new missiles and air-refueling capabilities, were now ranging as far south as the Larak and Lavan terminals, thus placing all Iran's oil terminals in the Gulf at risk.

In response, Iran had threatened *in extremis* to close the Strait of Hormuz and, in the meantime, targeted those Gulf states known to be actively supporting Iraq's war effort, particularly Kuwait. Iran's accusation that Kuwait served as a transshipment point for arms destined for Iraq, and that the sheikhdom with its financial subsidies and anti-Iranian policies was in effect an undeclared belligerent, was not seriously contested. But none of the superpowers (nor the GCC states) were prepared to admit Iran to target shipping destined for the Gulf sheikhdoms as a legitimate response to Iraq's attacks on Iran's shipping. This ran counter to the outside powers' policy of containing the Gulf war (as it had by now become) and defending the other Gulf states.

The more sustained became Iraq's attacks on ships serving Iran, the more acute became the pressure on Iran to submit passively or to exert pressure militarily on the Gulf states. The dilemma posed did not admit of a solution. Unable to find Iraqi targets in the waterway, Iran attacked the next best thing and found itself playing into Iraq's hand by antagonising its immediate neighbours as well as the superpowers. (Iran's retaliation against third-party shipping for attacks sustained from Iraq thus played into Iraqi hands by bringing in outside powers against Iran.)

By mid-1987 the result of this attack on shipping was seen on two levels: a virtual schism between Persian and Arab in the Gulf after the Mecca incident in July. This schism was symbolised by the Arab summit conference in Amman in November, which, at the insistence of Saudi Arabia, gave priority for the first time to the Gulf war in Arab councils. The concerting of policies by the superpowers in the United Nations in the form of Security Council Resolution 598 was another indicator of the degree to which Iran's conduct of the war had aroused international concern and even stimulated a parallel response. For the resolution, despite all its apparently neutral terminology, was manifestly aimed at arresting *Iran's* continuation of the war, inasmuch as it threatened mandatory sanctions (in the form of an arms embargo) if a cease-fire was not accepted.

This is not the place to discuss Iran's relations with the superpowers, except to note that by mid-1987 it had done little to cultivate the friendship of either and much to push the two together in their efforts to contain and end the war. Soviet leaders, particularly Andrei Gro-

myko, repeatedly counselled Iranian officials that "three years of negotiation are better than one day of war." In December 1987 Gromyko
prophetically told the Iranian ambassador that the longer it takes Iran's
leaders to reach the conclusion that it needs to end the war, the less
favourable it will be for Iran.[10] Iranian leaders consistently overestimated both their own centrality in international affairs and the importance of oil, while remaining insensitive to the changing nature of
relations between the superpowers. At the same time, they were unable
to improve their margin for maneouvre between the superpowers simply
because Iran's ideological inflexibility shackled its diplomacy and prevented credible threats to "go toward the West" or "ally with the East."

If the internationalisation of the war, regional isolation, and the threat
of a future comprehensive arms embargo increased the psychological
pressure on Iran, the lack of success since Fao (in February 1986) had
also begun to diminish the domestic enthusiasm for the war, even
among the diehard *hezbollah* and the *mustazefin* (oppressed) class.
Thus in the second arena, domestic politics, the cost of continuing the
war without decisive results was beginning to be felt.

There were several indications that Iranian leaders were at least
reassessing their approach to the war as of mid-1987:

1. Iran's willingness to take up the gauntlet thrown down by the
   superpowers' decision to escort Kuwaiti shipping suggested that
   Iran somehow welcomed the diversion as a sideshow rather than
   concentrating on the serious prosecution of the war on land.
2. Iran's unwillingness to reject the Security Council resolution of
   July 1987 outright but willingness to seek modifications were also
   indicative of a change in attitude.
3. Iran's still-ambiguous war aims had nonetheless been modified
   over previous months: The demand for the removal of Saddam
   Hussein still stood, but the insistence on the removal of the Ba'ath
   party, reparations, and the installation of an Islamic republic had
   disappeared.
4. The stream of volunteers for the front had dwindled and Iran's
   leaders, notably Rafsanjani, had begun to talk publicly in mid-
   1987 of continuing the war *unless* (or until) it began to interfere
   with the political administration of society.[11]

Iran's leaders had begun to despair of a military solution to the
conflict by the autumn of 1987, but they were still far from devising
a diplomatic strategy for extrication from the war. For one thing the
war, whose importance had been repeatedly and irresponsibly inflated,
and equated with "Islam" and "our life," was clearly becoming costly

to continue, but who could guess what the political costs of ending it ignominiously would be? And who would be the courageous soul willing to convince Khomeini of the necessity, and of the change in the cost calculus, of protracted war versus negotiations? This was not made any easier by the fact that Iran's sense of aggrievement about the origins and hence blame for the start of the war was not shared by many permanent members of the Security Council, in part because of Iran's prolongation of the conflict since mid-1982. And the political collapse of Iraq now looked more remote and less likely a source of salvation. Furthermore, the U.S. fleet (together with that of five European allies) had taken on the appearance of a permanent fixture, less vulnerable and therefore less susceptible to political intimidation than the land presence in Lebanon (1982–1983) with which Iranian leaders erroneously compared it.

However, it was one thing for Iran's war effort to be running out of steam and quite another for it to collapse outright, precipitating the difficult, if unavoidable, decision on the part of Iran to sue for peace. The elements squeezing Iran's war effort were not such as to galvanise its leaders into making such a momentous decision in favour of peace. Only the perception that the continuation of the war would threaten the very existence of the Islamic republic, Khomeini's legacy, could have done so. Simply stated, two sets of events catalysed Iran's decision to seek a quick cease-fire in mid-1988: first, the intensive use by Iraq of long-range missiles on cities, and chemical weapons on the front; and, second (a consequence of the first), a change in the balance of power on the ground and, in particular, the shattering of the morale of Iranian forces.

Although Iran and Iraq had traded attacks on each others' city centres in the course of the war beginning in 1984, these attacks did not reach the intensity of the exchanges witnessed in the revived "war of the cities" in early 1988. Previously, Iraq had used its air superiority to take the war home to Iran by bombing Tehran (in the spring of 1985) in order to raise the political and economic costs of continuing the war. Although this effort had some political effect, it was not sustained enough to produce more than occasional panic and resentment. Iran had responded by proclaiming a programme for building air-shelters and by acquiring Soviet bloc supersonic missiles (SSMs) from Syria, Libya, and possibly China. These missiles, together with artillery, were to counter Iraq's air threat to Iran's inland cities, for Iran had the disadvantage of being within shelling range of Iraq's principal cities. The situation of mutual vulnerability might have been expected to produce an end to these exchanges, were it not for Iraq's perception in late 1987 of the need to intensify the war against Iran during the period of its maximum vulnerability.

Reference has already been made to the widening gap between the two adversaries' military equipment. Nowhere was this more evident than in the next phase of the war, when Iraq launched 150 SCUD-B missiles (modified for extended range allegedly by East German technicians, at the cost of reduced payload[12]) in a period of five weeks starting at the end of February. In the same period Iran fired one-third the number. Less significant than this ratio was the fact that Iraq felt confident enough of the numbers at its disposal to engage in such barrages, and that Iraq, with uncontested advantage in fixed-wing aircraft, was now being supplied with apparently unlimited numbers of SSMs as well. The effect of these indiscriminate terror attacks was to instill panic in the urban populations. (It may be that Iranian leaders' attempts to publicize these attacks for propaganda advantage inadvertently led to the amplification of their terror effect.) Later, after the war, Rafsanjani was to claim that, of the 133,000 deaths resulting from the war, 10,000 to 11,000 were attributable to air and missile attacks on cities.[13]

The effect of these attacks was doubled by Iraq's resumption of the use of chemical weapons at the front, notably during the attack in February 1988 on the town of Halabja in the north. Again, the psychological effects may have been worse than the military ones. But it did not escape notice in Iran that the international outcry over documented uses of these banned substances was relatively restrained when Iranian soldiers or villages were targeted. Rafsanjani was later to tell the Revolutionary Guards that the war had shown chemical and biological weapons to be "very decisive," and that "all the moral teachings of the world are not very effective when war reaches a serious position."[14]

The turning point in the war came soon after, I believe, in the double blow sustained by Iran on April 17–18 with the loss of Fao to Iraq and several boats to the U.S. Navy. Fao, of course, was politically and psychologically significant. It had been the major tangible symbol of Iranian success in the war, and its loss would leave Iran virtually empty-handed after six years of prolonging the war. But more important still was what Iraq's recapture of Fao signalled, in terms of the shift in the psychological balance that had taken place. Iraq had dumped its "defence only" policy, its policy of leaving the initiative to Iran, of hiding behind static defences, and of seeking to limit casualties in engagements. By seizing the initiative and striking out with counteroffensives, Iraq not only complicated Iran's defence planning but served notice of a new and unsuspected confidence.

Certainly Iraq's newfound confidence and belligerence on the battle-field came as a surprise to the Iranians, who were accustomed not so much to reacting as to dictating the time and place of engagements. A week before Iraq's recapture of Fao, President Khamenei was depicting the "war of the cities" as a logical outgrowth of Iraq's incapacity to do anything else militarily: "The Iraqi regime lacks the power even to defend itself. For years it had lost the power to mount an offensive on the battlefield. Today it does not even command defensive forces, as is evidenced by Halabja."[15]

In Iranian eyes, the double blow was too suspiciously coincidental in timing to have happened accidentally. After all, it was generally known (and admitted) that the United States was already providing Iraq with detailed intelligence data to aid Iraqi bombing runs on Iranian targets. Furthermore, both the range of Iraqi aircraft and the accuracy of their bombing against Iran's oil refineries and terminals had suspiciously improved of late. It was but a short step from there to seeing the actions on April 17–18 as being coordinated and even jointly planned. Rafsanjani accordingly depicted them as a plot.[16]

The fact nonetheless remained that Iraqi troops had wrestled the initiative away from Iran (which for the first time since the start of the war had been unable to mount an offensive in the appropriate season) and forced its troops to flee. Coming as it did on the heels of the missiles and chemical weapons, this outcome finally cracked morale on the Iranian side. The one asset on which Iran had relied to com-pensate for inferiority in every other area had simply dissolved. This fact was of decisive importance because morale, commitment, zeal, or dedication (whatever its label) could not, by its very nature, be recon-stituted overnight. Unlike a shortage of aircraft or spare parts, it could not be made good or topped-up by outside suppliers.

Indicative of this shift in the respective motivation of the two sides were the tremors of discontent that were again emanating from within Iranian society. In May, Mehdi Bazargan, the head of the Liberation Movement of Iran, the only opposition party allowed by the Islamic republic, made a scathing criticism of the government's policy of con-tinuing the war. What distinguished this from earlier criticisms by the same source were the echoes it now audibly evoked in many sectors of society. For the stoical populace of the Islamic republic, economic hardship and other privations such as fuel rationing and electricity cuts were tolerable in the cause of victory, but not otherwise. Now there was evidently precious little optimism about this goal, even among the high priests of war.

The scene was thus set for a radical rethinking of policy. What lent it urgency was the evidence that Iran's soldiers were unwilling and unable to continue the fight. Even in those cases where impending Iraqi attacks were publicised, as in Majnoon, the Iranian troops' commitment to defence was a shadow of their earlier performance. (The lack of supplies and ammunition had clearly aggravated the deficiency in morale.) The string of Iraqi military victories after Fao, Shalamcheh, Mehran, and Majnoon, among others, only hastened Rafsanjani's determination to get Khomeini's approval for Iran's acceptance of a cease-fire.

The destruction of an Iran-Air airbus by a U.S. naval vessel's missile in early July provided a convenient occasion for the announcement of the decision to accept the cease-fire. It gave Iran's leaders precisely the moral cover of martyrdom and suffering in the face of an unjust superior force to camouflage the comprehensive defeat of their political goals. Even Khomeini could not dissemble the depth of the defeat.

If the war and the revolution had imperceptibly merged into one, and if the war had proven virtually the only achievement of the revolution in nine years, what possible verdict on the revolution could now be passed? Judged from the standpoint of traditional diplomacy, Iran's war effort had been a valiant but pointless exercise. Having elevated self-reliance to an absolute goal, Iran had found through its own immoderation that it was no longer just a goal but a reality, and a constraint with which its war effort had to struggle. Self-reliance, self-sufficiency, a nation tempered and forged in war, and similar such romantic notions were the most that could be salvaged from a war that should never have occurred. Iran's inattention to the military balance had made war attractive to its rival neighbour. Similar inattention to the business of making peace at the optimum time ensured that Iran was to reach the conference table at the point of its maximum weakness.

The major casualty of the war has been the credibility of the Islamic republic among its own rank and file. It will no longer be able to effectively call upon its populace for crusades and sacrifices, but will have to act more like a normal state. It is for this reason that Hashemi Rafsanjani has indulged in preemptive self criticism of past policies. It is for this reason, too, that reconstruction policies are particularly important. A peace dividend must be found for the supporters of the revolution if the virus of discontent is not to spread and affect the very legitimacy of the revolution. Regardless of whether future generations commemorate the war as a glorious chapter in the revolution, the present generation may be forgiven for not doing so. Indeed, the palpable sense of relief felt in Iran at the end of the war has been followed by a silence that may turn out to be a prelude to the sense of disgust at the waste and be followed by a demand for an accounting from the leadership.

The war, which provided Iran's revolution with a focus and a sense of unity and in which politics were submerged, has been followed by a resurfacing of contentious issues long left dormant or unresolved. The course of the revolution and its priorities are now the objects of political competition, and the struggle for power sharpened by expectations of Khomeini's imminent demise is likely to exacerbate the differences among the Islamic republic's leaders. In this sense the war, by providing the Islamic leadership with a convenient alibi, postponed the very real difficulties facing the revolution—difficulties that still have to be faced. Only now they must be faced in the wake of an inglorious and costly war.

NOTES

1. For a more detailed discussion see Shahram Chubin and Charles Tripp, *Iran and Iraq at War*, Boulder, Colo.: Westview Press, 1988.

2. Martin Wight, *Power Politics*, edited by Hedley Bull and Carsten Holbraad, Harmondsworth: Penguin, 1979, pp. 89–90, 91–92.

3. See my longer discussion of this problem in Shahram Chubin, "Les Conduites des Operations Militaires," *Politique Etrangere*, Vol. 2 (Special Issue on Iran-Iraq: La Diplomatie du Conflit), 1987, pp. 303–317.

4. Jeffrey Record, "The OS Central Command: Toward What Purpose?" *Strategic Review*, Spring 1986, p. 44, fn 4.

5. See Edward Luttwak's *Strategy: The Logic of War and Peace*, Cambridge, Mass.: Belknap Press, 1987.

6. These ratios were taken from *World Military and Expenditures and Arms Transfers 1986*; they were also quoted in "Overview of the Situation in the Persian Gulf," Hearings and Markup Before the Committee on Foreign Affairs, May–June 1987, pp. 230–231.

7. See "War in the Gulf," a staff report prepared for U.S. Committee on Foreign Relations, Senate (Committee Print), Washington, D.C.: Government Printing Office, August 1984.

8. Tehran television, 22 September, in BBC/ME/0267/A/3, 27 September 1988.

9. Unless otherwise stated, these figures are derived from the annual International Institute of Strategic Studies (IISS) *Military Balance*, 1984–1988. Saddam Hussein recently boasted about this: "Our people who began with 12 divisions at the beginning of the war, now have about 70 divisions at the end of the war. The entire world has never seen such a development." See Baghdad Home Service, 14 November, in BBC, Summary of World Broadcasts, ME/0311/A/9, 17 November 1988.

10. *Pravda*, 5 December 1987; *Izvestiya*, 8 December 1987.

11. Chubin and Tripp, op. cit., pp. 73–74 and citations therein.

12. See *The Independent*, 22 March 1988; and *Washington Post*, 10 March 1988.

13. See Rafsanjani's speech in Qom, 24 September, broadcast by Tehran radio on 25 September and excerpted in BBC/ME/0267/A/4, 27 September 1988.

14. Tehran home service, 6 October, excerpted in BBC/ME/0277/A/2, 8 October 1988.

15. President Khamenei, Sermon, Tehran University, 8 April, excerpted in BBC/ME/0122/A/3, 11 April 1988.

16. See Rafsanjani's interview with Tehran Television, 18 April, in BBC/ME/0130/A/6, 20 April 1988.

8

The Legacy of the Iran-Iraq War

John Sigler

INTRODUCTION

Few analysts were prepared for the rapid end to the Iran-Iraq war. It came with the dramatic announcement from Teheran on 18 July 1988 that Iran accepted unconditionally the United Nations' terms for a cease-fire in the long war, which had lasted just one month short of eight years. Indeed, it was one of the twentieth century's longest wars, although it was not, as the *Economist*, 23 July 1988, called it, "the world's largest war since 1945." That dubious distinction goes to the Korean war, which lasted thirty-seven months and took an estimated 2 million lives in combat (Small and Singer, 1982: 92). It was closely followed by the Second Vietnam war, which lasted just over ten years (1965–1975) and took an estimated 1,216,000 lives in combat. The estimates on battle deaths in the Iran-Iraq war range from 420,000 (Cordesman, 1987) to one million (U.S. Department of State, 1988:1). Each side went to extraordinary lengths to minimize its losses, including Iraq's reported procedures for holding bodies in cold storage and re-leasing them over time to grieving families. If the lower figures are used, the war is outranked by the Sino-Japanese war of 1937–1941, which resulted in an estimated 1 million battle deaths. But it would still place fifth in severity in all interstate wars since 1815, exceeding the Lopez war of 1864–1870, which took the lives of 310,000 Argentinians, Brazilians, and Paraguayans. The rapid growth in military technology since 1815 has greatly increased the efficiency of the killing fields, so that one can really say that the Iran-Iraq War was the most severe in human history. What distinguishes it from the Vietnam and Korean conflicts is the minimal degree of outside intervention (given 37 American battle deaths in the Iraqi Exocet attack on the USS Stark on 17 May 1987). In the tanker war in the Gulf, 474 merchant seamen also lost their lives in the 548 attacks by both sides on commercial shipping (*Christian Science Monitor,* 12 August 1988).

In material terms, the cost of the war to the combatants was more than $200 billion dollars through 1986, according to Israeli experts cited by the *Washington Post*, 18 August 1988. The same figure has been used by the Stockholm International Peace Research Institute. The *New York Times*, 10 August 1988, estimated the total cost at more than $400 billion dollars. This includes lost revenues, damaged and destroyed buildings, industrial plants, ships, and military equipment. Kiyotaki Tsuji (*Washington Post*, 18 August 1988) of the Japanese Institute of Middle East Economic Studies estimated that lost oil revenues were $23 billion dollars for Iran and $65 billion for Iraq. *La Tribune* of Paris, August 1988, estimated Iran needs $80 billion and Iraq $30 billion to rebuild the basic economic and social infrastructure destroyed in the war. Oil refineries costing billions of dollars were destroyed on both sides. The *Economist*, 13 August 1988, estimated that rebuilding oil installations alone will cost $25 billion dollars. Iraq began the war with $35 billion in reserves and now owes an estimated $110 billion, although half of this is owed to Kuwait and Saudi Arabia and will probably not be repaid. Iraq owes an estimated $26 billion to European, Japanese, and Soviet bloc creditors that will have to be repaid, with interest. Iran had tried to avoid foreign borrowing, but in the later years of the war it ran up $5 billion in short-term loans from foreign banks. By 1988, Iran was spending 30 percent of its total budget on the war, with unemployment and inflation rates of over 30 percent. Iraq was spending 60 percent of its budget on the war.

The psychological toll is far more difficult to assess. The war caused an estimated 1.5 million refugees to flee the scenes of devastation. In the north, Iraq has again followed a scorched earth policy, just as it did in 1975 when it punished the Kurds for the aid they gave to the Iranians during the war. (Large numbers of Iraqi troops were engaged in battles on the southern and central fronts.) Iraq's increasing use of chemical weapons in the closing months of the war, particularly against civilian populations, increased the stress on the Iranian population. Iranian publicity on the Iraqi gas attacks on the civilian Kurdish population at Halabja in March 1988 may have boomeranged by increasing the fears of the urban populations of Iranian cities that the Iraqis might arm their medium-range modified SCUD-B missiles with chemical warheads. Both Gary Sick and Robin Wright (*New York Times*, 22 July 1988) cited the Iraqi gas attacks as having had a major impact on Iranian civilian morale. The Strategic Bombing Surveys of World War II reported that civilian morale was not greatly undermined as had been feared, but the preliminary evidence from Iran in the intense "war of the cities" suggests this conclusion may need to be modified in light of the experience of this war. During the 52-day missile exchange in February and March 1988, Iraqi rockets are estimated to have killed at least 2,000 civilians in Teheran alone and to have caused up to half the city's population to flee the city. A leading U.S. expert on Iran, James Bill (*Washington Post*, 28 August 1988) reported the severe damage that Iraqi bombing has wreaked on the great Islamic monuments of Isfahan—damage that has contributed to the breaking of Iranian resolve to continue the fighting.

IRAN'S DECISION TO LEAVE THE WAR

The surprising Iranian announcement came after weeks of reporting from Iranian experts on the deep divisions within Iran in the power struggle for the succession to the ailing Ayatollah Khomeini. The so-called pragmatists under Parliamentary Speaker Hashemi Rafsanjani apparently convinced a highly reluctant Khomeini to sanction the withdrawal from the war on the argument that its continuation was now a major threat to the survival of the Iranian Revolution. In the long war of attrition, it was the larger and more zealous party, Iran, that finally showed the greater signs of exhaustion, although this was far from predictable even a year before. How do we account for this rapid decline in Iranian resolve?

The reasons that have been put forward by commentators include the following:

1. *A series of rapid Iraqi military victories.* These include the recapture of the Fao peninsula by units of the elite Presidential Guards in April 1988, followed by the defeat of the Iranian Revolutionary Guards at Shalamcheh in May on the central front, the overrunning of the Maj-noon islands in June, the 40-kilometer thrust into Iran in the Zubaidat area, and the capture of Dehloran. In explaining these surprising Iraqi victories, analysts have pointed to the fear engendered in Iranian troops by the increased Iraqi use of chemical weapons, and to reports just before the Iranian acceptance of the cease-fire that Iraq was massing fifteen armoured divisions for a major assault into Iran.

2. *A breakdown in Iranian military command, a shortage of supplies, and an inability to raise new recruits.* For Anthony Cordesman (*Newsweek*, 1 August 1988: 29), "the anvil that broke the Iranian hammer" was the failed offensive against Basra in late 1986 and early 1987. The Iranians lost as many as 70,000 men in their human-wave charges against Iraqi defenses. RAND analyst Frank Fukuyama (*Los Angeles Times*, 20 July 1988) argues that the Iranians were unable at Basra to maintain a pipeline of weapons to front-line troops, and they suffered

tremendous losses of noncommissioned and junior field officers. The Basra offensive went as well as it did because the Iranians had the last of the high-technology weapons acquired from the United States in the "arms-for-hostages" deal. After that, they were forced to rely on Eastern Europe, China, and North Korea for fewer and lower-quality weapons. Israeli experts (*Wall Street Journal*, 22 July 1988) claimed that Iran had no anti-aircraft missiles left in its inventory, was down to only 40 serviceable fighter aircraft (compared to Iraq's 600), and had reached a "red line" on most military systems. Credit was given to the tough new application of Operation Staunch by the U.S. administration.

3. *The loss in civilian morale due to the missile attacks in February and March, and the effects on civilians of the use of chemical weapons in Kurdistan.* An estimated 300,000 young Iranians had gone into hiding or exile to avoid conscription.

4. *Economic deprivation.* Shireen Hunter (*Newsweek*, 1 August 1988: 28) calculated that Iran needed a minimum of $10 billion annually to purchase arms, food, and other essentials abroad, but the country expected to earn only $6 billion in 1988 from the export of oil.

5. *U.S. Fleet intervention.* The U.S. shootout with the Iranian navy in April 1988 came simultaneously with the Iraqi victory at Fao. The confrontation caused a deep split within Iranian ruling circles, with the hardliners demanding attacks on U.S. targets. The resulting shootout destroyed a good part of the Iranian fleet. Rafsanjani, who opposed the hardliners, was able to show the dangers to Iran in taking on the Americans.

6. *The Airbus tragedy.* In announcing the acceptance of the cease-fire, Iranian President Ali Khamenei cited the 3 July downing of the Iranian Airbus flight by the *USS Vincennes*. The resulting 290 deaths were a "clear manifestation" that the war was now "engulfing innocent civilians." Gary Sick (*Wall Street Journal*, 19 July 1988) said that "in its own peculiar way, [the Airbus attack] may have added to their sense of frustration, and their sense, that they were, in effect, surrounded and had a superpower at war with them." Rafsanjani (*Washington Post*, 20 July 1988) said that the Airbus attack was the "turning point" that led to serious Iranian discussion of accepting the cease-fire, inasmuch as Iran interpreted the attack as a deliberate U.S. warning that it would permit "immense crimes" if Iran persisted in the war.

7. *Effective UN diplomacy.* Throughout the long history of the war, the only mediator who retained any credibility with both sides was UN Secretary General Perez de Cuellar. In the early years, however, the great powers behaved very cautiously toward the conflict; the dominant view was the cynical one expressed by Henry Kissinger to the effect that it was in their interest for the war to continue and "both sides

lose." There was a dramatic shift in U.S. policy following the embarrassment of the Iran-Contra scandal. A whole new team of experienced officers came to the White House under Frank Carlucci and led a turnaround in U.S. policy on the Gulf war. On 23 January 1987, President Reagan announced a new two-track policy of exerting diplomatic pressure on Iran to sue for peace and bolstering U.S. military support for the Arab Gulf states. Most important, the President announced that the United States was determined to bring the war "to the promptest possible negotiated end, without victor or vanquished." The offer of reflagging Kuwaiti vessels followed in March, but so did a very active U.S. diplomatic effort to develop a broadly shared and comprehensive peace plan, culminating in UN Security Council Resolution 598 on 20 July 1987. As the U.S. tilt toward Iraq accelerated, the United States did push for an arms embargo against Iran, but it was resisted by the UN secretariat and the other permanent members, particularly the Soviet Union, which argued for more time to press Iran to accept the Resolution 598 package. U.S. handling of the Airbus attack in the Security Council succeeded in passing what Iran called the "litmus test" for fairness to its concerns. In the debate, George Bush criticized both Iran and Iraq for refusing to agree to a cease-fire, particularly with regard to attacks by both nations on Gulf shipping. President Saddam Hussein criticized the Bush line as "twisted logic," but it was the first time that Iran had heard an even-handed approach. The expressions of regret and offers of compensation to families also aided in this process. Iran may have sensed its own strong diplomatic isolation when it failed to get a sponsor for a resolution condemning the United States for the attack, but behind the scenes the United States worked with Paulo Nogueira-Batista of Brazil, the President of the Council, for compromise language acceptable to Iran. Ironically, both the Iran-Contra affair and the Airbus attack, which were deeply embarrassing to Washington, drove the administration to work more constructively through the United Nations. Since the acceptance of the cease-fire, Iran has succeeded in working effectively within the UN framework and putting Iraq on the diplomatic defensive.

THE LESSONS OF THE WAR

Even great tragedies rarely result in broadly shared "lessons." These lessons are filtered through prevailing value systems. We see what we want to see, and we learn what we want to learn. Partisanship plays a critical role as well. We are all citizens of a particular state, and the lessons may reflect what serves the particular parochial interest of that state, or the one with which we sympathize. In the prevailing debate on philosophies of international relations, academics frequently identify three contending schools: the realist, the liberal internationalist, and the radical (McKinlay and Little, 1986) schools. It is not surprising that the lessons put forward thus far more or less conform to the principal values of these schools of thought.

For the realists, the principal value is the preservation and promotion of the interests of the state. Both Iraq and Iran are committed to transnational ideologies, which claim identities and loyalties beyond that of the existing nation-states that they run. Part of the Iraqi motivation for the war was to assert its pan-Arab claims on the Arabic-speaking province of Khuzistan. Similarly, the Iranians made a pan-Islamic radical claim on the loyalties of primarily Iraq's majority Shi'ite population. One lesson of the war on both sides was the limited effect of these trans-border appeals to what were seen as like-minded people on the other side. The Arabic-speaking population of Khuzistan did not rally to the Iraqi cause, and the Shiites of Iraq largely behaved in a loyal manner, obeyed the call to arms, and fought well. The territorial borders of the state took on real meaning, and each side fought best when it was defending its own national territory. In this sense, the Western territorial state system emerged intact from a war between two regimes that ideologically made much larger claims for their political ambitions than the narrow territorial state that they led. As Ayoob (1985: 584) points out, Iran is "a much stronger state in social, psychological, and political terms than its neighbors across the Gulf." The Iraqi regime has a much greater challenge in establishing strong state mechanisms and regime legitimacy. In this sense, perhaps Christine Helms (*New York Times*, 5 August 1988) is right in arguing that the reason Iraq insisted so strongly on face-to-face negotiations in the initial UN cease-fire implementation talks was to have clear recognition from the Iranians that they accepted the legitimacy of the Baath regime.

Both Iran and Iraq turned inward as the war progressed and are now strongly committed to the reconstruction and revival of the territorial state and its institutions. What this means abroad for Iran is a defeat, at least for the moment, of the militants who pressed for the export of the Revolution, and the scaling back of the promotion of a radical pan-Islamic vision in Lebanon and the Gulf. Ahmad Abdulgahi (*New York Times*, 24 July 1988), an Egyptian diplomat in Baghdad, said:

> It is the beginning of the end for militant Islam. Fundamentalists in the region had two sources of support. Morally they looked upon Iran's defiance of the world and its success in the war as an inspiration for

their own movements, and they took money from the Iranians to fund their activities. Both have now evaporated.

Other Israeli analysts are less confident of this view. Amatsia Basria (*Wall Street Journal*, 22 July 1988), from the University of Haifa, thinks there will be no lessening of Iran's revolutionary fervour:

> I think that what we are seeing is a replay of the Russian Revolution. Khomeini is a new Lenin, Montazari is the new Trotsky and Rafsanjani is the new Stalin. Just as with the Bolshevik Revolution, the three will now work at trying to consolidate the revolution from within, strengthening the army and helping underground movements abroad, especially in Saudi Arabia and Lebanon.

Other Arab analysts say that Iran has changed its tactics in the export of the revolution. The emphasis now will be on trying to establish an attractive alternative form of government and to promote greater contacts with the area's Shiite Muslims, many of whom have been alienated by the experience of the Revolution and the use of violence abroad. Philip Robins (*Christian Science Monitor*, 25 July 1988), an analyst with the Royal Institute of International Affairs in London, believes that the Iranians will continue to try to export the revolution but that they lack the ability to destabilize the smaller Gulf states.

Realists place major emphasis on the importance of the armed forces as a key agent in the coercive instruments of the state. Iraq is generally seen as the military victor in the conflict, because of its string of victories in the last six months of war. It emerged from the war with fifty well-trained, well-led, well-equipped, and battle-hardened divisions. Iraq's reputation in this sense has been enhanced; it is seen as both influencing its friends and intimidating its enemies. The cease-fire came as a particular surprise in Israel, which had supported Iran during the war; despite the Revolution's strong anti-Zionist views, the war was seen as a means of tying up and weakening Iraq, one of the Arab world's potential leaders. In the previous Arab-Israeli wars, Israel had had relatively little difficulty in neutralizing the poorly led and inexperienced Iraqi units. Since the end of the war, a major campaign mounted from Israel and echoed in the American press hypothesizes that Middle East peace is now seriously threatened by the new sophistication and capability of Arab states, led by Iraq, in mid-range ground-to-ground missiles, complemented by their new sophistication and experience with chemical weapons (the poor man's nuclear equivalent) and by the particular danger of chemical warheads on missiles targetted on Israeli cities. The Israelis were particularly worried about Egyptian-

Iraqi cooperation with Argentina to develop the Condor II, a state-of-the-art intermediate-range missile equivalent to the U.S. Pershing II, destined for destruction under the new Intermediate Range Nuclear Force (INF) agreement with the Soviet Union. Indeed, the United States convened the Missile Technology Control Regime (United States, France, U.K., West Germany, Italy, Canada, and Japan) in Rome on 8–9 September 1988 to try to block the Condor II as well as other Third World missile acquisition projects (*Washington Post*, 19 September 1988).

Israeli Foreign Minister Shimon Peres (*Washington Post*, 19 July 1988) said that the cease-fire meant an important shift in the regional military balance, and that the Gulf countries might decide to compete for prestige by menacing Israel rather than by rebuilding their countries. Brigadier General Aharon Levran (*Christian Science Monitor*, 20 July 1988), head of the Middle East Balance project at the Jaffe Centre of Strategic Studies at Tel Aviv University, said that the end of the war posed no immediate threat to Israel inasmuch as Iraq will be reluctant to take on new military adventures and will have to keep a wary eye on Iran. For the longer term, Israel fears that Iraq's new strength may limit Israel's ability to make a preventive strike against Saudi missile installations and to occupy the East Bank of the Jordan. The latter move would now certainly provoke a serious Iraqi intervention (Leviticus, 1988:6). The end of the war also revived the debate within Israel as to whether it should not have taken a more positive attitude toward Iraq by trying to move it into the Mubarak-Hussein moderate camp. Whatever opportunities might have existed for a better understanding with Iraq, the country was now seen as likely to return to its leadership of the anti-Israeli Arab coalition. Michael Ledeen (*New York Times*, 19 July 1988), the U.S. National Security Council consultant (1984–1986) who played a key role in linking the White House with Israeli officials to win influence in Teheran, returned immediately to the idea of a Washington-Teheran rapprochement. Charles Krauthammer (*Washington Post*, 16 September 1988) also called for a "decisive [U.S.] geopolitical tilt toward Iran." The idea of reviving the Washington-Jerusalem-Teheran axis is strongly supported in Israel, particularly by Mossad and the top echelons in the military (Leviticus, 1988:6), because such an axis would prevent closer U.S.-Arab relations. As Andrew Gilmour (*Christian Science Monitor*, 1 August 1988), an analyst with the Center for Strategic and International Studies in Washington, put it: "[T]he one constant in Israeli foreign policy . . . has been to drive a wedge between the U.S. and the Arabs." The speed with which an organized Kurdish/Israeli lobby secured the condemnation by George Shultz of the Iraqi use of chemical weapons on the Kurds, and the subsequent

Senate and House embargos on trade with Iraq, suggests how quickly the wedge can be driven. Iraq turned sharply on the United States, mounting huge demonstrations outside the U.S. Embassy in Baghdad and running long footages on Iraqi television of the devastation at Hiroshima and Nagasaki. The attack on Iraq raises few domestic problems, but drawing closer to Iran remains a highly sensitive issue in U.S. politics. The White House was reported (*New York Times*, 22 September 1988) to have blocked efforts by middle-level officials in the State Department to lift U.S. economic sanctions against Iran.

Israeli Reserve Army Major General Sholom Gazit (*New York Times*, 24 July 1988), former head of military intelligence, said that "[o]ne can say with certainty that the Iraqi Army will reach our border and will fight in a much more comprehensive way than we've known in the past." The Israeli Knesset's foreign and defence committee went into immediate hearings on why the intelligence services had failed to predict the imminence of an Iraq-Iran cease-fire. Defence Minister Rabin suggested that the Iran-Iraq war may not turn out to have been such a good thing for Israel because both sides acquired sophisticated weaponry that might in the future be turned against Israel.

Several U.S. commentators were more bluntly realistic in their assessment. Charles Krauthammer (*Washington Post*, 22 July 1988) wrote:

> In fact, the major reason for Iran's capitulation is Iraq's recent military successes. . . . Nevertheless, one crucial cause of Iran's decision to call off the war was the United States. Its massive presence in the Gulf and its policy of preventing Iran from carrying out its side of the tanker war gave Iraq an overwhelming advantage at sea. . . . What is it to us if two barbaric countries—one specializes in terrorism, the other in poison gas—stop killing each other? . . . The work is done and the big stick did it. . . . The key was not keeping the weapons from getting into Iran . . . but keeping the oil from getting out. The tanker war (and other Iraqi bombings) did that. The Iraqi air force supplied the sword, the U.S. Navy the shield. The rest is history and a valuable lesson about what a superpower with an immense military can do when it has the nerve.

Other analysts are skeptical about the conclusion that the U.S. Gulf presence played such a decisive or even positive role. Brian McCartan (*Washington Post*, 20 July 1988), of the Center for Defense Information in Washington, points out that the Gulf fleet did not reduce the number of attacks on shipping in the Gulf. Iranian attacks doubled from 64 in the year before the fleet presence to 117 in the year of the fleet's presence. Krauthammer agrees that the U.S. fleet did not ensure freedom of navigation. On the contrary, it took no action against stepped-up

Iraqi attacks on Gulf shipping in the same period; but it was the economic strangulation of Iran that the U.S. fleet assisted by defending the Arab states against Iranian retaliation. The fleet operation was highly controversial even within the Pentagon, however. The operation cost over $20 million a month and diverted important naval resources from their other missions, which were left uncovered. Marine General George B. Crist, the head of the U.S. Central Command with overall authority on Gulf operations, told the House Appropriations Defense Subcommittee that even though the United States was a winner in the Gulf, this end was not accomplished with the right kind of equipment for low-intensity conflict at sea. U.S. Defense Secretary Carlucci (*Washington Post*, 25 July 1988) defended the dispatch of the *Vincennes* to the Gulf, saying that such sophisticated electronic equipment was necessary to deal with the threat posed by the Iranian Silkworm missiles installed at the Strait of Hormuz. Another military commander said: "How come we have to keep 30 ships in the Gulf when the Russians do their escorting with a couple of minesweepers?" We can be sure that one of the lessons of the war for the U.S. military will be new requests for equipment that can handle low-intensity conflict in "brown water" areas of the Third World. Ware (1988) of the Air Defense University, using Iran-Iraq as one case study, argues that the United States should recognize that its East-West focus has blinded it to the requirements for increased frequency of operations against hostile forces in the Third World—forces that have no links with Moscow. At its 1988 annual meeting, the International Institute of Strategic Studies also talked of the prospect of heightened warfare in the Third World.

William Tuohy (*Los Angeles Times*, 22 August 1988) provided a lengthy assessment of the legacy of the war:

1. Iraq has emerged as the most powerful force in the region.
2. The failure of the Iranian military has dulled the luster of the Shia Muslim revolution.
3. Syrian President Hafez Assad's continuing support of non-Arab Iran in the war has made him one of the conflict's big losers, rendering him a choice target for Iraqi diplomacy and propaganda.
4. The Arab Gulf states no longer have to fear takeover by elements influenced by Iran, but they may come under the hegemony of Iraq.
5. It was in Israel's interest for the war to continue; their favorite, Iran, came out second-best and they are now considering quiet contact with the Iraqis.
6. Iraq may play a larger role in faction-torn Lebanon, supporting the Lebanese forces against Syria.

7. The Palestinians will receive additional support from Iraq and are net winners.
8. The superpowers will both profit from the end of the war because the potential for their being drawn into it would be removed.
9. The Europeans stand to profit from hefty contracts for rebuilding the infrastructure of both countries.

The *Economist* (23 July 1988) offered a set of clear lessons from the war: (1) armies matter more than territory; in other words, Iran should not have stopped and tried to negotiate after its first success but should have kept up the pressure. (2) Don't trust air power. Although Iraq cut Iran's oil revenue, it had no great military effect on Iranian infrastructure. (3) Poison gas works well. (4) Sea mines can cause havoc. (5) Merchant ships are easy targets. (6) The best attack may be good defence. And (7) war is hell, not just for soldiers. On this last point, the judgment was sweeping: "This entire dreadful conflict was in many ways a mistake from start to finish." Indeed, judgment on the utility of this particular war moved the realist criteria from military strategy and tactics to the liberal criterion of illegality as well as inefficacy of war in the modern technological age.

The liberal internationalists, particularly the global society variant (Banks, 1984), are concerned about legitimacy and respect for international law and international institutions. Richard Falk (1981: 75–76), Princeton Professor of International Law and Politics, has argued that the failure of the international community to condemn Iraq for its aggression against Iran was comparable to the betrayal of the League system by Britain and France in 1935 in failing to act against Italy for its aggression against Ethiopia. In both cases, short-term national interest overrode any respect for the requirements of international law and the obligations under the League Covenant and the UN Charter. Iran itself may have learned some important lessons in this regard. It chose to ignore the international community and the World Court in refusing to release American diplomatic hostages in 1979 and 1980, such that its claims to protection of the Charter in the fall of 1980 fell on largely deaf ears.

The liberal internationalist view has received little coverage in the American press since the end of the war. Andrew I. Killgore (1988a: 5–6), former U.S. Ambassador to Qatar, used the end of the war to provide a powerful critique of U.S. involvement in the region. He cautioned against repeating past mistakes, citing the overthrow of nationalist leader Muhammad Mossadeq in Iran in 1953, the punishment of Iraq's Colonel Qassem in his efforts to gain greater control over Iraqi oil concessions, Kissinger's agreement to involve the CIA in secret

Israeli and Iranian activities to support a Kurdish revolt in Iraq, the general abandonment of U.S. leadership in the Gulf to Israeli initiatives, Kissinger's agreement to sell the Shah a crippling $25 billion in U.S. arms between 1972 and 1978 as a pillar of U.S. influence in the region, the Iran-Contra affair, and the tilt toward Iraq to make up for these errors of the past.

Killgore argued for an even-handed U.S. policy in the area and equal treatment of all states—Iran, Israel, and the Arab states. Specifically, to help resolve the long-standing dispute over the Shatt al-Arab, he proposed that the United States use its influence to internationalize the waterway, under UN or other auspices, and ensure free movement of commercial traffic there (1988b:10).

Iraq's fears for the future have been clearly expressed since the end of the war by the reassertion of its claim to full sovereignty over the waterway and by its demand for guarantees that Iran will not again assert restrictive rights over access to the Gulf itself through the Strait of Hormuz. Iran initially insisted on the sanctity of the 1975 Iran-Iraq accord, which Iraq disavowed on 18 September 1988, four days before the outbreak of the war. It is now clear, however, that the treaty was imposed under duress; Iran agreed to end its support for the Kurdish rebellion in Iraq in exchange for Iraqi agreement to the long-standing claim of the Iranians for the river boundary to be set according to the Thalweg principle of the middle of the navigable channel of the river. Settlements that are imposed by the powerful on the weak have little legitimacy, and may in fact exacerbate the original grievances. The Iran-Iraq war is a classic case of the failure of coercive diplomacy as a technique in conflict resolution.

Shireen Hunter (*Christian Science Monitor*, 15 September 1988) has argued that the "international community's lack of respect for its own principles . . . prolonged the war. Had the United Nations condemned Iraq's aggression and pressed it to withdraw from Iran early in the war, it could have ended much earlier. International rules and principles must be treated as indivisible and applied irrespective of political preferences." Specifically, she cautioned Iraq against overconfidence and excessive ambition. Iran's first priority must be national reconciliation and the acknowledgment that it must live within the rules of the international system. Hunter also urged the great powers to restrain Iraq and to create and maintain a new balance of military and political power in the region, thus discouraging aggression and hegemonic tendencies.

Nikki Keddie (1988) has also argued for fairness and even-handedness in future great-power diplomacy in the area. She particularly deplores the crude anti-Sovietism that has dominated recent U.S. foreign policy in the Gulf. She also deplores outside manipulation of U.S. policy as seen in the Iran-Contra affair, during which the White House allowed itself to be manipulated by Israelis and Iranian leaders alike and "[profiteered] international arms salesmen who doubled as diplomats" (p. 31). She believes that U.S. intervention on the side of Iraq seriously delayed Iranian acceptance of UN Security Council Resolution 598. Written before the cease-fire, her arguments could be extended to the present: greater willingness to work with the Soviets on UN-sponsored mediation, accommodation to the interests of both Iran and Iraq, and avoidance of the unilateral use of force.

The radical perspective places major emphasis on the value of justice and argues particularly against imperialist economic, political, and social domination of the region. The radicals have little sympathy for any of the political regimes in the area, neither for Iran, Iraq, Israel, and Saudi Arabia, nor for United States, the Soviet Union, international capital, and the oil companies.

As radical commentary rarely makes any of the mainstream press, the reactions to the Iran-Iraq settlement and the lessons to be learned from it will have to await access to the specialized literature reflecting this point of view.

One of the most balanced summaries of the lessons of the war was provided by Richard W. Bulliet (*Los Angeles Times*, 20 July 1988), director of the Middle East Institute at Columbia University. Iraq, he wrote, had failed in its major goal of overthrowing the Iranian regime, but it succeeded in blunting the expansionist tendencies of the Iranian Revolution. For this it paid a terrible price in terms of human and material losses and colossal debt. Iran failed to defeat the Baathist regime and the overthrow of Saddam Hussein, but it can claim victory in having fought to a standstill an Iraq financed by Saudi Arabia and Kuwait, aided by the superb weapons of France and the USSR, and by the political and military support of the United States. Iraq's allies will now have to contend with a stronger and more dangerous Saddam Hussein. The United States can claim a victory for its diplomacy in that it wanted no winners. It has established military dominance in the Gulf and increased the dependence of the Arab states on the United States. OPEC has been weakened, and the Arab-Israeli conflict has been put on the back burner. Business can look forward to reconstruction and rearmament. But Bulliet also warns that "victory and defeat are chameleon concepts that change color with time and point of view. Ask the Germans, or the British, or the Japanese."

CONCLUSIONS

Bulliet's comments are wise in showing the limitations of commentaries written so quickly after major traumatic events. Abundant work is yet to be done by analysts in interpreting this war. There is, for instance, the nagging question asked by both Falk and Hunter as to why the great powers remained so silent in dealing with Iraq's initiation of the war. The proposed international tribunal will have its hands full in sorting out the competing claims of the parties on the origins of the war. Iraq argues that it was only responding to Iran's attempts to subvert the Iraqi regime, and to its provocations in initiating artillery and other attacks on Iraqi territory. It will claim that Iran violated the terms of the 1975 accord by failing to turn over the disputed border areas awarded to Iran in the 1975 settlement. Iran will insist on strict observance of the principles of the UN Charter, which require that such disputes be brought to the UN Security Council and not be solved by resort to war.

The final report of this tribunal will likely have much to say about the mutual responsibilities of both sides for the war, and for the responsibility of the international community in failing to observe its obligations for dealing with such threats to peace and security. With the new attention now given by the great powers to the United Nations and to the procedures established for the key role of the Security Council in handling threats to international peace and security, the report will probably have some impact, thus prompting other leaders to ponder the nature of their responsibilities in limiting the use of self-help procedures.

The great powers themselves have not set much of an example in recent history. U.S. commentators continue to insist on the efficacy of the U.S. intervention in Grenada, the mining of Nicaragua harbors, and the attack on Tripoli. The criticism from abroad has centred largely on the lack of justification for such acts under international law. When the great powers show such little respect for community standards, they should not be surprised when they are emulated by others. Criticizing the Israeli attack on the Baghdad nuclear reactor in the summer of 1981, the *New York Times* (14 June 1981) wrote: "The conduct practiced—and condoned—by the strong invariably shapes the ambitions of the weak."

Strategic analysts concerned with the continuing utility of war as an instrument of statecraft will need to contemplate the colossal miscalculation of Saddam Hussein in launching this war. The utility of war usually emerges unscathed from such analyses; instead, the emphasis is on the inability of certain decision-makers—because of inadequate information, prejudices, and emotional factors—to make the proper calculations. The stubborn fact that decision-makers have been increasingly unable to make the proper calculations in this century (as opposed to the nineteenth century) might on the one hand be interpreted as a commentary on the irrationality of our age, or on the more complex calculus required; on the other hand, one might pose the question, as Dyer (1985) and others have done, whether the sheer destructive power of modern instruments of war, even the conventional weapons used in the Iran-Iraq war, imposes costs that vastly exceed any of the alleged benefits of the war.

Questions must also be asked regarding the key turning points in the war. Why did Iran decide in 1982, after having expelled the Iraqis from Iranian territory, to further pursue the war and enter Iraq? There are parallels to the Korean war and to the drastic miscalculation by General Douglas MacArthur to cross the 38th parallel. Why did the effort by Saudi Arabia and Kuwait to buy off the Iranians also fail? Lawson (1983) has suggested that this use of positive sanctions, admirable as it was, failed because no new regional balance of power had yet been established and these actors lacked effective clout to reinforce their preferences.

Most of the analyses reflected above are locked into a foreign policy perspective; that is, the judgments are made according to the interests and advantages of each of the principal actors. No doubt Bulliet is correct in saying that each of the major actors will try to put the best possible interpretations on the outcomes in question. But we have a major analytical—and ethical—problem here. Rapoport and Chammah (1965) and others have pointed to non-zero-sum game theory in their analyses of a common paradox of rationality: What is rational at the unit level is far less than optimal at the system level. The United States continues to believe that some "invisible hand" (in the case of international relations, the function is assumed by the so-called balance of power) will enable us to continue to pursue individual and short-term self-interest and have it all work out for the best at the system level. In the nuclear age, however, the continued reliance on this thinking may indeed be suicidal. The U.S. is again at a critical turning point in international relations. From the Iran-Iraq war, Americans have new evidence of the folly of the use of force as a basic instrument of statecraft. We are also faced with the dawning realization again, as after World Wars I and II, that some new concern with community standards and shared community interests is all that can save us from the prisoner's dilemma and the challenge of the paradox of rationality.

REFERENCES

Ayoob, Mohammed (1985), "The Iran-Iraq War and Regional Security in the Persian Gulf," *Alternatives*, 10:581–590.

Banks, Michael (1984), *Conflict in World Society*, Brighton (UK): Wheatsheaf Books.

Cordesman, Anthony (1987), *The Iran-Iraq War and Western Security, 1984–87*, Jane's Fighting Ships, London.

Dyer, Gwynne (1985), *War*, New York: Crown.

Falk, Richard (1981), "The International Order and the Prospects for Humanity in the 1980s," in Canadian Council on International Law, *International Law and Canadian Foreign Policy in the 1980s*, Ottawa: CCIL, 75–83.

Keddie, Nikki R. (1988), "Iranian Imbroglios: Who's Irrational?" *World Policy Journal*, 5:29–59.

Killgore, Andrew I. (1988a), "The United States and the Persian Gulf: Avoiding Past Mistakes," *The Washington Report on Middle East Affairs*, 7, No. 5:5–6.

———. (1988b), "Towards a Lasting Iranian-Iraqi Peace: Internationalize the Shatt al-Arab River," *The Washington Report on Middle East Affairs*, 7, No. 6:9–10.

Lawson, Fred H. (1983), "Using Positive Sanctions to End International Conflicts: Iran and the Arab Gulf Countries," *Journal of Peace Research* 20:311–328.

Leviticus (1988), "Iraq: Soon a Major Player," *Israel and Palestine Political Report*, No. 143 (August):5–7.

McKinlay, R. D., and R. Little (1986), *Global Problems and World Order*, Madison: University of Wisconsin Press.

Murphy, Richard W. (1988), "US Role in the Persian Gulf and the Middle East Peace Process," *Current Policy*, No. 1062 (22 March).

Rapoport, A., and A. Chammah (1965), *Prisoner's Dilemma*, Ann Arbor: University of Michigan Press.

Small, Melvin, and J. David Singer (1982), *Resort to Arms: International and Civil Wars, 1816–1980*, 2nd ed., Beverly Hills: Sage.

Ware, Lewis B., et al. (1988), *Low Intensity Conflict in the Third World*, Washington, D.C.: U.S. Government Printing Office.

PART FIVE

Iran and the Superpowers

9

Double Demons: Cultural Impedance in U.S.-Iranian Understanding

William O. Beeman

INTRODUCTION:
THE PROCESS OF DEMONIZATION

The decade from 1979 to 1989 marks one of the most remarkable chapters in the history of international foreign relations—the era of troubled and difficult relations between the United States and Iran. The period is remarkable, first, because of the extraordinary degree to which the two nations lacked perspective on the cultural basis for each other's political motivations and strategies in the international arena and, second, for the degree to which each side was able to use vilification of the other as a political stratagem for domestic political purposes.

For both nations this was the longest period of direct wrangling with a nation outside of their own immediate geographical sphere in the twentieth century. The difficulties faced by the two nations went beyond simple misunderstanding or conflict of interests, and their differences were essentially cultural. Each nation, led by governmental leaders, constructed a mythological image that served to "demonize" the other.[1] Paradoxically, each fulfilled the worst expectations of the other, playing true to the image being created for it.

For Iran, the United States became the Great Satan, an external illegitimate force that continually strove to destroy the pure, internal core of the Iranian Revolution. For the United States, Iran took on another demonic form—that of the "crazy outlaw" nation whose activities were illegal, unpredictable, and irrational.

This "mythology of the other" was complemented by each nation's mythology of itself and its role in world affairs. For Iran, the revolution of 1978–1979 assumed this mythic status. For the United States, a more complex structure (which I term the "U.S. Foreign Policy Myth") held sway.

U.S. MYTHS

The "U.S. Foreign Policy Myth"[2] is an extremely powerful and pervasive belief system about the nature of foreign policy, its conduct, and its effect on American life. This belief system is troublesome because of the hold it has on shaping political strategy and defining "normalcy" in foreign affairs, even when it falls far from the mark in reflecting reality. At best, the foreign policy and military strategy based on this system of belief are ineffective. At worst, they are detrimental to U.S. interests.

The United States is not alone in espousing such a system. Indeed, virtually every nation operates in the foreign policy realm from an equally inaccurate base of beliefs. (I will deal with Iranian myths below.) It is natural for this to be so. Nations, like individual human beings, develop habits of thinking, often based on real short-term experience or shaped by a particularly powerful leader, that are difficult to break. When these habits become institutionalized in the bureaucracy, they become especially pervasive. In this case, the U.S. foreign policy myth is narrowly applicable. It works fairly well when dealing with Western industrialized nations, including the Soviet Bloc. It may also have been serviceable in dealing with the rest of the world in the immediate post–World War II period. However, it has become woefully outdated for dealings with the global community in the past two decades, and it will become even more outdated as humankind moves into the twenty-first century. As a further point of contrast, those who have memories of earlier periods in U.S. history will be able to see how the current belief system differs from that of previous periods.

THE FIVE PRINCIPLES OF BELIEF

The five principles are, briefly as follows.
1. **The world consists of nation states.**
It is not surprising that the United States should come to believe that the world consists entirely of nation states with basically homogeneous populations whose primary identity (and homogeneity) derives from identification with their common nationhood. The United States was, after all, the first great nation founded on this principle.

Of course, there are very few nation states in the world. One can think only of a few European countries, of Japan perhaps, and of certain new Pacific island states. The majority of the people of the world do not identify primarily with their nationhood, and they certainly do not identify with the central governments that rule the nations in which they happen to live. The notion that one would sacrifice one's life for one's president or prime minister is a patent absurdity in virtually every nation on earth.

2. **The East-West power struggle is the most important event in world politics. All other political relationships must be ranked in terms of it.**

Before World War II, even the United States accepted the belief in a multipolar world structure. Now the United States has accepted a basically bipolar model, and it tends to structure the entire world order within this framework.

Of course, for most nations on earth the East-West struggle is very nearly irrelevant for the conduct of everyday life, except as an enormously bothersome obstacle that they must confront at every turn. The possibility of nuclear destruction is of course a paramount concern for thinking people everywhere; but it is the height of bitter irony that the majority of people who would be destroyed in a nuclear holocaust have absolutely no interest in the ideological struggle that will be the basis for that holocaust.

Few nations would accept the U.S. belief that all nations must eventually assign themselves to one camp or another, and some, like India, have had to work very hard to stake out an independent position.

3. **Economics and power are the basis of relations among nations.**

Power politics as a philosophy has been with the United States only a short time. It was articulated in an extremely effective way by Hans Morganthau, perhaps the principal teacher of the current U.S. politicians who are exercising executive power in the U.S. foreign policy community. Former Secretary of State and National Security Advisor Henry Kissinger was perhaps its most celebrated practitioner.

For anthropologists it is particularly galling to see that in the United States' conduct of foreign policy, almost no attention is paid to cultural differences between nations. The general assumption is that wealth and military might are universal levellers, and that little else matters. Occasionally, religious feeling, ideology, pride, greed, and altruism are recognized as factors in the course of human events, but such matters are often dismissed as unpredictable.[3]

4. **Nations are ruled by a small group of elite individuals.**

It is difficult to understand why the United States, with its strong internal ethic supporting democracy and broad-based grass-roots participation in public affairs, finds it so difficult to take these same broad-based processes seriously in other nations.

Yet again and again, one finds that the conduct of U.S. foreign policy is based on the identification and support of narrow political structures: elite elected officials, elite dictators, and elite religious officials.

Clearly, power is thought to inhere in these narrow structures. An office is the chief sign of this power, perhaps reflecting the aforementioned belief that the world consists of nation states. Thus the United States cannot easily see the underlying cultural processes that contribute to social change; or, if it does see such processes, it feels them to be automatically negative in nature because they threaten the established order.[4]

5. **The normal conduct of foreign policy thus consists of the elite leaders of nation states meeting in seclusion and discussing matters of power and economics, presumably in the context of the East-West conflict.**

This final point is not a separate belief but, rather, the conglomeration of the preceding beliefs into one scenario—a scenario that in fact, describes much of the conduct of foreign policy carried out by the United States in recent years.

NORMALCY

As mentioned above, the U.S. foreign policy myth is a definition of normalcy—of expectations about how actors in the world behave and are motivated to act. Nations and actors that do not fit this mold are relegated to residual cognitive categories: "irrational," "crazy," "criminal," "unpredictable," and "deviant."

The United States had indeed become accustomed to pursuing serious foreign policy negotiations over economic and military conflict exclusively with other Western industrialized nation states. "Third world" and "developing" nations were traditionally dealt with in offhand, summary fashion. The legitimate needs and desires of the peoples of these countries, especially when they were in conflict with the recognized elite leadership structures, were never a part of U.S. foreign policy considerations. Indeed, such factors were regularly ignored or seen as directly opposed to U.S. strategic interests, inasmuch as they were viewed as "destabilizing forces."

The "Kissinger doctrine" in U.S. foreign policy, which still pervades the policy community, was opposed to attempts to understand the needs of other nations, the assumption being that it was their job to represent their own needs to the United States. Policy was often carried out with the aid of elite leaders ("plumbers") who had been co-opted through a combination of economic and military force.[5] Indeed, until the conflict in Vietnam in the 1960s and early 1970s, it had been possible to deal with conflict in these nations almost exclusively through co-optation, military threat, or economic pressure.

The Vietnam conflict should have been a warning to Americans that the basis for international relations in the world was changing. Unfortunately, Vietnam was treated as an aberration—as a defeat to be ignored and forgotten as soon as possible. The basis for U.S. involvement in the conflict was unqualified U.S. support of a dictatorial regime that was out of contact and out of favor with its own population. That support arose from the United States' need to carry out its own foreign military strategies, based on the popular domestic political posture of containing Communism.

Iran played a role in U.S. foreign policy similar to that of pre-conflict Vietnam. It was one of the "twin pillars" of U.S. defense in the Gulf region (the other being Saudi Arabia). In the immediate postwar period, oil supplies from the Gulf region were critical for the United States; and the spectre of Gulf oil falling under the domination of the Soviet Union, however unrealistic that scenario might be, was enough to justify a massive foreign policy effort aimed at shoring up friendly rulers in the region ("more plumbers") who could be counted upon to carry out U.S. foreign policy with little need for U.S. officials to involve themselves in great depth with the nations in question.

Shah Mohammad Reza Pahlavi was an ideal "plumber" in U.S. eyes. He was restored to his throne in 1953 through the efforts of the U.S. Central Intelligence Agency, following a coup d'etat engineered by Mohammad Mossadeq that U.S. officials feared would allow greater Soviet influence in Iran. Thereafter the shah became one of the United States' chief political and military clients. He purchased billions of dollars of advanced military equipment from the United States and provided a fertile economic climate for Western investment in the Iranian economy.

The shah was an extremely clever client. The money for all of his purchases and economic improvements came from the sale of oil to Western nations, the price of which was jacked up some 400 percent in 1973 by the Organization of Petroleum Exporting Countries (OPEC), largely due to the shah's influence. Thus the United States and its allies were actually paying for economic improvement and arms purchases by Iran through the increased price of oil.

Iran's pattern of dealing with the United States during the postwar period was a continuation of a century of similar dealings with other great powers. Iran had been in conflict with other industrialized nations—Great Britain and Imperial Russia in the nineteenth century and the Great European Powers in this century. However, it had always been powerless to resist either militarily or economically in any significant way. The Pahlavi shahs, like the Qajar shahs before them, were alienated from their own populations. Strapped for ready cash, they cleverly decided that cooperation with the Western powers and Russia in economic and military matters was far more prudent—and profitable—than defiance. They sold concessions to foreigners on almost every national resource: agricultural, industrial, mineral, commercial, and transportational. In the process they became wealthy themselves.

It was possible for the Pahlavi shahs to do this by establishing a very special foreign relationship with the United States and other Western nations—namely, a type of cultural insulation whereby the West was largely prevented from coming into close contact with Iranian culture and civilization. The United States, as Iran's chief ally in the West, was most affected by this policy in the post–World War II years. Mohammad Reza Pahlavi insisted that all U.S. military and commercial dealings with Iran be passed through Iranian government channels. The CIA was active in Iran, but it could not pass reports on Iranian internal affairs back to the U.S. government, of which the shah did not approve. With few exceptions, embassy staff members did not speak Persian until the period immediately following the revolution, and in any case they were kept from meeting with the bulk of the Iranian population.[6]

The Iranian Revolution marked a dramatic watershed in this state of affairs. After a brief six-month period of secular nationalism, the government was taken over by religious forces. The secular nationalists were out of power and Iran became an Islamic Republic. Suddenly the rules for interaction between Iran and the United States changed. Iran's leaders adopted an independent set of international relations goals, summed up in the phrase "neither East nor West." They expressed the desire to establish a true Islamic Republic based on religious law. They became deeply suspicious of U.S. motives, fearing that, as in 1953, the United States would attempt to reinstate the monarchy in order to regain the economic benefits enjoyed during the reign of the shah.

More disturbing for U.S. politicians was the attitude of the new Iranian leaders. Having assumed an air of moral superiority, they were not interested in cooperation with Western nations on Western terms. Moreover, they seemed comfortable in committing acts that outraged the United States, with no apparent thought as to the possible consequences. This kind of behavior was inexplicable for most Americans.

To add to these difficulties, the Iranian leaders in the immediate post-revolutionary period were not in full control of their own nation. Though identified by U.S. policy makers as elites, they had very little capacity for independent action on the foreign policy scene. As will be seen below, their ability to act vis-à-vis the United States was especially limited.

In short, post-revolutionary Iran violated every tenet of the U.S. policy myth. Iran looked like a nation state, but its political structure, both under the shah and today, was far more tenuous than that of any Western nation. After the revolution it was not concerned with the East-West struggle, preferring to reject both sides. Its national concerns transcended matters of military and economic power; it was often far more concerned about questions of ideology, morality, and religious sensibility. Its elites were and continue to be informal power brokers and balancers of opinion rather than powerful actors able to enforce their will directly on the population. Moreover, they have had to be extremely careful about contact with foreign powers, because their offices do not protect them from political attack as a result of such contact.

All of this has tried the patience of U.S. leaders. Iran does not conform to the set model of international behavior with which the foreign policy community is prepared to operate. As a result, the Iranians have been labelled "crazy outlaws."

IRANIAN MYTHS

For American citizens one of the most difficult aspects of the Iranian Revolution was comprehending the blanket condemnation levelled against the United States by Iranian officials and revolutionary leaders. Their vituperative, accusatory rhetoric seemed to be aimed at indicting all U.S. leaders since World War II for unacceptable interference in Iranian internal affairs and destruction of the Iranian culture and economy.

For most Americans it seems incredible that such a blanket condemnation of the United States could have any substance in fact. Didn't the United States want to help Iran develop in the 1960s and 1970s? Weren't U.S. industrial firms invited into the country by the Iranian people? Wasn't the U.S. interest in developing Iran's military strength during this period also in Iran's best interest? From an American standpoint it seems that the United States could be accused of no worse than wanting to make an honest dollar in a fertile market.

In the light of disinterested hindsight, however, it seems that there was indeed real justification for the complaints of Iran's revolutionary leaders. At the time of the revolution, Iran was left with a demoralized population, a sprawling economy that was out of control, and a repressive, autocratic government that allowed its citizens no influence whatsoever in policies that affected them directly—not even the right to complain.

But according to the assessment of the Iranian people themselves, a far more serious development had taken place in Iranian society: The civilization had lost its spiritual core. It had become poisoned—obsessed with materialism and the acquisition of money and consumer goods. For pious Iranians, hardships can be endured with the help of one's family and social network as well as through faith (*tavakkol*), the ultimate reliance on the will of God. But to lose one's own sense of inner self—to be a slave to the material world—is to be utterly lost.

Understanding why Iranians came to feel this way about themselves, and why the United States came to be blamed for causing this phenomenon, requires a close analysis of Iranian cultural and ideological structures. Iranian ideology was expressed during the revolution and after in religious terms.

However, using "religion" or "religious fervor" as a label for Iranian opposition to the United States is far too simplistic. Anti-U.S. feeling was widespread during and after the revolution, and was not confined to people who followed the clergy. It was also acutely felt among secularized members of the middle and upper classes, who cared not a fig for the mollahs and Ayatollahs. More significant, it was expressed by many highly religious persons who actually *opposed* the clerical leadership of Iran and were convinced that the United States was supporting that leadership.

The reason for the violent expression of anti-U.S. sentiment, which wreaked havoc on relations between the two countries and eventually led to the taking of a whole embassy full of American hostages in November 1979, lies in the symbolic role played by the United States vis-à-vis the Iranian nation, from the Iranian perspective.

Taking their clue from Ayatollah Ruhollah Khomeini, the Iranian revolutionaries delighted in referring to the United States as the "Great Satan" in public street demonstrations. Although this epithet seems a bit hyperbolic, it provides an important clue as to the symbolic conceptions being invoked. In this case it is significant that the term *Great Satan* was used, and not another.

In order to understand the full significance of this seemingly straightforward linguistic usage, we must examine Iranian inner symbolic life.

INTERNAL AND EXTERNAL:
THE MORAL DIMENSION

Religious doctrine often serves as the most tangible concretization of the core symbols of society. In so doing, it not only makes statements about the truth of the conceptual world in which society exists but also prescribes for society's members what they should do and avoid doing. Furthermore, religion serves as a formal statement of symbolic categorizations in cultural life. It helps individuals regulate their lives by placing certain aspects of life at the core of their value and action systems and by relegating other aspects to the periphery.

Religious systems, like all systems of patterned symbolic elements, are not merely static arrangements of idealizations. They are dynamic, and occasionally make their dynamic nature explicit. Such is the case with Iran.

The central symbolic pattern in Iran—a pattern that renders all human actions, both great and small, as indicative of life for Iranians—is the struggle for the inside (the internal or core) to conquer the outside (the external or periphery).[7] The contrast between the pure inner core and the corrupt external sphere in Iranian ideology is explored in depth in a recent study by M. C. Bateson, *et al.*[8] In this paper Bateson discusses the differences between the exemplary traits of *safa-yi batin* ("inner purity") and the bad traits of the external world, which lead one to become *bad-bin* ("suspicious, cynical, pessimistic"). The bad external traits—epitomized in adjectives such *zerang* ("shrewd"), *for-sattalah* ("opportunistic"), *motazaher* or *do-rou* ("hypocritical"), *hes-abgar* ("calculating"), and *charbzaban* ("obsequious" or "insincere")—are qualities that Iranians feel they must combat in themselves as well as in the external world.

Iranians during the Pahlavi era, especially during the final ten years, often expressed regret over behavior they felt was unduly at odds with the good qualities desirable for one with a pure and uncorrupted inner core. A doctor of my acquaintance, in a village outside of the city of Shiraz, once went into a long disquisition on the difficulties of living in what he assessed as a corrupt world:

> They are all corrupt, all of my superiors. They are stealing all the time, and not just from the government—they also steal from the poor people who come to them for medicine and treatment. God help me, in this system they *force* me to be dishonest as well. They will give me medical supplies, but only if I pay them some bribe. When I ask them how I am to get the money, they tell me to charge the patients. So you see I have no choice I must steal too if I want to carry out this job. I hate myself every day of my life for being dishonest, and I wish I didn't have to be, but I can't help it.

Iranian concern with this problem is reflected extensively in expressive culture. One of the principal themes of Iranian literature, films, and popular drama shows characters caught between the drive toward internal morality and the external pull of the corrupting world. This, in fact, is one of the central concerns in the doctrine and practice of Sufism, in which the killing of one's *nafs* ("passions") is one of the prerequisites to achieving mystic enlightenment. Display of one's concern for the depth of feeling that accompanies the drive toward the pure inner life is highly valued throughout Iranian society. This concern leads individuals to disdain that which is superficial or hypocritical. In the tension between the internal drive toward morality and the external pull of the corrupting world, one of the highest compliments one can pay another is to say, "His or her inside and outside are the same."[9]

INTERNAL AND EXTERNAL:
THE LEGACY OF HISTORY

The struggle between the pure forces of the internal and the corruption of the external exists not only in the idealization of individual morality; it also is a principal theme in the popular view of the history of Iranian civilization.

For ordinary Iranians, the external conquests that have buried their land over the centuries—conquests by Alexander and the Greeks, the Arabs, Ghengis Khan and the Mongols—are as fearsome as if they happened yesterday. The British/Russian partition of the country into two spheres of influence in 1907 continued the pattern of cycles of conquest. Finally, as will be argued below, the economic domination of Iran by the United States in the post–World War II period seemed to extend the age-old pattern into the modern period.

Nevertheless, every time Iran was conquered by one of these great external powers, the nation subsequently rose like a phoenix from the ashes and reestablished itself. The times between these conquests were peak periods in Iranian culture, during which literature, art, philosophy, mathematics, artisanry, and architecture flowered.

Thus the struggle between inside and outside, when painted on the canvas of Iranian history, can be seen as a struggle between the destructive forces of external invading conquerors and the reproductive growing forces of the internal core of Iranian civilization. The internal core has thus far been the victor.

The struggle between inside and outside has also been encapsulated in the central myth of Shi'i islam—the martyrdom of Imam Hosain, third Imman of Shi'i Moslems and, significantly, grandson of the Prophet Mohammad.

Hosain's father, Ali, was the only caliph to be recognized by both Shi'ites and Sunnis. Following his death, his son Hasan was convinced to resign his claim to leadership by Sunni partisans, who then usurped the caliphate, bestowing it on the ruler of Damascus, Mo'awiyeh. Upon his death, it passed to his son, Yazid.

Hosain was called upon to recognize the leadership of both Caliphs of Damascus, but he refused—and this act set the stage for his subsequent martyrdom. In the legendary act of refusal, Hosain came to represent for Shi'i Moslems the verification of the truth of the spiritual leadership of Ali and his bloodline (as well as the bloodline of Mohammad), through his willingness to be martyred when his own right to succession to leadership of the faithful was challenged.

Thus Hosain represented for Iranians the struggle between internal and external forces. In death, he became an eternal symbol of the uncompromising struggle against external forces of tyranny, the defender of the faith, the possessor of inner purity and strength, and the great martyr in the name of truth.[10]

Yazid and his henchmen, on the other hand, became the supreme symbols of corruption. Not only are they murderers, but they also represent false doctrine—imposed from without. The sufferings of the family of Hosain, who survived the slaughter of their patriarch, are laid to Yazid's account, as are, by extension, the sufferings of all Shi'ite followers in subsequent history. To this day, a cruel, corrupt individual who brings ruin to others is labeled "Yazid."

From this exposition, it should be clear that in Iranian society the source of corruption is external to the individual, and to society itself. If civilization or individuals become corrupt, it is because they do not have the strength to resist forces from without that are impinging on them at all times. This particular directionality gives a specific bias to Iranian political psychology. As internal conditions within the country become more and more difficult, the tendency of the population is to search for conspiracy from an external source. This was a distinct feature of the Pahlavi regime, which saw opposition to the central government as a Marxist-inspired plot. The same bias inspired the efforts of the oppositionist forces, who saw the central government policies as inspired by non-Iranian considerations. The confrontations that led to the revolutionary events of 1978–1979 and to the ouster of the shah took place in an ironic context: Both the shah and his opposition viewed themselves as defending the inner core of the civilization against the external forces of corruption and destruction. Thus, the revolution can be seen as a battle of definitions: He who could make his vision of the inner core valid for the population as a whole could control the nation.

The duty of a righteous Muslim is to resist corruption and promote the good. Any action is justified against a corrupting force. Thus the ouster of the shah was presented as a religiously justified action, as was the persecution of those who supported the shah.

For post-revolutionary Iran, the United States fit perfectly into the cultural mold reserved for corrupt forces. It was an external, powerful, secular force. It supported a regime that revolutionary leaders had designated as corrupt. It gave the shah refuge and refused to allow verification of his claim of illness, thus raising the possibility that it was plotting against the revolution.[11] When the Iran-Iraq war began, the United States seemed to "tilt" toward Iraq, a second corrupt external force, and demonstrated again and again in its actions in the Gulf region that it was working against Iran's interests in the course of the war. It was thus easy for Iran's leaders to apply the epithet "Great Satan" to the United States and make it stick.

SINCERITY, POLITICAL RHETORIC, AND CULTURAL IMPEDANCE

Iranian and U.S. leaders have accused each other of manipulative and insincere dealings with each other. Such accusations are extremely difficult to evaluate in a multicultural context.

First, it must be understood that, in their foreign relations decisions and pronouncements, both sets of leaders are appealing primarily to their domestic constituencies. Thus they attempt to say and do things that make themselves look good, whatever they may actually believe about a particular situation.

U.S. leaders, for example, were opposed to negotiations with Iran over the release of the embassy hostages held in 1979–1980 for nearly a year, partly because they did not want to see Iran, an "outlaw nation," in a relationship of seeming equality with the United States. They also wanted to look for more traditional solutions through economic and military threats, and thus searched for "plumbers" to effect the hostage release. It is somewhat ironic that the hostages were released in the end through a mediated negotiation.[12]

Iranian leaders have had difficulties dealing directly with U.S. officials since the revolution because of the taint carried by such relationships. Through their vilification of the United States, they effectively denied themselves any access to these officials, even though such access might have been important for the ongoing progress of the revolution. The threat to their careers—indeed, to their lives—was very real. In the first three years of the revolution they could not be known to be talking to or receiving messages from Americans. Indeed, to avoid accusations of collusion with the United States during the hostage crisis, nervous

Iranian leaders opened "secret" messages from U.S. officials and read them in public.

The fact the Iranian and U.S. leaders do talk on occasion when necessary indicates that, at some level, the officials in both nations understand the difference between pragmatic dealings and public symbolism. Yet even this understanding does not eliminate the cultural impedance that prevents full comprehension by one side of the actions of the other.[13]

As most Iranian leaders have had no experience in dealing with international politics prior to assuming power, it has taken them some time to understand how to behave in a way that the Western world will find comprehensible. The United States did not crumple at being called the Great Satan, nor did it cease pursuing what it considered its own strategic interests—even in the face of Iranian curses and gadfly tactics.

An important change in Tehran, attendant upon the cease-fire in the Iran-Iraq war, has been the search for an international voice for the Islamic Republic. As a result, Iran may be projected as more of a nation state than it really is (certainly not an uncommon strategy among newer nations); or certain issues, such as economics, which are easier for the United States and its allies to deal with, may come to be emphasized over ideology and religious sensibility. The Great Satan epithet seems to have been laid to rest at this point. If this process continues, the revolution may be "Pahlavized," particularly as Iran once more insulates its true cultural feelings behind a patina of Western-oriented international communication strategies.

The United States for its part should realize that this period of stress in dealing with Iran constitutes an invaluable lesson for the international relations of the future. Most nations in the world do not conform to the narrow U.S. mythology of foreign relations. As world politics becomes more multicentered in the next decades, U.S. politicians must increasingly deal with the nations of the world on a one-to-one basis, taking their cultural sensibilities into account. Labelling nations and their leaders "criminal," "outlaw," or "crazy" because the cultural underpinnings for their actions are difficult to understand does nothing to promote real solutions to the political differences creating problems in the world today.

NOTES

1. I borrow this term from Professor R. K. Ramazani's insightful book, *The United States and Iran.* See also his *Revolutionary Iran* and James Bill's remarkable account of U.S.-Iranian relations, *The Eagle and the Lion.*

2. I have elaborated on the U.S. foreign policy myth at greater length in other publications (Beeman [1986b, 1986d]).

3. Nowhere is the structure of this belief so clearly seen as in the composition of U.S. Embassy staffs. There are economic attaches and political attaches, but in no embassy in the world is there a single officer whose primary duty is to interpret cultural differences that could cause misunderstandings between nations. This lack is reflected in mistake after mistake committed by U.S. diplomatic personnel everywhere—events I hardly need to detail for readers here. In fairness, however, I must note that the United States is hardly alone among nations in having some unskillful diplomats and foreign policy advisors or in being unable to analyze cultural differences. I should further note that the sensitivity that *is* demonstrated by talented, diligent persons at the working levels of the foreign policy community is often obscured in the recommendations and observations that reach the White House, where action decisions are made by persons with minimal direct experience in dealing with the cultural realities of the non-Western world. As an anthropologist I cannot resist stating that I think the world could use many more anthropologically trained individuals in foreign policy positions everywhere, to compensate for those who believe that money and guns constitute the only basis for international understanding.

4. As the world knows, of course, when broad social movements prove important in terms of the United States' interpretation of the East-West struggle, then great significance is attached to them.

5. Given the United States' extraordinary economic and military resources compared to those of the developing world, especially in the immediate post–World War II decade, this "superpower" mentality was perhaps understandable; but the increasing sophistication of the educated people of the world (many of whom were educated in the United States) has made this view seem naive and anachronistic.

6. James Bill (1988) documents this isolation quite effectively.

7. The account of the opposition between the internal (*baten* or *batin*) and the external (*zaher*) is somewhat simplified for the purposes of this discussion. It should be pointed out that Iran is by no means unique in maintaining a distinction between "inside" and "outside" dimensions in symbolic culture. The Javanese and Japanese cultural systems also employ this distinction, albeit within a context very different from that of Iran. For additional discussion on this point see Beeman (1986a). Nikki Keddie (1963) points out that the *zaher* need not be identified merely as the locus of evil. It also can be seen as a zone that contains and excludes those evil forces that may attempt to intrude on the pure *baten*, which should not be open to outsiders.

8. See Bateson et al. (1977:257–273).

9. Ibid., 269–270.

10. See Fischer (1980:147–156) for an account of the meaning of the figures of Hosain and his father, Ali, in present-day politico-religious discourse. Fischer refers to the cultural symbolic complex of Hosain and his death as the "Karbala paradigm."

11. This, of course, was the immediate cause of the capture and holding of U.S. Embassy personnel for 444 days in 1979–1980.

12. The hostages were released only after the negotiations had been taken over by a group of U.S. government officials completely different from those who had directed the operations during the previous year.

13. The arms-for-hostages negotiations in 1986–1987 are a case in point. The need to reestablish relations with Iran was correctly acknowledged by the Reagan administration, but the means used to achieve this end were naive. For example, U.S. negotiators failed to recognize the danger these means constituted for Iranian officials. The only way these officials could "deal" with the Americans and not risk the charge of collusion with an enemy by their political rivals was to best the United States in the deal.

BIBLIOGRAPHY

Bateson, M.C., J.W. Clinton, J.B.M. Kassarjian II, and M. Soraya Safvi (1977), "Safa-yi Batin: A Study of the Interrelations of a Set of Iranian Character Types." In L. Carl Brown and Norman Itzkowitz, eds., *Psychological Dimensions of Near Eastern Studies*. Princeton, New Jersey: Darwin Press.

Bill, James (1988), *The Eagle and the Lion*. New Haven: Yale University Press.

Beeman, William O. (1986a) *Language Status and Power in Iran*. Bloomington: Indiana University Press.

——— (1986b), "Anthropology and the Myths of Foreign Policy." In Walter Goldschmidt, ed., *Anthropology and Public Policy: A Dialogue*, Special Publication No. 21. Washington, D.C.: American Anthropological Association.

——— (1986c), "Iran's Religious Regime—What Makes it Tick? Will it Ever Run Down?" *Annals of the American Academy of Political and Social Science*, Vol. 483 (January); pp. 73–83.

——— (1986d), "Conflict and Belief in American Foreign Policy." In Mary LeCron Foster and Robert A. Burenstein, eds., *Peace and War: Cross-Cultural Perspectives*. Rutgers: Transaction Books.

Fischer, Michael M.J. (1980), *Iran: From Religious Dispute to Revolution*. Cambridge: Harvard University Press.

Keddie, Nikki (1963), "Symbol and Sincerity in Islam." *Studia Islamica*, Vol. 19, pp. 27–64.

R. K. Ramazani (1982), *The United States and Iran: The Patterns of Influence*. New York: Praeger.

——— (1986), *Revolutionary Iran*. Baltimore: Johns Hopkins University Press.

10

The Soviet Union and Iran: Changing Relations in the Gorbachev Era

Carol R. Saivetz

When Mikhail Gorbachev became general secretary of the Communist Party of the Soviet Union in March 1985, he inherited a policy toward Iran that was a product of several factors. First, the Soviet Union, and Russia before it, had long declared its interest in its southern neighbor. Throughout the years since 1917, the USSR negotiated a treaty with Teheran in 1921 and in 1946; and in one of the first postwar crises, Soviet troops remained in Iran after the expiration of the World War II occupation agreement. In the 1960s and 1970s, the Kremlin and Teheran enjoyed a period of blossoming economic and political ties.

Second, by all indications, the Soviets were as surprised as the West was with the weakness and final collapse of the Peacock Throne. Despite their good relations with the Shah, they moved to take advantage of Iran's strident anti-Americanism and apparent anti-imperialism.

Third, between September 1980, when the Iran-Iraq War broke out, and the Gorbachev succession in March 1985, the Kremlin steered a course designed to balance the USSR's somewhat attenuated ties with Iraq with its desire to cultivate the Islamic Republic of Iran. Moscow's policy was generally successful—in that the USSR avoided having to take sides—although it was fraught with difficulties stemming from the fortunes of war, the superpower balance, and intra-Arab complications.

Parts of this chapter have been adapted from my book, *The Soviet Union and the Gulf in the 1980s,* Boulder, Colo.: Westview, 1989.

At the same time, the new Soviet leader brought to the Politburo new ideas and new energies. He set out, first of all, to revitalize the ailing Soviet economy, and *perestroika* became the economic watchword. And in an effort to harness the creative energies of the Soviet state, he enunciated a policy of *glasnost'*, or openness. In the foreign policy realm, Gorbachev began to speak in terms of *navoe myshlenie*, the "new political thinking," which translated into political detente with the West coupled with a search for resolutions to regional conflicts.

It is against this background—the tangled history of Soviet-Iranian relations especially since 1979 and the fundamental changes taking place within the Soviet Union—that one must examine the bilateral relationship between Moscow and Teheran. This chapter will analyze the Soviet-Iranian relationship in the Gorbachev era. It will first look briefly at the historical context of Moscow's links with Teheran and then examine how Soviet policy toward the Gulf War affected the bilateral ties. Finally, it will assess the current status of the relationship. The oscillations in Soviet-Iranian relations since March 1985 can be explained as the interplay of three factors: the superpower relationship in the Gulf, the Kremlin's perceptions of regional politics, and the domestic political context in both Teheran and Moscow.

THE HISTORICAL CONTEXT

With Joseph Stalin's death in 1953 and Nikita Khrushchev's accession to power, the USSR pursued a new Third World policy designed to cultivate anti-Westernism and to establish the Soviet Union as a true world-class power. Leonid Brezhnev basically continued the policies of his erratic predecessor.[1] Thus, in the mid-1960s, the Soviets offered Iran a $300 million credit and signed agreements to build a steel mill at Isfahan and a gas pipeline from the gas fields of Sarajeh to the USSR. Soviet-Iranian economic relations flowered in the wake of these agreements. As with the early steel mills in India and the Aswan Dam in Egypt, the pipeline deal was implemented only after the United States had refused to help the Iranians construct it. The agreement enabled the Soviets to sell their native supplies to the East European countries while using Iranian gas domestically. After the completion of the pipeline in 1970, Iran became the USSR's primary supplier of natural gas. In the fall of 1972, during an official visit of the Shah and his wife to Moscow, the two countries signed a fifteen-year economic treaty. The provisions of this agreement included several industrial projects and contained the pronounced intention to increase economic cooperation.

In 1974 a major natural gas pricing dispute jolted the bilateral ties. As international oil prices rose, the Iranians attempted to force the USSR to pay the going rate. However, the Soviets not only refused to agree to Iranian demands but also claimed that the Iranian price increases were instigated by Western imperialists. Ultimately, Moscow agreed to a compromise price that was below the world rate but higher than that previously paid.

The return to "business as usual" was disrupted by the Iranian Revolution. Although the Soviet media reported events in the final days of the Shah's regime, every effort was made to downplay the political upheaval and ultimately also the revolutionary leadership of the Shi'i clergy. From the outset, most Soviet observers concluded that repressive conditions in Iran precluded the rise to leadership of groups other than the clergy. Calling Islam a "catalyst of nationalist attitudes," Soviet observers, at the time, went so far as to claim that the Iranian Revolution was in no way a religious movement.[2] And Leonid Brezhnev, in his speech at the 26th party congress in 1981, said: "Despite its [the Iranian revolution's] contradictory nature, it is basically an anti-imperialist revolution. . . . The liberation struggle may develop under the banner of Islam."[3]

There can be no doubt that the Soviets misunderstood the nature of the Iranian Revolution in Teheran. Yet, their misconceptions notwithstanding, the Kremlin leadership clearly hoped that what had been a significant loss for the United States could be turned into a major gain for the USSR. Thus, despite their misgivings about Khomeini's Islamic vision, they made significant efforts to cultivate Iranian anti-Americanism. At first, it appeared as if the Soviets' job would be easy: The seizure of U.S. diplomatic personnel in Teheran signalled to Moscow that a major opportunity awaited. Few reporters mentioned the illegality of the seizure itself. In fact, the official Soviet line was openly sympathetic to Teheran. As a correspondent wrote in *Pravda:* "To be sure, the seizure of the American embassy in and of itself does not conform to the international convention concerning respect for diplomatic privileges and immunity. However, one cannot pull this act out of the overall context of American-Iranian relations."[4]

A second opportunity—the outbreak of the Iran-Iraq War—presented itself in September 1980. Although (as noted above), Moscow had to be careful not to rupture its ties to Baghdad, the chance to show at least tacit support to Khomeini proved tempting. Publicly, the USSR proclaimed its neutrality. Soviet propaganda stressed that the war benefited only the imperialists and Zionists; however, the record presents a contrasting picture. When Iraqi Foreign Minister Tariq Aziz flew to Moscow to request military assistance, the Soviet leadership was not terribly forthcoming. Some Soviet-made spare parts did arrive in Baghdad, although they were probably already in the arms pipeline. No new major arms deals resulted from the trip; in fact, the USSR, still the primary Iraqi supplier, held up military shipments to Baghdad during the first winter of the war. But in an effort to keep the Saddam Hussein regime on the line, Moscow simultaneously permitted its Warsaw Pact allies to increase significantly their military sales to Iraq.

On the Iranian side of the ledger, military assistance began to flow from Libya and Syria. In both cases the deliveries were of Soviet equipment, and it is presumed that the Kremlin approved the transfers. While all observers agree that during the initial stages of the war, Moscow's professed neutrality tilted toward Teheran, a few see evidence of more direct Soviet support. Shahram Chubin, for example, writing in *Foreign Affairs*, alleged that Soviet backing of Teheran was nothing less than a warning of the impending attack, a means of easing Iranian concerns regarding the USSR's intentions so as to permit reassignment of Iranian troops, and a way to provide satellite information.[5]

This tacit Soviet tilt toward Iran did not seem to provide any tangible results. With the end of the hostage crisis in January 1981, a potential obstacle to U.S.-Iranian rapprochement was removed. In February 1981, Prime Minister Raja'i, during a meeting with the Soviet ambassador, criticized the continuing occupation of Afghanistan and chided the USSR for not condemning the initial Iraqi attack. And in addition to the Iranian rhetoric that labelled the USSR "the lesser Satan," press reports in Teheran began to evidence a distinctly anti-Soviet flavor. The Soviets responded in broadcasts to Iran that they possessed only a friendly attitude. Moreover, the stalemate on the battlefield until mid-1982 meant that it would be increasingly difficult for the Soviet Union to hold up arms shipments to its client Iraq, thus increasing the costs of the pro-Iranian stance.

As the war continued into 1982, the political leanings of the clergy in Teheran became increasingly important and distressful to the Kremlin. As early as March 1982, reporters noted problems in Soviet-Iranian relations, including the non-accreditation of Soviet correspondents, the disbandment of Soviet-Iranian cultural groups, and the closure of the Soviet consulate in Resht. Moreover, as *Pravda* correspondent Pavel Demchenko, a veteran Middle East observer, wrote:

> We know that the Shi'ite clergymen who hold the reins of government in Iran are not uniform in their political beliefs or social positions. There are various conservative factions . . . with extreme right-wing views. It seems that it is these groups who want to put up obstacles to the expansion

of Soviet-Iranian relations even though such action could harm the Iranian economy and Iran's ability to fight imperialist pressure.[6]

Also in March 1982, a new stage of the war began when Iran sent 200,000 troops into the north; then, in May, the Iranians expelled Iraqi troops from Khorramshahr. In June, endangered Iraq declared a unilateral cease-fire and withdrawal from Iranian territory. Baghdad also announced its readiness to negotiate without conditions. In July, Iranian troops crossed into Iraq. In these new battlefield conditions, the USSR's tilt toward Iran became increasingly untenable. Iranian anti-Sovietism, coupled with Soviet fears of an Iranian victory in the war, led to a reinstatement of the arms connection between Moscow and Baghdad. And Moscow publicly applauded Iraq's willingness to negotiate an end to the costly war. The following February, the Khomeini regime cracked down on the pro-Soviet Tudeh party (communist); and in May of that year, it expelled eighteen Soviet diplomats. In response, Soviet propaganda issued increasingly strident denunciations of Iran's intransigence (i.e., given its unwillingness to consider negotiation) and the Kremlin increased its arms assistance to Baghdad.

This shift to a more pro-Iraqi position was coupled with the enunciation of the policy of "reciprocity." In mid-June, then Foreign Minister Andrei Gromyko said in a speech before the Supreme Soviet: "We have friendly relations with Iraq. We are *for* normal relations of friendship with Iran as well." He added: "In short the USSR will act with regard to whether Iran wishes to *reciprocate* its actions and maintain normal relations with us or whether it has different intentions."[7] Gromyko's policy of reciprocity remained in effect until 1985.

GORBACHEV AND THE GULF WAR

Between November 1982, when Leonid Brezhnev died, and March 1985, the USSR underwent three succession crises. The uncertainty in the leadership meant that Soviet policy, as outlined above, basically drifted. Mikhail Gorbachev thus inherited the legacy of his predecessors' policy while facing intensifying regional complications. The USSR not only exercised caution so as not to disrupt its ties with Baghdad while cultivating Teheran, but it also grew increasingly concerned over the shifting superpower balance in the region and the realignments in the Arab world—all caused by the war. Gorbachev's first year in the Kremlin saw the USSR alternate between condemning Iran's domestic affairs and its refusals to negotiate, on the one hand, and exchanging several diplomatic and economic delegations, on the other. On the battlefield, Iran and Iraq engaged in the most intense fighting to date, including attacks on civilian population centers.

One of the first personnel changes effected by Gorbachev was the "promotion" of Andrei Gromyko to the presidency of the Soviet Union. His replacement by Eduard Shevardnadze allowed Gorbachev greater flexibility in foreign policy. Specifically, Gromyko was associated with several long-term Middle East policies, and his elevation allowed Gorbachev to try out new approaches. Shevardnadze's inexperience in foreign policy permitted the new General Secretary a free hand with which to mould Soviet foreign policy, and his appearance and polish— in contrast to Gromyko's dour visage—facilitated a new Soviet image abroad.

In terms of relations with Iran and the Gulf War, Gromyko's promotion allowed Gorbachev to abandon the policy of reciprocity. This meant the pursuit of intensified economic contacts despite events in the Gulf and despite Teheran's continuing anti-Soviet rhetoric. In July representatives of the Iranian Chamber of Commerce visited Moscow, and in September the long-planned meeting of economic delegations took place in Moscow. These contacts culminated in the trip of Soviet Deputy Foreign Minister Georgii Kornienko to Teheran. While there he met with Iran's Foreign Minister Ali Akbar Velayati and Speaker Hashemi Rafsanjani. According to Iranian dispatches, the discussions were "extensive" and Kornienko emphasized the Soviet's interest in expanding relations between Moscow and Teheran. Further discussions were then held on the resumption of Iranian natural gas exports to the USSR.

It is entirely possible that this 1986 renewal of contacts was designed by Teheran. Iranian reports indicated that Kornienko traveled to Iran at Iranian invitation. Although a new natural gas deal and further economic contacts would be mutually beneficial, Teheran may have hoped to convince Moscow of the importance of improved relations. Indeed, the promise of an ameliorated economic relationship may have been dangled in front of the Soviets in return for a limitation on the Soviet arms shipped directly to Iraq. Further evidence for this line of reasoning may be gathered from the timing of the February 1986 Fao offensive, in which some 30,000 Iranian troops crossed the Shatt-al-Arab and occupied the Fao Peninsula.

The late 1986 revelations that the United States had sold arms to Teheran—Irangate—provided Moscow with a tremendous propaganda opportunity; yet they also clearly alarmed the Kremlin. All Soviet commentary emphasized the duplicitous nature of the U.S. foreign policy. Moscow attempted to portray itself as the true friend of the Arabs while discrediting U.S. statements about neutrality in the Iran-

Iraq war. Because the disclosures sent such shock waves throughout the Arab world, the Soviets felt constrained once again to deny reports that they, too, were dealing arms to the Iranians. Underneath the bravado, however, lay a very real concern that Iran might indeed reestablish diplomatic relations with the United States. As unsuccessful as the Soviet Union had been in cultivating the Khomeini regime until then, it could at least draw comfort from the fact that until the November 1986 revelations, there were few known contacts between Teheran and Washington. Nonetheless, Soviet-Iranian economic contacts continued: The standing commission on economic cooperation was convened for the first time since 1980.

In the beginning of 1987, Moscow continued to condemn certain Iranian activities while pursuing bilateral economic agreements and high-level political contacts. In mid-February, Iranian Foreign Minister Ali Akbar Velayati traveled to Moscow, where he met with Eduard Shevardnadze, Andrei Gromyko, and Nikolai Ryzhkov. It is clear from both Soviet and Iranian coverage that the talks were less than successful: Soviet sources described them as a "frank, businesslike exchange of opinion," thus indicating sharp disagreements. The Soviets took the opportunity once again to urge the Iranians to negotiate an end to the war. For his part, Velayati chided the Soviets about their continuing assistance to the Iraqis.[8]

The actual extent of disagreement between Velayati and the Soviets with whom he met was detailed in the Kuwaiti press. *Al Ra'y Al 'Amm* claimed that Moscow, in agreeing to Velayati's trip, responded to an urgent plea from Teheran. The Iranian reportedly went to the USSR to urge the Kremlin to cease its supply of weapons to Baghdad and to pressure Saddam Hussein to end the bombing of Iranian cities. But "the sources said the Soviets rejected the Iranian minister's request and told him they were prepared to suspend arms supplies to Iraq and to pressure it to stop bombing Iranian cities if Iran responds to peace initiatives, ends the war, and issues an official communique in that regard." Not only did Velayati reject this proposal, but he also threatened that Iran would turn "openly" toward the United States if the bombardment did not cease. The article went on to allege that Moscow, too, had issued threats—specifically to the effect that its unhappiness with the Iran arms deal would lead the Kremlin to "take a different stand on the war."[9]

By spring, Soviet concerns centered on Kuwait's requests to both superpowers to protect its shipping from Iranian raids. As Kuwaiti ships came increasingly under Iranian attack, and as Kuwait found that it was itself a target for Shi'i terrorism at home, it sought international protection for its tankers. The negotiations with both superpowers came at a time when the dangers of the war were becoming increasingly evident: One Soviet ship was attacked by Iranian gunboats, another hit a mine, and the USS *Stark* was hit by Iraqi missiles.

While the United States debated about its response, Moscow offered to lease three tankers. From the Kremlin's perspective, the request from Kuwait—a long-term friend—could not have been denied. Moreover, the approach to Moscow provided the USSR what it had long sought: an invitation for its presence in the Gulf. By the same token, the Kuwaiti appeal to the United States provided further legitimacy for U.S. naval activity. Washington for its part agreed to reflag eleven tankers and to provide them escort through the waters of the Gulf. Moscow could not condemn the reflagging operation *per se* without calling into question its own assistance to the Kuwaitis. As Moscow's Domestic Service claimed: "Incidentally, the actual intention of the United States to raise the U.S. flag, at Kuwait's own request, over its tankers is hardly objectionable."[10]

Because of the double-edged nature of the Kuwaiti effort to garner international protection for its shipping, Moscow renewed calls for the withdrawal of all foreign forces from the region. An additional problem for Gorbachev was that neither the demilitarization proposals nor the superpower aid to Kuwait was well received in Teheran. In response to the withdrawal proposal, Teheran's Domestic Service commented that the Soviet Union had by implication "excluded its own military presence from [its] statement."[11] After the first reflagged convoy sailed, Rafsanjani stated in a speech: "The Americans conspired with the Kuwaitis, reached agreement on reflagging ships, and told the Kuwaitis to invite the Russians to lease their ships. The Russians, who have always dreamed of establishing a foothold in the Persian Gulf, would be only too eager to come in as soon as possible."[12]

The complications of diplomacy and of the balancing act—between Iraq and its supporters and Iran—led the USSR to join with other members of the UN Security Council to vote for a cease-fire resolution. This marked a significant shift in prevailing Soviet attitudes toward the United Nations. In contrast to earlier nonsupport for UN activities, Moscow was now touting the United Nations and expressing support for Secretary General Perez de Cuellar's trip to the war zone. Moreover, CPSU General Secretary Mikhail Gorbachev, in a major article appearing in both *Pravda* and *Izvestiia*, called for enhancing the powers of the United Nations and particularly the International Court of Justice.[13]

Although the Soviet Union voted for UN Security Council Resolution 598, it also (almost simultaneously) undertook independent mediation efforts. In mid-June 1987, Deputy Foreign Minister Yuli Vorontsov was sent to Teheran as Gorbachev's personal emmissary. The meetings in Iran dealt with both the war and the status of Soviet-Iranian bilateral relations. According to reports, Vorontsov proposed an end to the tanker war and to negotiations. Despite Teheran's objections to parts of this plan, Vorontsov was then sent on to Baghdad. These Soviet initiatives proceeded with discussions in Moscow between Andrei Gromoyko and both Iranian and Iraqi officials. Concomitantly, parallel discussions led to the strengthening of the bilateral economic relationship, including a new pipeline agreement.

The renewal of diplomatic and economic ties with Iran led many to question who benefited most from the proposed pipeline agreement. Observers also questioned who was manipulating whom? For Iran, faced with a potential embargo and Iraqi attacks on its tankers, the Soviet Union was the major outlet for its oil. One need only think back to the 1979–1980 period, when the USSR permitted transit of Iranian goods over its soil. On the political level, once the Iran-Contra scandal broke, Iran was forced to distance itself from any dealings with the United States. In addition, it is entirely possible that Teheran again held out the prize of better economic and political ties so as to sway Moscow to lessen its support of Baghdad. In the meantime, better ties with Iran provided the Kremlin with several intangible benefits. If indeed the USSR under Gorbachev wished to play the mediator, then these new ties could furnish additional leverage in any negotiations. Moreover, the Kremlin may have viewed these agreements as a way to balance its aid to Kuwait and Iraq in Teheran's eyes. Last, it cannot be emphasized strongly enough that Iran remains the strategic prize in the region. Indeed, the answer to the question of manipulation may well be "both." Each for its own reasons sought to strengthen "good neighborliness."

Moscow's good neighbor policy apparently included criticisms of the U.S. escort operation and a refusal to back sanctions against Iran when it refused to accede to Resolution 598. Moreover, in the fall, Moscow shifted closer to the Iranian position on the resolution by calling for the cease-fire to occur concurrently with the investigation into responsibility for the war. The apparent tilt toward Teheran alarmed Iraq and attenuated the USSR's long-sought-after ties with the Gulf states and the moderate Arabs. As the Kuwaiti *Al Anba* noted: "The USSR, which has concluded important agreements with Iran and has appeased its regime at a time when its savageness has reached unbearable limits, is placing itself in the position of being almost a friend of that aggressive state."[14]

Throughout the summer and fall, as the Arab League took an increasingly anti-Iranian position, Moscow's support for the Arab cause was questioned. At the league's Amman summit meeting of November 1987, the Arab representatives focused on the Gulf War but, for the first time, not on the Arab-Israeli dispute. Even Syria acquiesced to a resolution that strongly condemned the Teheran regime for continuing the war and ignoring Resolution 598. The meeting also further legitimized Egypt's readmission into the Arab fold. The League agreed that, although as an organization it would not readmit Egypt, each of the members could reestablish diplomatic relations with Cairo. Most Arab states restored ties with Egypt without forcing Cairo to renounce the Egyptian-Israeli peace treaty. This was a setback to the USSR because as long as Egypt remained outside of Arab councils, the legitimacy of the U.S.-brokered Camp David Accords could be questioned.

Finally, the tilt toward Iran raised the question of whether the USSR could be dragged directly into the conflict. Although Iraq began the tanker war, Iranian attacks came under increasing criticism. Because Baghdad was no longer dependent on Gulf shipping to get its oil to world markets, the Iranian attacks on Kuwaiti and Saudi shipping, and on U.S. reflagged tankers, were viewed as politically motivated. At the same time, the Iraqi attacks were considered by many to be legitimate economic warfare.[15] Thus, as Iran raised the ante in the Gulf War in the fall of 1987, the question arose of whether or not Teheran was attempting to use the Soviets as a protective umbrella from which to attack.

In late 1987 and early 1988, Moscow therefore found it increasingly difficult to look aside and block sanctions after Teheran refused to agree to the cease-fire. Moreover, the actual conduct of the war potentially damaged the newfound ties between Iran and the USSR. In the winter of 1988, the so-called war of the cities was renewed. Each side seemed more determined than ever to make the war even more costly to the other's civilian population. Soviet concern over this round of escalation was magnified when Iranians in Teheran stormed the USSR embassy to protest Iraqi use of Soviet SCUD missiles to attack Teheran. The Iranian press agency reported that a group of worshippers, following Friday prayers, marched on the Soviet Embassy, chanting "Death to Russia."[16] Moscow claimed that the Iraqis themselves had modified the missiles to enhance their range. TASS reported a "crowd of unruly elements," while Moscow radio commentators spoke in Farsi about "provocative" actions against the Soviet Union. Moscow radio also issued a not-so-veiled threat to Teheran that these actions could undo the renewal of Soviet-Iranian economic relations.[17]

In the end, it took the United States' downing of the Iranian Airbus to trigger a change in the Iranian position on the war. The incident elicited very careful Soviet criticism. Although the USSR could, of course, blame the war and the massive U.S. presence for the disaster, there were echoes of the Soviet downing of KAL 007. Thus, in the aftermath of the shoot-down, Vorontsov met with Iranian Ambassador Mohammed Nobari in Moscow at the latter's request. The Supreme Soviet sent condolences, as did the Soviet Muslim board. Beyond using the incident to augment the by-now usual calls for a U.S. withdrawal, Moscow could not easily blast the United States without calling into question its own actions five years earlier.

Two weeks later, on July 18, 1988, Teheran announced its willingness to accept Resolution 598. At first, TASS issued only a terse announcement of the Iranian position. The next day, Gennady Gerasimov, the Soviet Foreign Ministry spokesman, expressed "profound satisfaction" at the turn of events.[18] Simultaneously, Yuli Vorontsov traveled to the war zone. He arrived in Baghdad on July 17 and spent the 20th through the 22nd in Teheran. According to several reports, Vorontsov offered the auspices of the USSR to mediate between the two combatants. Iranian officials rejected the offer. In the words of Ali Mohammad Besherati: "In this way [through the mediation offer] the Soviet Union wants to give the appearance that it is impartial in this war. . . . The point is that not only are they not impartial in this war, but by the blatant and hidden support for the Baghdad regime, they have encouraged Saddam . . . and therefore, the Russians are a partner to and share in Saddam's crimes."[19]

GORBACHEV AND KHOMEINI

Following the cease-fire, and despite the Iranians' rejection of the Soviets' mediation offer, the trends previously seen in Soviet-Iranian relations were accelerated. In fact, January 1989 seemed to usher in a new era in Soviet relations with Khomeini's Iran. The Ayatollah Javadi Amoli met with Gorbachev to present him with a message from Khomeini. Although the by-now famous letter was anti-Communist, it did offer the prospect of better relations between the two neighbors. According to Teheran television: "Since assuming his position, Mr. Gorbachev has been engaged in a new round of revision, development, and facing up to world realities. Therefore, his holiness the Imam regards Gorbachev's courage, boldness and bravery as praiseworthy." The letter also contained the following: "It is clear to all that henceforth communism must be sought in the museums of world political history and that it is not possible for materialism to save humanity from the crisis of lack of spiritual conviction."[20]

Mohammed Javad Larijani, the Foreign Ministry official in charge of ties with the West, was in Moscow at the same time. Two days later a new trade agreement was announced. Then on January 12, the Soviet deputy gas minister arrived in Teheran to discuss the actual reopening of the Soviet-Iranian pipeline. The flourish of diplomatic activity continued with a meeting between Velayati and Shevardnazde in Paris. Following this meeting, the Teheran press hinted broadly at a forthcoming significant improvement in bilateral ties.

There were several reasons for the alteration in the fabric of post-revolution Soviet-Iranian relations. First, there can be no doubt that the August 20th cease-fire was welcomed in Moscow. The end to the Iran-Iraq War, at least on the battlefield, lessened the pressure on the USSR to choose sides and reduced the likelihood that the Kremlin could be denounced for tilting openly toward Teheran. It also allowed Moscow greater flexibility in pursuit of the mutually beneficial economic relationship with Teheran.

This view is in keeping with Gorbachev's "new political thinking." His *glasnost'* and *perestroika* translated into political detente with the West, coupled with the acknowledgment that the U.S.-Soviet relationship was central in overall foreign policy. The new General Secretary argued that the Soviet Union needed an international environment conducive to economic reform and political change. This meant, first of all, an amelioration of the superpower relationship, including arms control, verification procedures, increasing economic and political exchanges, and trade. In what might be called a cyclical pattern, Gorbachev's attention to U.S.-Soviet relations necessitated concessions on regional conflicts. At the same time, the momentum of improved relations between Moscow and Washington may well have induced the Kremlin to be more conciliatory.

Indeed, in the USSR today a significant reevaluation of past foreign policy mistakes is being undertaken. Observers, in this era of *glasnost'*, candidly admit that regional conflicts impinge on the superpower relationship. In the words of Vyacheslav Dashichev, an eminent historian:

> We are wrong in assessing the global situation. . . . Though we were politically, militarily (via weapons supplies and advisors), and diplomatically involved in regional conflicts, we disregarded their influence on the relaxation of tension between the USSR and the West. . . . [Soviet] interests lay by no means in chasing petty and essentially formal gains associated with leadership coups in certain countries.[21]

This theme—that the USSR somehow lost sight of its priorities—has been repeated by many Soviet commentators. As Boris Piadyshev, the editor-in-chief of *International Affairs* (Moscow), stated: "We were involved in a whole number of problems having little relevance to our key national interests. . . . [O]ur attention was focused largely on the periphery of international affairs."[22]

The new approach to regional conflicts will make the West European countries more comfortable with an enhanced trade relationship and, as has already proven the case, more willing to provide credits to help finance *perestroika*. Moreover, the new Soviet thinking will facilitate the search for trading partners that is definitely part of the Gorbachev agenda. Moscow's desire to improve relations with Japan, for example, can be explained not only in Asian political terms but also as an effort to attract Japanese investment in the USSR and a desire, perhaps, to buy Japanese technology. One might also speculate that the overtures to Israel have a trade-based motivation. Other examples include increasing trade with the newly industrializing nations of Latin America and with Saudi Arabia. Indeed, renewed trade with Iran in oil and natural gas will facilitate *perestroika* as well.

Second, it could be argued that the height of danger for the Soviet tilt toward Iran was the fall of 1987. At the time, one may recall, it looked as if Iran were attempting to use the USSR as a protective shield so that it could strike in the Gulf with relative impunity. It was also at that point that the Arab world demonstrated an unprecedented degree of anti-Iranian unity. The Palestinian uprising that began in December 1987 eased the Soviets' dilemma in that it refocused Arab attention on the Arab-Israeli dispute and away from the Gulf War. Although Soviet dealings in the Arab-Israeli-Palestinian nexus were not always successful, Moscow seemingly felt more secure in its initiatives in that arena than in confronting the Iranian question. Moreover, the Soviet stance on the Rushdie affair (see below) in all probability eased some Arab discomfiture with Moscow.

Third, the announced end to the Kremlin's occupation of Afghanistan also eased the tensions inherent in the Soviet-Iranian relationship. In January 1988, Gorbachev announced that a Soviet withdrawal from Afghanistan could begin May 15, if a UN-sponsored agreement among Afghanistan, Pakistan, the United States and the USSR could be reached by March 15. Although the original deadline was not met, the Soviets continued to seek a way out. Finally, after an April mini-summit between Afghan Party Secretary Najibullah and Gorbachev in Tashkent, the two announced agreement on the terms of a withdrawal. The UN-sponsored settlement called for both a Soviet withdrawal by February 15, 1989, and the resettlement of refugees. In addition, the USSR has, at the least, attenuated the link between its prestige and the fate of the Najibullah government.

Initially, Iran condemned the UN accords because they meant less support to the mujahedeen. Moreover, Teheran charged that the agreement illustrated the collusion between the two superpowers to achieve world domination.[23] In the months between the signing of the withdrawal accords and the actual Soviet withdrawal on February 15, 1989, it became increasingly clear to all that the USSR did indeed intend to get out. Moreover, Yuli Vorontsov, Gorbachev's Middle East trouble shooter, was appointed ambassador to Kabul. As the man on the spot, Vorontsov was in a unique position to oversee this transitional phase. Finally, Shevardnadze has met more than once with representatives of the several tribal groupings in order to effect a coalition government acceptable to all. Vorontsov, too, has negotiated with the mujahedeen; indeed, some of those meetings have taken place in Teheran.

Despite the initial Iranian opposition to the agreement, the withdrawal of the Red Army troops from Afghanistan does remove one of the long-term irritants in the Soviet-Iranian relationship. By the same token, Moscow's demonstrated willingness to negotiate with the mujahedeen—and in Iran—further facilitates the Soviet-Iranian relationship. From Teheran's perspective, this willingness means that they can pursue the links to Moscow without appearing to abandon the mujahedeen. Conversely, the Kremlin can use its dealings with the tribal councils and so on to show Khomeini that it takes the Iranian-backed forces (and others) seriously.

The USSR welcomed not only the amelioration in Soviet-Iranian relations but also the improvement in Teheran's ties with the Western European countries. Soviet media praised the "moderation" in Iranian foreign policy. For example, *New Times*, in a biographical sketch, applauded Rafsanjani and described him as a "moderate." (The word was written out in English.) The press also responded favourably to the Ayatollah Montazeri's push for a more even keel on Iranian policy.[24]

The evolution of Iranian policy and the Soviet response to it was jolted by the publication of *The Satanic Verses*. Khomeini's response, including the death threats against the author, led to a reversal of the apparent trend toward moderation. Relations with the West were rebroken, and the Rushdie affair provided the context for a victory of the radical political forces within Iran. Montazeri was summarily dismissed as heir apparent, and Larijani, the architect of the renewal of ties with Europe, was fired.

Moscow's handling of the Rushdie affair illustrates the ambivalence that continues to characterize Soviet-Iranian relations. At first, Soviet statements were critical of the publicity given to the affair and leary of the impact on the course of Iranian politics. Yet, while condemning the death threats against Rushdie, the Soviet press urged the West to be sensitive to Muslim sensibilities.

In the middle of the scandal, Eduard Shevardnadze arrived in Teheran, the last stop of his extensive and highly significant Middle East tour. The trip was the culmination of all of Gorbachev's Middle East initiatives. The Soviet Foreign Minister met in Cairo with Egyptian President Hosni Mubarak, Israeli Foreign Minister Moshe Arens, and PLO Chairman Yasir Arafat. He flew on to Damascus to meet with Syria's President Hafiz al Assad, to Baghdad to hold discussions with Saddam Hussein, and finally to Teheran where he met with the heads of the Iranian leadership, including Khomeini himself. By all accounts, the meetings in Teheran were successful. Gorbachev, through Shevardnadze, sent a return letter in which he characterized Soviet foreign policy and indicated Soviet interest in an improvement in bilateral ties. The Teheran press characterized the exchange of letters as a turning point in Soviet-Iranian relations.

While in Teheran, Shevardnadze raised the question of the scandal over *The Satanic Verses.* He even offered to "mediate" between Khomeini and the West. From the Iranian perspective, the Rushdie affair afforded the perfect context for an amelioration of ties with the USSR. Claiming, in effect, that the West did not understand Islamic sensitivities, the radicals in Teheran bolstered their indignation by turning more openly toward the Soviet Union. Gennady Gerasimov stated that Moscow was concerned over the unpredictability of the scandal, and it was therefore natural that Shevardnadze should raise the issue on his trip.[25]

Following the Soviet Foreign Minister's trip, the pace of the rapprochement that started with Khomeini's letter accelerated. In March Velayati traveled to Moscow, and in May Vorontsov met with Iranian officials in Teheran. At the same time, the Iranian press announced new bilateral economic agreements, including a new natural gas agreement and the provision of Soviet credits to Iran totalling 1.2 billion rubles.[26] When the Ayatollah Khomeini died in early June, the Kremlin leadership sent condolences to the Iranian people and a delegation of Soviet Muslims traveled to Iran during the official mourning period. Commentary in the Soviet media praised Khomeini for his pursuit of an independent foreign policy and for the turnaround in relations with Moscow.

The high point came in late June, when Rafsanjani met with Gorbachev and other Soviet leaders in the Kremlin. The trip, which had been announced earlier, took place despite the death of Khomeini. The visit produced additional economic accords, reportedly an arms deal, and a declaration of principles governing relations between the two neighbors. The pronouncement of official friendship included pledges of mutual respect, economic cooperation, Soviet assistance in increasing

Iran's defensive capabilities, promises of exchanges, support for the North-South dialogue, and support for the United Nations.[27]

It should be noted that the language of the declaration approximates that in earlier friendship and cooperation treaties, especially the phrase "strengthening Iran's defensive capabilities." The Soviet Union never publishes details of arms agreements, but the Iranian and Gulf media did reveal some statistics. In early May, the Iranian news agency quoted First Deputy Foreign Minister Ali Muhammad Besherati when he announced that Iran and the Soviet Union were on the verge of signing a series of arms agreements.[28] Even earlier, *Keyhan* had reported Czech and Rumanian deals that included weapons production facilities as well as 180 tanks.[29] Finally, the Kuwaiti and Abu Dhabi media indicated that the Soviet Union had promised to sell Teheran sophisticated weaponry and advanced radar in return for Iranian pledges of noninterference in Soviet Muslim areas.[30]

Thus the spring of 1989 represents the culmination of the policy begun when Gorbachev fired Gromyko and abandoned the policy of reciprocity. The simultaneity of the Rushdie affair and Shevardnadze's trip provided Moscow with a major opportunity. Given that Teheran is the strategic prize in the region, it seemed logical that Moscow should take advantage of this anti-Western opening. The record of Soviet–Third World relations in the Gorbachev era reveals that, like his predecessors, the new General Secretary will move to reduce Western influence; yet unlike those before him, Gorbachev will do so only where it will not be overly provocative or costly.[31]

By the same token, the amelioration of the Soviet-Iranian relationship is not without its dangers. Until Khomeini's death, the potential reradicalization of Iranian foreign policy—as symbolized by the Rushdie scandal—could have proven detrimental to Gorbachev's goal of improved international relations. At the regional level, the Kremlin must continue to be concerned about its ties with the Arab world. Following the announcement of the declaration of principles, Soviet broadcasts to the Middle East were designed to allay Arab fears about the arms agreements. Moscow endeavored to highlight those parts of the declaration that upheld UN activities and to minimize the novelty of Soviet arms assistance to Iran. Simultaneously, Soviet diplomats met with their counterparts in Arab capitals to soothe any ruffled feathers.

For the moment, at least, the evidence would seem to indicate that Moscow has decided to gamble on post-Khomeini Iran. It appears that in the Kremlin's view, the potential benefits, especially economic benefits, must outweigh the risks. Given Gorbachev's overwhelming economic priority, the lure of a return to pre-1979 mutually beneficial economic relations is quite strong.

NOTES

1. For a long discussion of the changes between Khrushchev and Brezhnev, see Carol R. Saivetz and Sylvia Woodby, *Soviet–Third World Relations* (Boulder, Colo.: Westview Press, 1985).

2. N. Prozhogin, "Stormy Time," *Pravda*, January 7, 1979, p. 4, quoted in *Current Digest of the Soviet Press*, Vol. XXXI, No. 1, January 31, 1979, p. 15.

3. *Pravda* and *Izvestiia*, February 24, 1981, quoted in *Current Digest of the Soviet Press*, Vol. XXXIII, No. 8, March 25, 1981, pp. 7, 8.

4. A. Petrov, "Display Prudence and Restraint," *Pravda*, December 5, 1979, p. 5, quoted in *Current Digest of the Soviet Press*, Vol. XXXI, No. 49, January 2, 1980, p. 26.

5. Shahram Chubin, "The Soviet Union and Iran," *Foreign Affairs*, Vol. 61, No. 4 (Spring 1983), p. 934.

6. Pavel Demchenko, "USSR-Iran: In the Interests of Good Neighborliness," *Pravda*, March 9, 1982, p. 4.

7. As reported in *Pravda*, June 17, 1983 (italics added).

8. Teheran Domestic Service, February 14, 1987, quoted in FBIS MEA 87 032, February 18, 1989, p. 14.

9. *Al Ra'y Al 'Amm* (Kuwait), February 15, 1987, pp. 1, 18, quoted in FBIS SOV 87 036, February 24, 1987, pp. H5-H6.

10. Moscow Domestic Service, July 6, 1987, quoted in FBIS SOV 87 129, July 7, 1987, p. E2-3.

11. Teheran Domestic Service, July 6, 1987, quoted in FBIS MEA 87 129, July 7, 1987, p. S2.

12. Teheran Domestic Service, July 24, 1987, quoted in FBIS MEA 87 143, July 27, 1987, p. S1-5.

13. Mikhail S. Gorbachev, "The Realities and Guarantees of a Secure World," *Pravda*, September 17, 1987, pp. 1–2. See also *Izvestiia*, September 1987.

14. *Al Anba* (Kuwait), August 20, 1987, p. 1, quoted in FBIS MEA 87 163, August 24, 1987, p. J3.

15. As of October 12, 1987, the Iraqis had hit 214 ships whereas the Iranians had attacked 139. See *Armed Forces Journal International*, November 1987, p. 76.

16. IRNA (Iranian News Agency), March 4, 1988, quoted in FBIS NES 88 042, March 4, 1988, pp. 55–56.

17. TASS, March 6, 1988, quoted in FBIS SOV 88 044 March 7, 1988, pp. 23–24; and Moscow Radio in Persian, March 7, 1988, quoted in FBIS SOV 88 045, March 8, 1988, pp. 17–18.

18. TASS, July 19, 1988, quoted in FBIS SOV 88 139, July 20, 1988, p. 9.

19. Interview with Ali Mohammad Besharati, Teheran Domestic Service, July 27, 1988, quoted in FBIS NES 88 145, July 28, 1988, p. 36.

20. Teheran Television, January 4, 1989, quoted in FBIS NES 89 003, January 5, 1989, p. 40.

21. Vyacheslav Dashichev, "East-West: Quest for New Relations," *Literaturnaia Gazeta*, May 18, 1988, p. 14 quoted in FBIS SOV 88 098, May 20, 1988, pp. 7–8.

22. Roundtable discussion, "PERESTROIKA, the 19th Party Conference and Foreign Policy," *International Affairs*, No. 7, 1988, p. 5.

23. Teheran Radio commentary, April 14, 1988, quoted in FBIS NES 88 073, April 15, 1988, pp. 55–56.

24. *New Times*, No. 2, January 10–16, 1989.

25. TASS, March 1, 1989, quoted in FBIS SOV 89 040, March 2, 1989, pp. 27–28.

26. See details in IRNA, May 13, 1989, quoted in FBIS NES 89 092, May 15, 1989, p. 50.

27. See the text in *Pravda*, June 24, 1989, p. 1.

28. IRNA, May 1, 1989, quoted in FBIS NES 89 082, May 1, 1989, pp. 46–47.

29. *Keyhan*, March 30, 1989, quoted in FBIS NES, May 4, 1989, pp. 50–51.

30. *Al Qabas*, June 26, 1989, p. 22, quoted in FBIS SOV 89 124, June 29, 1989, p. 15; and *Al-Ittihad*, June 25, 1989, pp. 1, 21, quoted in FBIS NES 89 125, June 30, 1989, pp. 37–38.

31. See the discussion in the concluding chapter of Carol R. Saivetz, ed. *The Soviet Union in the Third World* (Boulder, Colo.: Westview Press, 1989).

PART SIX

Conclusion

11

The Internal Struggle,
the Rushdie Affair,
and the Prospects for the Future

Miron Rezun

GENERAL REMARKS

Sweeping generalizations are all too often made in regard to Iran. In our forecasts of the country's future we are often inordinately judgmental, and we fall into this pitfall either by design or by accident. Indeed, it is almost a foregone conclusion to say that Iran is a country riddled by dissension, fraught with confusion and uncertainty; that it is mysterious and baffling in its conduct, especially when viewed through the filter of Western stereotypes. In a world where there is increasing detente and arms reductions, amid talk of building a United Europe, of free trade blocs, perhaps even of a convergence of ideologies, Iran may sometimes seem an egregious maverick irreverently opposing international law and order. Not long ago it could be said that, while it was able to command or contest the approaches to the Gulf, Iran was considered to be strategically the most important country in the region. It is likely to continue playing that part in the coming years, even in view of the diminishing role of the Gulf itself.

But equally important is the fact that Iran has been able to project a resounding appeal to the Islamic world, encompassing Sunni and Shi'i alike. Iranians have also developed for themselves a distinct national character, or political culture, that sometimes mesmerizes, sometimes defies, and often challenges the work of Western international relations experts. The most consistent aspect of Iran is its inconsistency. As often as not, Iran has demonstrated its willingness to sacrifice domestic priorities for the sake of foreign policy objectives. Yet, the opposite is also true; otherwise Iran would not have ended its war with

Iraq. The acceptance of UN Resolution 598 (the cease-fire resolution) in August 1988 suggests that Khomeini himself recognized the need to tone down the ideological fervour of the Islamic Republic or jeopardize its very survival. The Gulf War was no longer synonymous with the survival of the revolution, for, as was often said during the war, Iraq could not win it and Iran could not lose it. What was needed, in effect, was a consolidation of the revolution, so as to secure the political future of the Islamic Republic long after the disappearance of Khomeini from the scene.

IS THE RUSHDIE AFFAIR
A FITTING CONCLUSION?

All of the chapters in this book thus far have dealt with Iran's relations with regional and major powers. Conspicuously absent is any mention of its relations with Western Europe and Japan. Equally absent is a more comprehensive and detailed analysis of the contemporary domestic environment. As I stated in the "Introduction" to this book, with Khomeini's death the internal situation in the country will determine external or foreign policy priorities. Even before Khomeini died, the internal power struggle in Teheran had already started. Nowhere is its salience better observed than in the "Rushdie Affair," which occurred just a few months before Khomeini's passing, at a time when he must have been gravely ill. The Rushdie Affair is a cogent illustration of how religious dogma, internal factionalism in the country, a slur on the Islamic faith by an Indian-born novelist, could ultimately make an impact on world politics and influence the policies of Western Europe and particularly Britain. It points up the fragility of the international system as long as there are states whose philosophy and culture are not rooted in Western liberal/secular traditions.

How does the Rushdie Affair fit into a long-term assessment of Iranian foreign policy? Might it be only a function of the domestic squabbles in Iran, having little to do with Salman Rushdie's book, *The Satanic Verses*, or with Islamic morality? And where precisely does Iran stand in the wake of this imbroglio? The international controversy caused by the publication of Rushdie's was entirely unprecedented. To be sure, the banning and the burning of books is nothing new in itself; but a death sentence pronounced on the strength of the *Velayat-e-Faqih*,[1] which allows the Imam Ruhollah Khomeini to issue a decree (*fatva*) against a foreign national, was sensational. By Khomeini's order Iran offered a bounty of as much as $5.2 million to Rushdie's assassin, preferably a Moslem. The Rushdie Affair thus set Iran and the West at odds, despite Rushdie's formal apology to the effect that he did not intend his book to be an insult to Islam.

THE NOVELIST AND THE PROPHET

Thus *The Satanic Verses*, written by an Indian-British novelist, a lapsed Moslem, may or may not have been designed from the outset to be controversial. Of particular interest is the fact that the publisher, Penguin-Viking, was contacted by the U.K.'s Action Committee on Islamic Affairs and warned that the book, if released, would be political dynamite. The Action Committee's liaison and cultural advisor for Indian affairs at Penguin-Viking warned the committee in October 1988 that the contents of the book were "lethal" and that it should not be published. Penguin-Viking went ahead despite this advice and decided to publish it anyway. It is often said that one must not judge a book by its cover. In my opinion, the novel is clearly mediocre in both form and content; parts of it are stylistically unintelligible, verbose, and relevant only to a British-Indian environment and the subcontinent's peculiar modes of colloquial speech. Much was made of the fact that the title is essentially the most provocative element about the book. Strangely enough, some of those who later were quick to judge and condemn the work had actually never read it, least of all the Iranian ecclesiastical-political leaders.

The Satanic Verses refers to an incident alleged to have occurred during Mohammed's life. According to writings more than a thousand years old, chiefly attributed to Ibn Sa'ad Al-Tabari, Mohammed (the prophet of God), in his struggle to bring the word of Allah to pagan Mecca, initially claimed that Allah had permitted Mecca's three major goddesses to act as intermediaries in worship. According to Al-Tabari, Mohammed later deleted this "divine permission" from the Koran, and Al-Tabari claimed that Gabriel had not communicated the word of God but, rather, that it had been Satanically inspired.

Islamic scholarship does not consider this story to be authentic in the least. It must be remembered that to all of Islam's followers, the Koran is not merely divinely inspired, as Christians would regard the Bible; for them, the Koranic verses were dictated by God to the Archangel Gabriel, who gave God's word to Mohammed. It was then dictated by Mohammed to his scribes without human editing and written down on whatever primitive materials were available: camel bone, palm leaves, parchment, wood, and so forth. Modern scholars, using methods adapted from Biblical analysis, have been suggesting for some time now that the Koran, as we know it, might well have been assembled some time after the Arab conquest of the Middle East, from

a large body of oral literature as a result of continuing polemics with
Christians and Jews. The incident of *The Satanic Verses* may be
admitted to have occurred, but the authenticity of Mohammed's education by Gabriel is suspect.

That Rushdie recounts the blasphemous tale of "The Satanic Verses"
in his book is bad enough. To a follower of Islam, particularly in the
Middle East, the term *satanic verses* could be taken as a slur on the
entire Koran. One therefore begins to wonder whether this international
incident would have occurred at all if the publisher had insisted on a
less inflammatory title. Indeed, there are dozens of scholarly books in
university libraries throughout Europe and North America, and even
in the USSR, that are far more subversive of Islamic morality than
this work of fiction. And there are works of fiction, in Arabic, published
in Egypt and Lebanon, that are far more offensive to Islam—but that
do not bear sacrilegious titles.

Rushdie's earlier books have been both critically acclaimed and
steeped in controversy. In 1981 his second book, *Midnight's Children*,
established Rushdie as a literary figure by winning him Britain's most
prestigious literary award, the Booker Prize. However, in its treatment
of Indian politics, this work aroused the anger of Indira Gandhi and
ended in a libel suit against him. Undeterred, in 1983 Salman Rushdie
went ahead with his next novel, *Shame*, which was also nominated for
the Booker Prize (albeit unsuccessfully); it was banned in Pakistan for
its fanciful recounting of the power struggle between Zia-ul Haq and
Prime Minister Zulfikar Ali Bhutto.

Rushdie admitted he was aware that *The Satanic Verses* would
provoke the Moslem community, but he added that he did not regard
the book as being blasphemous.[2] There is indeed much within *The
Satanic Verses* to provoke the consternation of Islam. For instance, the
novel refers to the "prophet" Mahound, which was actually a Christian
medieval name for the devil. It portrays Mohammed as a man of loose
morals, a chauvinist who refuses to "pick on women his own size."
Furthermore, Rushdie ridicules the *Shari'a* and wrongly states that
Islam approves of sodomy. The author's point in doing so is to ridicule
the concept that God would make any laws regarding sexual acts among
mankind. In addition to the shocking portrayal of Mohammed's wives
as whores, there are other references, typical of the Manichean, alle-
gorical tradition, that could offend sincere and devout Moslems. One
passage that has often been ignored in the international debate over
whether *The Satanic Verses* can be considered blasphemous is a passage
dealing with "The Imam." (In Iran, Khomeini was called an Imam.)
Like much of *The Satanic Verses*, that passage is part of a dream

sequence, a blending of past and present. The point that Rushdie is apparently trying to make is that Khomeini himself is comparable to the devil and cares nothing for mankind.

> "No tyranny on earth can withstand the power of this slow, walking love" [says the Imam]. "This isn't love," Gibreel, weeping, replies. "It's hate. She has driven them into your arms." The explanation sounds thin, superficial. . . . "They love me" the Imam's voices say, because I am water. I am fertility and she is decay. They love me for my habit of smashing clocks. . . . [A]fter the revolution there will be no clocks; we'll smash the lot. . . . Gibreel understands that the Imam, fighting by proxy as usual, will sacrifice him as readily as he did the hill of corpses at the palace gate, that he is a suicide soldier in the service of the cleric's cause.[3]

The "Imam" Rushdie refers to is Khomeini, not any of the other twelve Imams of Twelver Shi'ism.[4] Even though the direct slur on Khomeini had occurred in a religious context, the Imam Khomeini did not respond. In fact, Iran and Khomeini were not prepared to denounce the "blasphemy" of the book until such time as a series of other electrifying events had overtaken Iran—events that were sparked on the international scene.

England's Islamic Society for the Promotion of Religious Tolerance wrote to Penguin-Viking on October 12, 1988, saying the book was "an insult to Islam." Its chairman, Hesham Eli Essawy, added: "I would like to invite you to take some kind of corrective stand before the monster you have so needlessly created grows, as it will do worldwide, into something uncontrollable."[5] Penguin-Viking's own Indian Affairs advisor was soon to give the same advice as noted earlier—"Do not publish."

THE INTERNATIONAL DIMENSION

As soon as the book appeared on the market, Pakistan and South Africa were the first to ban it. To stop further exports of the novel to Moslem countries, the new London-based Action Committee wrote to all the Moslem ambassadors in the United Kingdom, explaining the offensive character of the novel and urging them to immediately proceed with a ban on importing it into their countries. Ahkunzaden Basti, the Iranian chargé d'affaires in Britain, was among those who received the letter. November 1988 slipped by without much more being said and done about this whole affair. But the Action Committee, desperate for publicity, decided to organize a book-burning demonstration in Bolton on December 2 in which 7,000 demonstrators took part. The book burning was ignored by both the government and the media in the U.K. The incident did, however, elicit some concern from the ambassadors of Pakistan, Somalia, and Kuwait, who contacted the British Home Office Minister, John Patten.

Another book burning occurred in Bradford on January 14, 1989, but this time even greater international action was elicited. Thousands of letters were sent to the American publisher before the release of the book in the United States. Loud demonstrations in India and South Africa took place, and a more violent riot erupted on February 12 just outside the United States Information Centre in Islamabad. That riot resulted in the deaths of six protesters as police turned machine guns on the crowd.

It is in Islamabad that the political significance of *The Satanic Verses* was first exploited for domestic (Pakistani) purposes. Why indeed did this demonstration take place outside an American cultural information centre? One wonders: Salman Rushdie, after all, is not an American. The claim by the demonstration organizers, that it was organized to stop the Americans from publishing the book, is untenable. The architect of the demonstration, Moulana Kausar Niazi, a former Minister for Information and Religious Affairs under Zia ul-Haq, surely knew that foreign agitation would hardly stop anything from being published in the United States. Niazi had in effect orchestrated the campaign in Pakistan, where the book was banned, ostensibly in an attempt to stoke the religious and cultural ferment of the people and rally them against Western values. Indirectly, the Islamabad demonstration was attacking the new Pakistani Prime Minister, Benazir Bhutto, whose gender would thus be construed as a symbol not of progress but of cultural imperialism. As Bhutto herself noted after the demonstration: "[T]he old order always likes to give a few kicks before it goes to rest."[6]

Whether Khomeini actually was aware of the furor over *The Satanic Verses* prior to the Islamabad riot will never be known. The timing of the Iranian reaction may or may not be important. At the end of January 1989, the *New York Times Magazine* featured the first cover story anywhere on Rushdie. The author, Gerald Marzorati, called it "Fiction's Embattled Infidel." Khomeini must have been repeatedly told of the publication of this novel in England and of the reaction to it by Moslems in Britain and elsewhere. Fred Halliday, a leading expert on Islam at the London School of Economics, called Khomeini's tactics "band-wagoning,"[7] seeing in it a pretext to reassert Khomeini's claim to leadership of the worldwide Islamic movement. The chargé d'affaires in London tried to downplay the whole situation in London. But the death sentence (*fatva*) against Rushdie was issued over Radio Teheran on the afternoon after the Islamabad riot:

> In the name of God Almighty, there is only one God, to whom we shall all return. I would like to inform all the intrepid Moslems in the world that the author of the book entitled *The Satanic Verses*, which has been compiled, printed, and published in opposition to Islam, the prophet and the Koran, as well as those publishers who were aware of its contents, have been sentenced to death. I call on all zealous Moslems to execute them quickly, wherever they find them, so that no one will dare to insult the Islamic sanctions. Whoever is killed on this path will be regarded as a martyr, God willing.[8]

In doing so, did Khomeini believe he was being overtaken by events in which Iran was not playing an active role? An explanation of Khomeini's *fatva* was promptly released. Rushdie's book was judged by the Ayatollah to be "the result of years of effort by American, European and Zionist so-called experts on Islam gathering in international seminars and conferences on the religion with the aim of finding the best way to insult and undermine Islam's highest values and traditions."[9]

On February 15, an Iranian mullah announced that there would be more than martyrdom as a reward; $2.6 million would be paid to the assassin if he was an Iranian, $1.0 million if he was not. On February 16, private contributors from Rafsanjani's hometown (at the time, Rafsanjani was still the Speaker of the Parliament) raised the bounty to almost $6.0 million.

Against this background, however, why should Khomeini have gone so far as to order the execution of a foreign national over a book? Not surprisingly, the Western news media began denouncing the *fatva*, and the issue carried all the trappings of a great saga: East versus West, censorship versus free-speech, religion versus the secular state. It was not out of character for Khomeini to have reacted in this way. Nor was it the first time that Iran was willing to directly confront Western values. As to the morality of ordering the death of someone who had renounced Islam (i.e., an apostate, which Rushdie admits he is) and attacked Islamic beliefs in print, there is no reason to believe that Khomeini considered it morally wrong or in conflict with Islam. Indeed, throughout the revolution, tens of thousands of innocent people had been killed or persecuted at the hands of the revolutionary courts for lesser crimes against Islam. One among many examples is the murder and imprisonment of Baha'i apostates who, as Iranian nationals, were ostracized for having quit Islam and starting a completely new religion.

THE INTERNAL DIMENSION

The point I wish to make is this: The issue may have little to do with Salman Rushdie and *The Satanic Verses*. The motives behind the death sentence lie in the complex, unpredictable, and misunderstood dynamics of Iranian factionalism. Iranian politics has been dominated by this factionalism since the fall of the Shah, and this factionalism will continue into the future. There is at present in Iranian society an underlying ideological conflict between the general issues of economics and political revolution.

The economics issue itself seems to be split into two camps. One, the laissez-faire side, advocates private development and minimal state intervention in the economy. Certainly Ali Akbar Hashemi Rafsanjani, the Speaker of the Majlis and Commander-in-Chief of the Armed Forces, has at times supported the laissez-faire camp, but this support may have been due to political reasons and not his own convictions. Rafsanjani has been quoted as saying that "state domination of the economy was a war measure that is no longer necessary."[10]

However, the most ardent laissez-faire supporters are the reactionary mullahs within the Council of Guardians. Over the years this body has blocked reformist legislation. The Council of Guardians is the body within Iran which ensures that the legislation of the Majlis is in accordance with the tenets of Islam; it is constitutionally allowed to veto such laws that it deems are in conflict with Islam. The conflict between the Majlis and the Council has been based on the Islamic tenet respecting private property. As Islamic tradition holds that private property is a Koranic principle, the Council has blocked all attempts to redistribute wealth among Iranians. For example, land reform legislation has been blocked repeatedly, thus preventing no more than 3 percent of arable land from being transferred to the poor.[11] This policy of blocking reform has brought the Council into conflict with Moussavi, the Prime Minister, resulting in a restructuring of the Council's power over economic issues. The new Economic Council has the support of the secular authorities.

Prime Minister Hussein Moussavi was always in opposition to the laissez-faire policies of the Council. Officially, the economy of Iran fell within his jurisdiction. Moussavi was therefore eager to use the powers of the State to intervene in the economy and, in the process, to garner support from the people. Again, the conflict between Moussavi and Rafsanjani on the issue of state intervention in the economy may have been a political battle for power, not a battle arising from convictions. To complicate the domestic scene even further, the ultra-revolutionary ex-Minister of the Interior, Hojatoleslam Ali Akbar Mohtashemi, is an inveterate capitalist when it comes to economic matters. Yet he is also extremely anti-American and consistently in favour of exporting the Shi'i revolution abroad, though he is more aware of Moslem upheaval in the Arab lands than in the Islamic parts of the USSR. Thus, whereas this popular Minister was noted to be an ally of Moussavi on revolutionary ideals (i.e., foreign policy), Mohtashemi appears to be an opponent of Moussavi on economic policy.[12]

The other issue is revolutionary zeal, or revolutionary romanticism, for lack of better terms. How profitable has this revolutionary fervor been? Was this religious ferment important to the preservation of the revolution itself? The idea of the revolution, to begin with, centered on "Islamic morality and law." Most observers have understood this idea to mean a backlash against Western values and a return to the Shari'a. However, revolutionary zeal has consistently led Iran to alienate the West and the Arab states, as the revolutionaries have tried to export their revolution. From this perspective, it is possible to see the revolutionary ideologies split three ways: First there are the ultra-revolutionaries, who have much in common with "Trotskyites" insofar as they wish to export the revolution. It is this group that must be viewed as the "enemy of the West"; it favors Islamic commitment in Iran and Islamic governments throughout the Middle East. Unquestionably, the ultra-revolutionaries are the ones responsible for state terrorism at home and abroad.

These ultra-revolutionaries have had various supporters within the Iranian government. The most notable among them thus far is Prime Minister Hussein Moussavi. The office of the Prime Minister no longer exists, and Moussavi, to be sure, is not likely to ascend as long as Rafsanjani leads the Government. Other notables include Khomeini's son Ahmed and, as indicated earlier, former Interior Minister Hojatoleslam Ali Akbar Mohtashemi. The weapon that has remained with the ultra-revolutionaries since the fall of the Shah has been the "Pasdaran," or Revolutionary Guards. In effect, significant elements within the Pasdaran still support the ultra-revolutionaries. Recognizing the Pasdaran's potential power, the progressives and pragmatists took steps, not so long ago, to bring it under the same ministry as that overseeing the armed forces[13] and to maintain some control over it.

Then there is the archetype of the more pragmatic revolutionaries. Such revolutionaries are concerned not with the export of the revolution but with the consolidation of the gains that revolution has been able to make at home. Needless to say such revolutionaries can be unpredictable, and it is into this category that I believe Ayatollah Hussain Ali Montazeri, Khomeini's demoted heir-apparent, falls. Montazeri had never been a moderate; in fact, he was very much a pragmatist (defined loosely) insofar as the goals of the revolution were concerned. There seemed an abiding belief in the Western media that Montazeri, by speaking out against political repression in domestic politics, was against violence of any kind, and that he was therefore a friend of the West. We must not forget that it was Montazeri who consistently condoned international terror tactics as retribution against the United States for the downing of the Iranian airliner in the Gulf.[14] Some analysts have labelled Montazeri a conservative. Contextually this might be true; but Montazeri is not cut from the same cloth as the Ayatollah's former opponent, Ayatollah Shariatmadari, whose roots were in Iranian Azerbaijan. So this label may be misleading, too, because Shariatmadari, in addition to being a conservative, was an Azeri nationalist with predominant support in Tabriz. Montazeri is feared for his strong Persian-ethnic views over and above his fundamentalist religious views.

The last group of revolutionary ideologists is frequently described as "moderate," or pragmatic. One could also call them progressive. Such leaders are interested in seeing Iran move ahead economically and domestically. What is left in Iran of the National Front of the Mossadegh era has supported this camp, for there is simply nowhere else for them to be. But the character of the progressives is not the character of a pro-West faction per se, and neither, lest we forget, was Mossadegh in the early 1950s.

Rafsanjani certainly belongs in this last category. He has consistently supported moves by the Iranian Government to curb the ultra-revolutionaries. This is why the latter threw their weight behind Mohtashemi, who became their spokesman when Khomeini passed away. But Rafsanjani clipped his wings by excluding him from the new Iranian Cabinet, an act that was resented by many in the Government. Because of the need for reconstruction, Rafsanjani, as his own power began to increase, set about curbing his Government's policies of alienating the West. It is Rafsanjani who was responsible for the pragmatic sensibility of a restrained Iran in the wake of the downing of the Iran Air flight 655 over the Gulf. It is Rafsanjani who finally persuaded Khomeini to agree to the cease-fire in the Gulf War. And, of course, it is Rafsanjani who led the way in suggesting Iranian mediation in freeing the hostages held by *Hezballah* in Lebanon in 1989, in exchange for the repatriation of Iranian assets still frozen in U.S. banks (some $11 billion, by official Iranian accounts).

The other prominent leader of the progressives is Sayed Ali Khamenei. His support, though influential, has been tempered by the largely ceremonial role that used to go with the presidency. When Khomeini died, it was President Khamenei who was chosen to succeed him.

Although he lacked Rafsanjani's popularity and the charisma and stature of the defunct Imam, he will probably end up supporting Rafsanjani and the new, enhanced status bestowed upon the office of the presidency.

On economic and domestic matters, therefore, it is possible to envision Moussavi and Rafsanjani at odds. Because Rafsanjani needs the help of the Council of Guardians, he has at times pushed for a laissez-faire policy within the Majlis. However, the economy has essentially been Moussavi's domain, and efforts to reduce the power of the state within the country's economy have diminished Moussavi's power. On domestic issues, Rafsanjani can skillfully use his allies in the Majlis, the bazaars, and the clergy for a "privatization" of the country's economy. A caveat here is that we must assess how much Moussavi will lose in influence within Iran as the move to a less state-controlled economy diminishes his power.

It must be remembered, however, that up until his death it was Khomeini who ruled Iran. It is he and he alone who delivered the *fatva* against Rushdie. Because many in the West have pretended otherwise, practical analysis of Iran's internal politics often seemed to leave Khomeini out of the picture. Since 1980, constant references to Khomeini as "alive but dying" colored most analyses of Iranian politics. In the entire post-revolutionary political equation, Khomeini remained the single most important committed ideologue of the revolution: It was, after all, very much *his* revolution. At times, of course, Khomeini might have been willing to referee between the factions in domestic disputes; but he never allowed foreign policy decisions to compromise the revolution internally. Up until 1990, reckless ultra-revolutionary policies or reckless progressive reforms were curtailed to protect the Iranian Revolution. As long as he was alive, Khomeini never allowed fundamentalist Islam to be undermined. The threat of such an outcome, perpetrated by either the West or the East, was like a nightmare to him. He therefore opposed any reassertion of Western liberal values in Iran.

KHOMEINI AS THE FINAL ARBITER
IN THE AFFAIRS OF STATE

Now that the ideals and possible motives behind the factionalism in Iran have been described, it is easy to see what prompted the Rushdie Affair. The Imam, in the waning years of the war, experienced sagging popular support within the country. His position degenerated into that of a referee between factions. Only on issues of "Islam" was he willing to exert control. He must have realized that at 89 he could not expect to be around much longer. He had been ailing and his heart was weak. The end of the war was a "bitter cup of poison" to him. For a time he was willing to let domestic politics run their course, provided that his revolution was not endangered. However, the rapprochement with the West since the close of the war, combined with "alarming liberalism," as Khomeini used to say, prompted him to seize the initiative after the Islamabad riots.

The furor caused by his death sentence against Rushdie was exactly what Khomeini needed to keep the embers of that revolution alive. What followed was a renewal of the "Pariah status" for Iran in regard to the West, as well as a renewal of popular support for himself at home.[15] Only a week after the incident, the Rushdie Affair was described by Khomeini as a "godsend" that helped Iran out of a "naive foreign policy." On the same day, Radio Teheran announced that Khomeini had spoken of a "Black Night" facing the Islamic Republic: "As long as I am alive, I will not let the Government fall to liberals. . . . I will cut off the influence of American and Soviet agents in the fields."[16]

Throughout the Rushdie Affair, Khomeini was clearly not trying to improve the situation. Rather, he was attempting to seize the initiative within the Islamic world and to outmaneuver the progressive elements within Iran. At this time, Khomeini actually acknowledged both the rifts within his own Government and the influence of those "misled liberals."[17] When President Khamenei indicated that an apology might defuse the situation, Salman Rushdie quickly complied. The Imam renounced the apology and insisted that even if Rushdie repented, he would still have to be executed. President Khamenei then reversed his position on Rushdie and reemphasized the death sentence. The chaos of crisis descended upon Teheran once more, but it was within this context that the power and leadership of the spiritual leader worked best.

The best parallel to the Rushdie Affair is, arguably, the hostage crisis of 1980. During that crisis the radical students, the "students of the Imam's line," grabbed the world's attention when they stormed the U.S. Embassy. Then, as in the Lebanon hostage crisis, which resulted from the Israeli kidnapping of Sheik Obeid almost a decade later, the Western press and governments searched for a solution. It was not customary for U.S. government specialists to research the history of Islamic doctrine regarding hostages. But they gave it a try, for the feeling was that if the U.S. Government could prove to Khomeini that hostage taking was contrary to Islam, then the hostages would be released.[18] The attempt was as naive as the efforts were vain.

THE ATTITUDE OF WESTERN EUROPE
AND THE UNITED STATES

Although the Western media explored the ethics and vicissitudes of the Rushdie Affair with predictable vigor, the Western public was wiser this time around than it had been when confronted with a crisis involving Iran and the United States. The Europeans (both the leadership and the public) seemed to understand, much better than the Americans, that, however serious the death threat and regardless of how unjustified it was on moral grounds, its principal motivating factor was the internal politics of Iran. This argument appeared in such German newspapers as *Die Zeit* and *Frankfürter Allgemeine*, in the Swiss *Neue Zürcher Zeitung*, and in the British *Manchester Guardian* and *The Observer*.

As soon as the war between Iran and Iraq ended, Iran turned its energies to postwar reconstruction—to the building of new industries, improving social initiatives, and land reform. By the fall of 1988 Teheran was prepared to spend billions of dollars for these purposes; it offered contracts to help rebuild the infrastructure (oil refineries, ports, dams, roads, and telecommunications) and even reequipped the armed forces. Not surprisingly, trade missions from Japan, Western Europe, South Korea, Canada, Australia, and Italy began flocking to Teheran. Iran announced that it was willing to spend more than $45 billion over the next four years (from 1989 to 1994), stating bluntly that it would be inclined to give preference in awarding reconstruction contracts to those countries that supported its position at the Geneva peace negotiations. Given Iran's existing trading patterns, Italy was favored for petrochemicals, Japan and West Germany for power and industrial projects. Australia's share appeared to be in the agro-industrial field. And India and Pakistan seemed likely to compete in the civil engineering field as well as in the expansion of port facilities.

But what can be said of the ramifications of the Rushdie Affair in the West? First, it immediately led to a reversal of the trend toward compromise and moderation. As the hysteria slowly began to die down, Western Europe's relations with Iran continued to be strained, although they were not beyond repair. The responses of Japan and North America were tempered by concern for trade in the Gulf and by domestic political pressure. These EEC countries did not sever diplomatic ties with Teheran altogether. Asked by Prime Minister Thatcher to support Britain's call for free speech, the EEC countries recalled all the ambassadors and chief envoys home from Teheran. The consensus of the recall, demonstrating a unity of action, seemed to communicate an appropriate signal both throughout the world and within Europe. The European consensus also demonstrated that, for Europeans, freedom of speech would remain an honoured Western value and that Western Europe would not compromise on these values.

France's François Mitterrand responded by associating the death sentence against Rushdie with an act of absolute evil. In general, the insults from Paris to the Iranian government were not very restrained. But given France's close relationship with Iraq during the Gulf War, this was not surprising. In fact, it was because of this close cooperation that French combat pilots flew low-risk missions on behalf of Iraq.[19] Although the French will not find themselves in a favorable position in the postwar investment bonanza, France stands at the head of the line for industrial contracts with Iraq.

Most significant in the Rushdie Affair was the reaction of the West Germans. West Germany is Iran's largest trading partner. Indeed, it has a trade relationship with Iran that goes back to the days of the Weimar Republic.[20] Although West German trade exports to Iran have fallen from the 1983 high of 7.7 billion marks to 2.8 billion, this decline should be attributed to a lessening of total Iranian imports, not to any major loss of markets to competitors. West Germany has always been anxious to acquire more contracts for reconstruction in Iran. It is for this reason that the West German cabinet urged the convening of the UN Security Council to consider the Rushdie Affair—a tactful side-stepping of hostile sanctions against Iran, not a dissenting voice within Western Europe.

Surprisingly, Iran's third biggest trading partner, Italy, was forceful in its condemnations of Iran. The *London Times* quotes an embassy spokesman for Italy as saying that Italy planned to postpone indefinitely a planned trade delegation to Teheran, and that the Rushdie Affair would change the picture of relations between the two countries.[21]

For Britain, the Rushdie Affair has completely destroyed the rapprochement that had been occurring between the two countries. After a lapse in formal relations since the revolution, diplomatic ties were reestablished in November 1988. In early 1989, however, the two countries again broke off diplomatic relations. Furthermore, the fate of British prisoners in Iran and that of the Archbishop of Canterbury's envoy to the Middle East, Terry Waite, are indeed bleak. By early 1990 things were just as bad as they were a year before. In February, one year after Khomeini's death, Teheran was still calling for Rushdie's head. Only time will sort out the diplomatic estrangement between Britain and Iran.

The Japanese response was deafening in its silence. Japan has been the second largest trading partner of Iran. Its exports in technology and steel are highly desired in the reconstruction effort. Japan, for its part, is strongly reliant on oil imports, and the Japanese are thus greatly concerned over any possible rift with Iran. Arguably, if any country will benefit from the Rushdie Affair (besides Turkey), it will be Japan. Japan was careful to keep all comments to a minimum level of controversy. Thus while Foreign Minister Sosuke Uno said that it was "outrageous to solicit murder, and that freedom of speech should be maintained," he also stated "that the customs of other states should be respected."[22]

The United States seemed to be reluctant to turn the controversy into a *cause célèbre* against the "Great Satan" and was restrained in its condemnations overall. This should be regarded as a diplomatic plus for the Bush Administration.

Equally restrained in its condemnations of the affair was the Soviet Union. Not surprisingly, the Kremlin waited patiently to see what the European and U.S. reactions would be like. It then cautiously declared that Iran's behaviour was rather irregular according to international norms. But it castigated Western Europe in its condemnation of Iran, thus preparing the way for a budding Soviet-Iranian relationship in which the USSR was increasingly seen as Iran's protector. After Khomeini's death, it was surmised that Rafsanjani had been given *carte blanche* to draw closer to Moscow. Teheran needed arms and a new market, and this is precisely what Rafsanjani set out to get when he concluded agreements with the Soviet government in the summer of 1989.

THE IMMEDIATE FALLOUT OF
THE RUSHDIE AFFAIR

The long-term effect of the Rushdie Affair is hard to determine. While Khomeini was alive, Rushdie was a marked man. With Khomeini gone, Rushdie may soon be forgotten in Iran and abroad. He cannot remain a subject for internal religious deliberations when there are other things to attend to. And it is doubtful that the ultra-revolutionaries would want to revive the subject just to keep Khomeini's image alive. Further provocation, along the lines of Iran actually having Rushdie killed, would likely result in sanctions that Iran simply does not need. However, the Rushdie Affair does seem to have left its imprint on the domestic politics of Iran. Both Ayatollah Montazeri and Deputy Foreign Minister Mohammed Javad Larijani were ousted from the Government, the official explanation was that they resigned. While Larijani's dismissal was perceived to be detrimental to the West, it was the fall from grace of Montazeri, Khomeini's chosen successor to the position of *Faqih* that appeared ominous for the future of Iran. (Larijani had in any case been able to get himself reinstated by Rafsanjani after Khomeini's death.)

Montazeri, a student of the Imam for years and described by Khomeini as "the fruit of my life," was unceremoniously removed in the last week of March 1989. He had been complaining in public that the economy was being mismanaged and that basic human rights were being trampled. Almost at once, Iran's Ambassador to the United Nations, Ahmad Mahallati, resigned. Everywhere in the country Montazeri's picture was quietly removed from its position alongside the Imam's. The dismissal of these pragmatic revolutionaries seemed to suggest that the fallout from the Rushdie Affair was going to be widespread in Iran.

Five questions arise from Montazeri's dismissal and Khomeini's demise: Will a new designated heir for the position of *Faqih* be found? What impact will an unacceptable heir to the position of *Faqih* have on Iran? What does Montazeri's fall imply for Rafsanjani? Will there be a struggle for power at some point between Rafsanjani and Ahmed Khomeini, the late Ayatollah's politically ambitious son? And, finally, what should the West expect from Iranian foreign policy?

A new heir to *Velayat-e-Faqih* will have to be named—that much is certain. Without a strong *Faqih*, Iran could experience a drift to secularism, following a new struggle for power. But there are other alternatives, other imponderables. Consider the alternative to one *Faqih*. When it is the case that one man of obvious qualifications for the position of *Faqih* is present, the Iranian constitution provides for a transfer of power to him from the Council of Experts. However, should such a person of obvious qualifications not be found by the Council of Experts, then anywhere from three to five Mujtahids will be appointed to a council to wield the powers of the *Velayat-e-Faqih*.

This fact means it is likely that a collective religious leadership could exercise Khomeini's spiritual authority. Khomeini's charisma would be impossible to replicate. Indeed, it was always questionable whether Montazeri would have been confirmed even when Khomeini was alive.

In addition, a power struggle of titanic proportions could occur, not immediately, but within a year or two after the Imam's death. It is during the coming power struggle that the fate of the revolution could be decided. I strongly suspect that this power struggle will be extremely violent and will produce yet another round of upheaval in Iran and the Gulf.

The outlook for Rafsanjani may not appear at first to be so dark. He is credited with having an uncanny ability to survive, both physically and politically. But, in my estimation, Rafsanjani will probably go down like all the rest before him. He will never have Khomeini's charisma, and his ecclesiastical credentials are weak; he is more the politician than the spiritual leader, and Iran still needs a spiritual leadership. Nevertheless, some observers predicted, after the Rushdie imbroglio, that Rafsanjani should be able to weather any storm.[23] But this view is overly optimistic and hardly consistent with the patterns of Iranian history. We know that in the summer of 1989 Rafsanjani became the new President by unanimous acclaim and that he picked the new Cabinet. But he still has to confront an increasingly determined Council of Guardians, which might undermine any economic or political reforms he tries to implement. In addition, Rafsanjani, or his substitute, will still have to win the support of the lower middle classes and the urban poor, those who have sacrificed most in the war and revolution and seen the least return for their efforts in terms of economic improvement. To stay in power, the new President of the Islamic Republic will also have to completely abolish the office of the premiership, if he wishes to address the economic ills that have plagued this land for more than a decade. If he knows what is good for him, he might even be forced, for the sake of survival, to physically eliminate the opposition. If he does not, that opposition—in the opaque world of Iranian politics—could find a way to get rid of him, be it Mohtashemi, radicals in the Army, or erstwhile supporters such as Khamenei.

By early 1990, contrary to the Geneva Conventions on Humanitarian Law, Iran was still bickering over the terms respecting a complete exchange of prisoners with Iraq. A new law was recently passed permitting the Iranians to arrest wanted Americans anywhere in the world, in response to the U.S. decision allowing American law-enforcement officials to arrest convicted terrorists outside the United States. On the first of November, 1989, a Saudi diplomat had been murdered in Beirut by terrorists linked to the pro-Iranian Hezbollah, in retaliation for the execution of 16 Kuwaiti Shi'i condemned for planting bombs in Mecca. Mohtashemi had been visiting Beirut and Hezbollah headquarters at the time. All this does not bode well for Rafsanjani, at least not in the short term.

The long-term prospects, however, remain optimistic. Sooner or later Iran will have to turn to the West. The demands of trade dictate that the country must deal with those who are able to afford Iranian oil and to provide Iranians with technology. In the short term, the Rushdie Affair and the passing of Khomeini will temporarily provide the revolution with a new lease on life. Efforts to predict future developments in the Islamic Republic are, like all predictions, conditional. Much will depend upon the outcome of important events and fortuitous occurrences that have yet to take place.

Iran is at a turning point in its history, with the potential to forge new relationships with its neighbours and with the superpowers. Whether Iran's foreign policy is to be likened to the proverbial behemoth run amok, with a singular, ideological world view, or whether it is a continuous reaction against ideological encroachment from the West, one overriding issue in the years ahead will be difficult to dispute— that it is locked in an internal power struggle that ultimately will determine this nation's foreign conduct.

NOTES

1. The Iranian Constitution adopted in December 1979 introduced a political-theological doctrine called *Velayat-e Faqih* ("rule of the jurist"), which Khomeini had invented while in exile. The "jurist" is, of course, Khomeini himself. The decree or legal pronouncement is called *fatva*.

2. *Newsweek*, February 22, 1989, p. 37.

3. Salman Rushdie. *The Satanic Verses*, London: Viking Press, 1988, p. 214-215.

4. For a clearer understanding of Khomeini as Imam and the Twelve Imams of Shi'ism, see Chapter 1 ("The Complexities of the Iranian Predicament") of this book.

5. *The Observer*, February 29, 1989, p. 15.

6. *Maclean's*, February 27, 1989.

7. *Newsweek*, February 27, 1989.

8. The text is from *The Observer*, February 19, 1989.

9. Radio Teheran, February 16, 1989.

10. *The Economist*, January 14, 1989.

11. *The Economist*, April 2, 1988.

12. *Newsweek*, February 12, 1989.

13. *The Economist*, September 17, 1988.

14. *The Economist*, July 9, 1988.

15. See my Chapter 1 in this book, "The 'Pariah' Syndrome: Complexities of the Iranian Predicament."

16. *The Times*(London), February 23, 1989.

17. *Time*, March 6, 1989, p. 35.

18. Afsaneh Najmabadi, "Iran's Turn to Islam: From Modernism to a Moral Order", *The Middle East Journal*, Vol. 41, No. 2, 1987, p. 202.

19. *Business Week*, August 3, 1987.

20. See the last chapter in my book, *The Soviet Union and Iran*, Westview Press, Boulder, 1988.

21. *The Times* (London), February 22, 1989.

22. *Ibid.*

23. *New York Times*, April 2, 1989.

Index